The Japanese Diet and
the U.S. Congress

A Westview Special Study

The Japanese Diet and the U.S. Congress
edited by Francis R. Valeo and Charles E. Morrison

The Japanese Diet and the U.S. Congress have in common many of the characteristics of democratic institutions, similarities that can be seen in the way the two legislative bodies are constituted, in what they do, and in how they do it. At the same time, there are disparities that stem from each nation's unique cultural background and political experiences. Both the similarities and the differences are treated in this unique study.

The authors, well-known Japanese and U.S. scholars, illuminate significant factors that not only underlie the differing roles of the Diet and the Congress in the two governments and the style of each government, but also help shape the nature of the interaction between Japan and the U.S.

Francis R. Valeo, now a consultant on government and Asian affairs in Washington, D.C., has been the secretary of the U.S. Senate and a staff advisor to the former Senate majority leader and to the current U.S. ambassador to Japan. *Charles E. Morrison* is a research fellow at the East-West Center, Hawaii, and at the Japan Center for International Exchange.

Published in cooperation with the
United States Association of Former Members of Congress
pursuant to a grant from the
Japan–United States Friendship Commission

The Japanese Diet and the U.S. Congress

edited by Francis R. Valeo
and Charles E. Morrison

Westview Press / Boulder, Colorado

A Westview Special Study

Copyright © 1983 by Westview Press, Inc.

Published in 1983 in the United States of America by
  Westview Press, Inc.
  5500 Central Avenue
  Boulder, Colorado 80301
  Frederick A. Praeger, President and Publisher

Library of Congress Cataloging in Publication Data
Main entry under title:
The Japanese Diet and the U.S. Congress.
  1. Japan. Kokkai—Addresses, essays, lectures.   2. United States. Congress—Addresses, essays,
lectures.   I. Valeo, Francis Ralph, 1916–   II. Morrison, Charles E.
JQ1656.J36   1982   328.52   82-13439
ISBN 0-86531-469-1

Printed and bound in the United States of America

Contents

List of Tables and Figures ix
List of Abbreviations x
Foreword, *Jed Johnson, Jr.* xi

Introduction
Francis R. Valeo and Tadashi Yamamoto 1

Part 1
The Japanese Diet

1. The Diet in the Japanese Political System
    Kan Ori 11

2. Political Parties and the Diet
    Hiroshi Yamato 25

3. Diet Structure, Organization, and Procedures
    Koichi Kishimoto 39

4. Diet Members
    Shoichi Izumi 61

5. The Diet and the Bureaucracy: The Budget as a Case Study
    Koji Kakizawa 79

6. The Role of the Diet in Foreign Policy and Defense
    Shuzo Kimura 99

Part 2
The U.S. Congress

7. Congress in the U.S. Political System
    James L. Sundquist 115

8. The U.S. Congress: Structure, Party Organization, and Leadership
   Robert L. Peabody 127

9. The Making of a Law: The U.S. Legislative Process
   Ralph D. Nurnberger 141

10. The Member of the U.S. Congress
    Susan Webb Hammond 155

11. The U.S. Congress in Budgeting and Finance
    Joel Havemann 171

12. The U.S. Congress in Foreign Relations, Trade, and Defense
    Charles E. Morrison 183

List of Conference Participants 200
List of Contributors 203
Index 204

Tables and Figures

Tables

3.1   Political Party Strength in the 94th Diet 42

3.2   Standing Committees of the Diet and Their Sizes 44

3.3   Bills Submitted and Passed, 1975–1980 52

5.1   Postwar Prime Ministers 82

6.1   Draft Resolutions Concerning Foreign Policy and Defense
        Issues Submitted December 1965–November 1980 107

Figures

5.1   Outline of the Budget Process in Japan 85

5.2   Changing Structural Dimensions of the Budget Process 93

Abbreviations

CBO	Congressional Budget Office
CGP	Clean Government party
DSP	Democratic Socialist party
GNP	gross national product
ITC	International Trade Commission
JCP	Japan Communist party
JSP	Japan Socialist party
LDP	Liberal Democratic party
NASA	National Aeronautics and Space Administration
OMB	Office of Management and Budget
PAC	political action committee
PARC	Policy Affairs Research Council
PRC	People's Republic of China

Foreword

Although much has been written about Japan and the United States and the policies and practices of their governments, one aspect of the relationship between the two nations has not been systematically explored. Until recently, there has been little awareness in the one country of the nature and role of the legislative body in the other. Yet it is increasingly apparent that the Diet and the Congress, each in its own way, are critical elements in determining the overall manner in which Japan and the United States interact with each other.

This gap in mutual awareness was perceived by the U.S. Association of Former Members of Congress and the Japan Center for International Exchange. Accordingly, with support from the Japan-U.S. Friendship Commission, the East-West Center in Honolulu, and other groups, the two organizations agreed to undertake a comparative study of the Japanese Diet and U.S. Congress. The study was designed by Francis R. Valeo, former secretary of the United States Senate and a consultant to the Former Members of Congress, which also directed the preparation of the U.S. papers. The Japanese part of the study was conducted under the guidance of Tadashi Yamamoto, director of the Japan Center for International Exchange.

Scholars and experts in both countries were commissioned to prepare the set of twelve integrated papers on the legislative systems of the two countries. These papers subsequently formed the basis for three days (February 12–14, 1981) of discussion at a binational conference at the East-West Center in Honolulu. Participants included the scholar-writers of the conference papers, sitting and former members of the Diet and the Congress, members of the staff of the East-West Center, and a number of other interested persons and observers.

The results of this joint Japanese-U.S. effort are reflected in this volume. The book includes the twelve conference papers and a brief commentary. A similar study is also being published in Japanese. The Japan Center for International Exchange and the Association of Former Members of Congress assume responsibility for offering these papers as a contribution to U.S.-Japanese understanding. Credit for substance, however, is attributable entirely to the authors. We wish to thank the members of the Advisory Board for their comments and suggestions. The special assistance of Charles E. Morrison, who served as editor for the Japanese papers, is also noted. Associated with the Japan Center and the East-West Center, Mr. Morrison also provided liaison and other assistance in making arrangements for the conference. Thanks go to Kazuo Ogura of the Japanese Foreign Ministry and the Johnson Foundation Conference Center, "Wingspread," at Racine, Wisconsin, for their contributions to the convening of a preliminary meeting of former members of Congress and of the Diet.

Mrs. Dorothy Bageant of the staff of the Former Members of Congress supplied the essential secretarial skills to produce the manuscript for publication in English.

Jed Johnson, Jr.
Executive Director
Association of Former Members of Congress

Introduction

Francis R. Valeo
Tadashi Yamamoto

In recent decades, Americans and Japanese have come to know a great deal of each other's ways. Scholars, scientists, writers, and others have examined the complexities and commonplaces of the two societies, and their observations have been widely disseminated in Japan and the United States. A great number of people — officials, tourists, businessmen, students, and professionals — have moved back and forth between the countries. Similarly, a vast tide of goods, services, and capital has flowed in both directions.

Japanese-U.S. relations are now characterized by a close interweaving of national interests and a high degree of interdependence. The ties between the two countries produce great mutual benefit. But inevitably, irritants and anxieties also appear from time to time. Looming large in recent difficulties are a heightening of economic competition between the industrial-commercial establishments of the two countries and conflicting viewpoints on matters of defense, especially with regard to nuclear weapons.

The economic difficulty is readily illustrated. When Japan pursues expansionist or anti-inflationary economic policies, Japanese export performance is affected, and, in turn, so too are U.S. industries producing goods like automobiles, steel, and color televisions. Conversely, U.S. monetary policies and banking deregulation can lead to capital outflows from Japan and, in turn, to pressures within that country for changes in its financial policies. U.S. agricultural policies influence the price and availability of food and feed grains in Japan because that country depends on the United States for approximately one-fourth of its total caloric intake. On the other hand, Japan's domestic agricultural subsidies and import practices can affect the prosperity of U.S. farmers, for whom Japan is the largest foreign customer. U.S. defense policies toward the world as a whole and Northeast Asia in particular affect in a major way Japan's security and defense needs, while Japan's defense policies and prohibitions regarding nuclear weapons influence the force levels and missions that are perceived to be required of U.S. forces in East Asia.

These interactions produce problems that are extremely complex and for which there are no panaceas. Nevertheless, Japan and the United States have generally managed to blunt sharp differences and, over the years, to maintain a high degree of bilateral cooperation. Traditional diplomacy, official missions, and ad hoc cooperative arrangements have been major factors in this fortuitous state of affairs. Another factor has been the large reservoir of trust built up after World War II. This trust is essential to the continuation of effective resolution of conflicts, and in great part maintaining it depends on the legislatures of the two nations. Sooner or later the major problems of U.S.-Japanese relations surface in the Congress and the Diet. What transpires in these bodies can calm or intensify the crosscurrents. But the Diet and the Congress remain, on the whole, reciprocal enigmas to the peoples of both countries, sometimes even to officials involved in U.S.-Japanese relations and to the legislators themselves.

Despite a growing number of face-to-face encounters, legislators of one country still find it difficult to appreciate with any depth the milieu within which their counterparts operate in the other country. It is common for these legislators to draw analogies based on their own experiences, but such analogies can be misleading. As the chapters in this volume show, there are many ostensible similarities between the two systems—for instance, the primacy of domestic politics, the importance of service to constituents, and the need for compromise or consensus as a basis for legislative actions. In many other respects, however, the legislative institutions are quite different—for example, the degree of autonomy of individual members, the relative importance given to oversight of government operations, and the manner through which compromises are made or consensus is achieved.

Many binational programs and exchanges have been directed at improving understanding of issues as they arise in the legislatures. Members of the Diet and of Congress have been among the active participants in these exchange activities. Although there is some mutual perception of problems, a deeper understanding of the inner workings of the two institutions and the part they play in influencing the U.S.-Japanese relationship is still absent.

The twelve chapters in this book are designed to help fill the gap. They illuminate the details of the two systems in an integrated pattern so as to permit comparative study. Beginning with James L. Sundquist's and Kan Ori's chapters, the Congress and the Diet are portrayed in the light of their histories and the places they occupy in their respective constitutional structures. The organization and distribution of power between and within each bicameral body form the substance of Hiroshi Yamato's and Robert L. Peabody's chapters. Kōichi Kishimoto and Ralph D. Nurnberger explain the process by which laws are actually made in each country, bringing into focus the great difference in the role of political parties in Japan and the United States. Shoichi Izumi and Susan Webb Hammond describe the human element, the nature of the tasks of the men and women who breathe life into the two legislative systems. Their chapters define the role of the individual members of the Diet and the Congress. They tell how these elected officials enter the two systems, what they do within their systems, and what the systems do for and to them.

Koji Kakizawa's and Joel Havemann's chapters on budgeting and finance set forth the complex procedures by which is discharged that most fundamental of legislative responsibilities, the taxing and spending of the people's money.

Finally, Shuzo Kimura and Charles E. Morrison provide insights into matters of defense, trade, and foreign policy. They show how the activities of the Diet and the Congress affect the overall relationship between Japan and the United States.

The twelve chapters reveal similarities between the Japanese and U.S. systems, some of which are superficial, others very deep. In nomenclature and in other aspects of surface structure, for example, the Diet and the Congress seem very much alike. Both legislatures are bicameral, and the "lower" organ in each is called the House of Representatives. Moreover, the two houses are similar in composition and even in procedures. In function, however, they are vastly different. In Japan the nation's political direction, for all practical purposes, in a constitutional sense, is in the hands of whatever party or group can command a majority within the House of Representatives. By contrast, the majority party in the U.S. House of Representatives is only one factor among several in the distribution of constitutional political power.

Superficial similarities are due in part to the fact that the present Constitution of Japan was adopted during the U.S. military occupation; U.S. specialists in government brought their own backgrounds to Japan and then played a significant role in the drafting of Japan's basic law. But U.S. influence is by no means, as has sometimes been suggested, the whole story. The fact is that a diet has been a part of Japanese life for a century or more. Japan did not start from scratch at the end of World War II in shaping its present Constitution and governmental structure. Rather, the roots of these developments go back to the Meiji period and the beginning of the Japanese modernization in the nineteenth century.

In a deeper sense, similarities between the two present systems stem from a common genealogy. Both have roots in British and European political systems. Both reflect a determination to anchor government in popular consent. Thus, while each system is a unique national expression, both are a part of the historic counterpoise of parliamentary pluralism to political authoritarianism.

The concept of people's sovereignty is expressed in sharply different ways in the U.S. and Japanese constitutional systems. In Japan, political power is fused around the Diet as the "highest organ of state power"; other governmental institutions are confined to peripheral or ceremonial functions. By contrast, political power in the United States is deliberately divided between the states and the federal government and additionally, within the latter, among several components. In the United States, the president and the Congress have come to share preponderant political direction of the nation. Both, however, are required to cooperate within the boundaries of the Constitution and law as interpreted by an independent court. As in Japan, moreover, in the United States the continuity of the quasiindependent and permanent bureaucracy also plays a highly significant, if unofficial, part in the political process.

The basic difference between the Japanese and U.S. systems, then, lies in the pattern of concentration of power in the former and that of diffusion in the latter. This difference is readily apparent in the inner structure of the Diet and the Congress. In Japan, for example, the "upper" House of Councillors and the "lower" House of Representatives seem to be cast in a juxtaposition similar to that of the U.S. Senate and House of Representatives. In reality, however, the scales are weighted overwhelmingly on the side of the "lower" house in the Japanese system, as they are in many other parliamentary structures, notably that of the United Kingdom.

The Japanese House of Representatives has the ultimate power to determine the course of government. It is there that all laws must be approved and, in critical matters, can be approved, if necessary, over the opposition of the House of Councillors. It is there, too, that the chief executive of the Japanese government, the prime minister, is chosen and held accountable by a majority vote. Together with the cabinet, he or she is subject to removal by a vote of no confidence.

By contrast, power is shared in the United States. It is divided, as has been noted, between an independent Congress and an independent presidency, with each having a separate claim to authority based on separate popular mandates. Moreover, the diffusion of power is carried even further in the U.S. system. Within the Congress, there is a roughly equal division between the House and the Senate. Unlike in Japan, where the lower house is supreme, neither body in the Congress can function without concurrence of the other.

Within the operating structure of each of the two houses there are still further divisions. Ad hoc groups based on regional, ethnic, occupational, or ideological interests form and reform across party lines to assert block power. Committees within each house also establish crisscrossing cores of power encompassing members of both major parties and, often, both houses. Of late, even subcommittees and their chairmen have tended in the same direction. Finally, there are the members themselves, 435 in the House and 100 in the Senate. Although they are usually identifiable as being of one or the other party, the members all act in virtual independence. They all owe election not so much to party as to individual effort in their constituencies and to support that more often than not is likely to cross party lines.

Members of Congress tend to be highly conscious of their individual constitutional role in a separate branch of government. They see their responsibility as that of a check and balance to the other branches. Although control of the White House and the Congress by the same party can mollify some of the conflict inherent in a system of separation of powers, it does not eliminate that conflict. Members of Congress tend to vote as individuals, and when constituency interests or personal judgments require members to vote against their party, they will often do so. Generally speaking, moreover, there are no party reprisals against such votes.

It is obvious from the above description that party is currently a weak source of unified political action in the United States. The party structures themselves are very fragmented. Party organization is separately determined in each house of Congress. Liaison between the party organization in the Senate and that in the House of Representatives tends to be casual and informal, and between both houses and the national party structure it is likely to be even more so.

In contrast, the Japanese Diet is tied together tightly by the knots of national parties, and members of the Diet vote by party. This practice is evident in the case of the Liberal Democratic party, which has retained majority control of the Diet for many years. Liberal Democratic Diet members are expected to and do support government-sponsored legislation.

The opposition parties are also heard in the Diet. They are expected to and do oppose the majority. But however much they denounce, decry, and delay, they can hardly affect significantly the outcome that has been predetermined by the majority party, voting as a unit.

Because of its long dominance of the Diet, the Liberal Democratic party has brought the bureaucracy into close affiliation with the majority. As a result, the bureaucracy and the cabinet dominate the Diet rather than the other way around. In these circumstances, the Diet as a body does not serve as a source of legislation, nor does it provide significant oversight of the bureaucracy.

Japanese political parties, including the Liberal Democrats, are not necessarily within themselves highly centralized. Most of them have factions centered around leading figures of the party. These factions are extremely important in bargaining within the party for the prime ministership and the cabinet offices. Factionalism notwithstanding, still fundamental to the Japanese parliamentary system is a capacity for individual legislators to repress their personal inclinations and work together in tight groups within a party system under a strong controlling leadership. In the United States the main characteristics of the system are almost the opposite. Although there are party structures, legislators can and do act on a freewheeling basis in pursuit of individually perceived goals. The power to act is widely diffused within the Congress. As a result, the responsibility for particular legislative acts is often obscured.

Notwithstanding sharp differences in the two systems, the men and women whose function it is to legislate in Japan and the United States have similar concepts of their roles and share many of the same trials. That resemblance is not surprising because, as elected representatives, they have characteristics quite common to popular politicians in democracies. The successful legislators are highly sensitized to local predilections and prejudices and to the economic, social, and other needs of their supporters. They are the ombudsmen of their respective constituencies. They are characterized by a readiness to serve the mundane interests of the people whom they represent and the nation's interests in international matters, interests sometimes viewed at a short range.

Whatever the differences between them, both the Japanese Diet and the U.S. Congress are democratic institutions. As in other democracies, in these countries, to function effectively, it is essential that legislative majorities be put together and sustained for reasonable periods of time. The development and retention of majorities in turn involves the reconciliation of pressures from within the society.

In Japan, the process of consensus building through the application of political judgment is made and completed outside the Diet, usually within the party machinery. This process continues, although there has been some evolution toward more active Diet debate and consideration of opposing viewpoints as a result of changes in party strength and the development of more realistic positions toward legislation by the opposition parties. Still, only about 20 percent of legislative proposals are amended in the Diet, and the amendments are largely of a technical nature. Since voting is by party rather than by individual member, the lobbying of the Diet is ineffective. Hence, pressure groups tend to concentrate on other centers of power, such as the bureaucracy and the various committees of the ruling party.

In both Japan and the United States, the task of consensus building is extremely difficult in matters of budgeting and finance. The budgeting systems of the two nations are similar in purpose and, to some extent, in machinery. They attempt to blend a vast array of current national requirements and a perception of future national needs with the special demands and supplications of numerous interest groups within the two societies. In the United States, the function of budgeting and finance is a many-step process. It is shared by the president and members of both houses of Congress. At various stages in the process, moreover, there is a vast input from the presidential advisers, the executive and legislative bureaucracies, legislative committees and staffs, and private pressure sources. A progressive reconciling of viewpoints takes place down to the final adoption of the last piece of relevant legislation. At the same time, the possibility of change exists down to the last vote in the U.S. system. In the Japanese system, the principal input from the bureaucracy and private sources takes place within the national structure of the majority party, with the final reconciliation of major conflicts the responsibility of the prime minister. Thereafter, once they are introduced into the Diet, budgetary measures for all practical purposes are in final form. The minority parties can spotlight flaws and challenge the division of the pie. In the end, however, the majority party in the House of Representatives cannot be gainsaid.

The formulation of trade, defense, and foreign policies in Japan follows essentially the same pattern. The inputs of the bureaucracy, private business, and local interests in these matters enters largely by way of the national party structure and the cabinet. The bureaucracy's role is particularly important in regard to defense and foreign policy. In part, this importance is due to its virtual monopoly of technical and confidential information in these highly complex matters. But here, too, the critical decisions are the prime minister's. When the prime minister presents a position to the Diet in matters of defense or foreign policy, that position is, for all practical purposes, final.

By contrast, it might be said that in foreign relations and defense, no major decision on U.S. policy can be final until it has been dealt with in the Congress or, in some cases, at least in the Senate. As does the president, the Senate has special constitutional powers in foreign relations. But the House of Representatives can and from time to time does insist successfully on a coequal role, notably when foreign policy decisions involve subsequent expenditures of money. Even in the critical areas of defense and foreign relations, then, it may be said that a prominent characteristic of the U.S. system in contrast with Japan's is diffusion of power and responsibility.

To sum up, the Diet and the Congress can be described as very different yet comparable institutions of representative and responsive government. Although few observers would deny that there are imperfections in both systems, the fact is that both have functioned essentially as popular institutions, subject to periodic tests in elections. They have been critical parts of governments that have generally been able to maintain orderly societies.

Like all other contemporary governments, those of Japan and the United States are hard pressed to deal with the monumental problems of contemporary times. However, both systems have been capable of making structural and other adjustments over the years. It may be that in the continuing evolution of the Japanese and U.S. systems, some of the experiences and practices of each legislature are relevant to the other. Continuing exchanges in legislative and parliamentary matters between the two countries might indicate ways in which both systems could be strengthened. In this way, as has already been the case in other areas, a growth in understanding could provide substantial benefit to Japan and the United States.

Part 1

The Japanese Diet

1
The Diet in the
Japanese Political System

Kan Ori

Japan's parliament, the Diet, has been in existence for over ninety years, even though it became a truly representative body of the Japanese people only after World War II (to be more precise, after the termination of the American occupation in 1952). In this chapter, after a brief discussion of the Diet under the Meiji Constitution of 1889, the role of the present Diet under the 1947 Constitution and the political functions it performs in the postwar political system will be examined. Recent changes and future prospects for the Diet will also be considered, and wherever possible, Japanese Diet practices will be compared with those of the U.S. Congress.

From the Imperial Diet to the National Diet

Historical Roots of the Diet

The imperial Diet was established in 1890 under the Meiji Constitution. Even though it is said that the Meiji political system was patterned after the Prussian model, it was "parliamentary" in name only. The original purpose of the Meiji Constitution was to create an emperor-centered state with Western "parliamentary" trappings. In fact, the Constitution stipulated that the emperor, in whom sovereignty was vested, exercise legislative power with the Diet merely assisting. Although laws were formally the product of the Diet, the emperor (and the cabinet) had the right to issue ordinances with the force of law. In addition, independent of the Diet the emperor controlled both the military and the civil bureaucracies, including their purse strings. The prewar Diet was composed of not only a popularly elected House of Representatives but also a House of Peers, having equal power, whose membership consisted of the nobility and those appointed by the emperor. In the beginning, the members of the House of Representatives were elected by a small electorate;

but the suffrage base was gradually enlarged, and universal male suffrage was achieved in 1925. (Female suffrage was not instituted until 1946.)

The three major functions the prewar Diet served were legitimization, political-role formation, and a kind of interest articulation. Although theoretically the chief function of the Diet should have been the making of laws, the prewar Diet never realized its full potential in this sphere. Very few bills actually originated in the Diet; in fact, most of the time, the prewar Diet was dominated by bureaucratic powers that had a monopoly over information. And yet every law needed the Diet's consent, and the Diet could initiate bills even though most of the time it simply voted on government bills drafted by the bureaucracy. The prewar Diet, then, was something more than just a "talking club," as some historians describe it, because the Diet had to legitimize legislative acts. The value of this legitimization function, even under the constraints of prewar Japan, should not be underestimated. More importantly, the House of Representatives served, however ineffectively, as a link between the people and the government. In the process, Diet members learned to represent their constituents, since their tenure depended on the voters. At the same time members got used to the workings of a legislature. In other words, prewar Diet members in the House of Representatives had ample opportunity to familiarize themselves with representative and legislative roles, and such political-role formation is essential for a working democracy. As for the interest articulation function, it is not an overstatement that the prewar Diet essentially represented the vested interests (be they those of landlords or financial concerns) of the day; that is, it represented the establishment. Some members attempted to work for much broader interests of ordinary people, but they were in the minority. And an even smaller number spoke for proletarian causes.

Despite performing these three major political functions, the prewar Diet was hardly effective as a parliament. Why was this true? Broadly speaking, there were three major types of constraints on the Diet in the prewar period: constitutional and formal constraints; political constraints; and cultural or social constraints. The constitutional and formal constraints alone were overwhelming. Every law had to be sanctioned by the emperor, and this power gave him an absolute veto over legislation even though he never exercised it. Only the emperor could convene the Diet and dissolve the House of Representatives. He alone could initiate constitutional amendments, whereas that is one of the imperative powers of the U.S. Congress. Individual ministers in the cabinet were personally responsible to the emperor, not to the Diet. More importantly, the prewar Diet had no real control over the budget. For example, even if the Diet failed to approve the budget, the government could carry on its business with the previous year's budget.[1]

The most important political constraint was the public bureaucracy. The bureaucracy and other oligarchical interests also had formal structures such as the Privy Council and Elder Statesmen (*genro*) to articulate their views to the emperor, counteracting the Diet. In addition, the military forces had their own channels of direct access to the emperor, their commander in chief. Despite these constitutional and extraconstitutional constraints, the Diet could have evolved into an effective legislative and representative body had there existed viable political parties reflecting the interests of the general public. But, except for a short period in the Taishō era (during the 1920s), the parties were weak, if not impotent, in the face of the bureaucracy. With a strong party system there might have even developed some sense of collective responsibility on the part of the cabinet, but this was never fully realized in prewar Japan.

Furthermore, cultural constraints were considerable. Although there was agitation for popular participation even before the establishment of the Diet (indeed, its establishment was in part due to this pressure) and more or less persistently throughout the prewar period, the public's dominant image of the government was that of a deity (*ōkami*), that is, something above and beyond daily concern. The government was, after all, the emperor's government, and his servants, not public servants, administered the country. In addition, it seems that the public firmly believed in the benevolent neutrality of government officials but, on the other hand, despised (and sometimes with good reason) the dirty politics and politicians associated with the popularly elected House of Representatives.

The Diet Under the Postwar Constitution

The most important accomplishment of the 1947 Constitution was the establishment of popular sovereignty. Sovereignty was transferred from the emperor to the people in the constitution. Thus, the Japanese political system was constitutionally changed from an emperor-centered structure to a truly democratic one. Accordingly, the postwar constitution designates the Diet as "the highest organ of state power," having "the sole law-making authority of the State."

Like the prewar Diet, the postwar Diet is bicameral, but with the significant difference that both houses are popularly elected. Presently, the House of Representatives consists of 511 members elected from 130 districts for a maximum term of four years. With the exception of 1 district (which elects a single representative), each district sends 3, 4, or 5 representatives to the Diet. (This system is in contrast to that of the United States, where every district is represented by a single member.) The House of Councillors is presently made up of 252 members. Of these, 152 are chosen in prefecture-wide elections. The number of seats is apportioned among the 47 prefectures in accordance with their populations; thus, the smallest prefectures elect 2 councillors each and the largest, Tokyo, elects 8. The other 100 councillors are elected from a single nationwide constituency. The councillors serve staggered six-year terms, half of them being elected every three years. The purpose of this arrangement is to assure some continuity in the House of Councillors, as is the case in the U.S. Senate.

In the Japanese Constitution, unlike the U.S. Constitution, there is no explicit enumeration of powers reserved for the Diet because Japan's political system is not federal but unitary. Also unlike the U.S. House, but like the United Kingdom's House of Commons, the House of Representatives is the dominant legislative body. Although laws require passage by both houses, if the House of Councillors disapproves a House of Representatives–passed bill (or fails to take final action on it within sixty days), the bill may still become law if it is repassed by the House of Representatives for a second time by a two-thirds majority of those present. Moreover, the budget must "first be submitted to the House of Representatives," and if "the House of Councillors makes a decision different from that of the House of Representatives, and . . . no agreement can be reached even through a joint committee of both Houses," or if "the House of Councillors [fails] to take final action within 30 days . . . the decision of the House of Representatives shall be the decision of the Diet." Similar provisions apply to the approval of treaties and, most importantly, to the designation of a prime minister. Thus, in the final analysis, the House of Councillors has only a delaying power.

Unlike the prewar Constitution, the 1947 Constitution envisages no other source of political power (beyond the electorate) than the Diet. The Diet is, constitutionally speaking, the supreme organ of government. Not only must the prime minister be selected by the Diet "from among the members of the Diet," but a majority of the cabinet ministers whom the prime minister appoints must come from the Diet. Actually, for political reasons, practically all postwar cabinet ministers have been Diet members. Following the canon of parliamentary democracy, the Constitution provides that, "the Cabinet, in the exercise of executive power, shall be collectively responsible to the Diet." But, in fact, the executive branch of government (that is, the cabinet and behind it the higher bureaucracy) dominates the legislative process in the Diet as in most other contemporary parliamentary systems. (This process is more fully discussed in Chapter 5.) If the House of Representatives passes a nonconfidence resolution, either the cabinet must resign or the House of Representatives must be dissolved. In addition, the postwar Diet has the formal power to investigate "in relation to government" and in pursuance of that duty can "demand the presence and testimony of witnesses, and the production of records." The Diet is also endowed with the power to impeach, as is the U.S. Congress; and it has the power to initiate amendments to the Constitution. (These require a concurring two-thirds vote of each house and ratification by the electorate.)

Whereas in the United States governmental powers are divided between Congress and the president, and thus the possibility of legislative-executive branch conflict is rather high, in Japan the governmental system is based on a fusion of the power of the Diet and the cabinet. Under this arrangement, the cabinet is responsible to the Diet constitutionally but actually takes leadership for legislation in the Diet along with the governing party. The parties and party factions maintain tight control over their members. In the Congress, on the other hand, the legislative process is highly decentralized, with semi-autonomous and powerful standing committees and little control over members by political parties. Another difference is that formal interpellation periods, during which cabinet ministers and bureaucrats are questioned in open session, are very important in the Diet, particularly in Budget Committee deliberations. The committee system in the postwar Diet is a hybrid of British-style parliamentary government and the U.S. system of standing committees on certain subjects. (For more on the Diet committee system see Chapter 3.) The Diet's standing committees, however, are much less autonomous than their U.S. counterparts because of a lower degree of functional expertise on the part of committee members and because of a different seniority system, particularly in the selection of committee chairmen. In Japan, committee assignments and continuity in the committee as well as appointments of committee chairmen are all closely controlled by party leadership.

The Diet in the Political System in Practice

Functions of the Postwar Diet in Japanese Politics

Interest articulation. Interest representation in the Diet is highly institutionalized in postwar Japan. As is well known, the Liberal Democratic party (LDP) articulates the interests of business, particularly big business, and the higher bureaucracy. The party is also mindful of farm interests the electoral support of which is essential, but its foremost commitment is clearly to the business and financial community. Not only does the LDP serve as a spokesman for the higher bureaucracy, but a high proportion of its members in the Diet are former government officials. By contrast, the Japan Socialist party (JSP) speaks for organized labor, or more precisely for the General Council of Trade Unions (Sōhyō), and former labor union officials compose about 70 percent of its Diet membership.[2] Like the Japan Socialist party, the Democratic Socialist party (DSP) represents the interests of labor, but not exclusively. While the DSP works for the interests of the Confederation of Labor (Domei), it also serves those of small and medium-size business and shop owners. The interests of the neo-Buddhist Soka Gakkai ("Value-Creation Society") are well represented by the Clean Government party (CGP). Practically all of the Diet members of the CGP are devoted followers of Soka Gakkai.

Of course, the interests that are most effectively represented are those channeled through the governing political party. Throughout almost the entire postwar period this has been the conservative Liberal Democratic party. Much interest articulation of this kind is done through the LDP leadership rather than through its individual Diet members or through the standing committees, as in the United States. In fact, dominant interests that have access to the LDP leadership do not have to pressure the Diet overtly or its standing committees. On the other hand, interests associated with the opposition parties are less effectively represented. Another distinctive aspect of interest representation in Japan should be mentioned: Diet members do not distribute benefits to their constituents through local pork-barrel legislation but serve, so to speak, as "pressure politicians," quite frequently on an individual basis, to influence the national bureaucracy through which local benefits are distributed.

Legislative. Does legislation originate in the Diet? If not, where do legislative ideas come from? Japan is a parliamentary system where the leadership on legislation is taken by the cabinet. Consequently, an overwhelming number of the measures introduced in the Diet are government bills. Even those put forward as members' bills are quite frequently initiated by the government or the majority party. In contrast, all legislative measures in the U.S. Congress are, at least in form, members' bills, even including those recommended by the administration. There is nothing in the Diet, moreover, like the members' private bills that are introduced in the Congress.

Thus, very few laws of any significance originate in the Diet or in its committees, although all legislative measures are formally introduced there. Many legislative ideas come from the higher bureaucracy; some originate with the cabinet and some with the Policy Affairs Research Council of the governing Liberal Democratic party in collaboration with higher bureaucrats and/or major interests such as big business. In fact, higher civil servants in the national bureaucracy conceive it as their role to draft legislation. Consequently the lawmaking process is dominated by the higher bureaucracy. Moreover, many former higher civil servants are in leadership positions in the LDP where they can exert considerable policy influence.[3] It should be remembered, however, that such dependence on the executive branch has become common even in the United States in recent years.

In the postwar Diet, as in the U.S. Congress, most important legislative deliberations and decisions occur in the standing (subject) committees. But even in these committees very few substantive debates take place.[4] The plenary sessions of the Diet are nothing but formalities or simply the acting out of roles in scripts that were written elsewhere. (This is because the LDP, which enforces strict party discipline, has had a majority in both houses ever since its formation in 1955.) What is crucial in postwar Japan is a sort of prelegislative process of negotiations, either among the LDP leadership or between the LDP and the government bureaucracy or opposition parties. Negotiations among the directors of each chamber's House Management Committee, who represent the positions of their respective parties on the Diet agenda, are also important, as are those negotiations that take place among directors of subject committees, who also reflect their parties' positions. (Each Diet standing committee has a board of directors [*rijikai*] that assists the committee chairman in running the committee and serves as the spokesman for, and is part of, its respective parties' leadership. Positions on committee boards of directors are normally apportioned in accordance with each party's overall strength in the house in question.) Thus, in contemporary Japan, not only do legislative ideas originate outside of the Diet but legislative negotiations and deliberations also take place outside or before the Diet session ever starts.

What role, then, does the Diet perform in the Japanese legislative process? It is too simplistic to say that the Diet merely rubber-stamps or ratifies legislative decisions already made elsewhere, or that it serves only as a safety valve.⁵ What the diet does is to examine—however superficially—criticize, publicize, and, with good luck, revise or block legislative measures introduced by the government. The opposition parties also try to embarrass the government during the question periods with the intention of drawing public attention to legislative issues or (even more often) exposing government predicaments. These are important functions of any legislature, and the fact that the Diet has a final say over legislation should not be taken lightly. Particularly important in this context is the matter of legislative judgment—judgment as to the amount of public concern, the probability of enactment due to the intensity of opposition, and the degree of controversy about a particular measure are all critical aspects of the legislative process of postwar Japan just as they are in most parliamentary democracies.

Fiscal. Whereas the prewar Diet was impotent in this sphere, the 1947 Constitution gave the postwar Diet the important function of control over the purse strings of government. The Diet has not lived up to expectations in this area, however, and its ineffectiveness in fiscal control is due as much to this legacy as to the fact that Japan has a parliamentary system of government. (This topic is discussed fully in Chapter 5.)

Policy issue resolution. Is the postwar Diet a forum for the resolution of public policy issues? If not, where are significant policy issues finally decided? In general, as far as the parties are concerned, the Diet is more a place for the articulation of issue positions than a forum for the resolution of issue differences. One reason for this is the importance of parties and their *ideological* orientations on policy issues during the postwar period. Political parties in Japan are well disciplined as far as legislative behavior is concerned, and so their Diet members vote along strict party lines. It should also be noted that the conservatives have controlled both houses of the Diet for the entire postwar period except for a brief interregnum in 1947–1948. In contrast, major parties in the United States are not ideological, nor do they have centralized congressional parties to control rank-and-file members.

Some policy issues are resolved through deliberation of the committees on house management or the standing committees, but usually the principal figures on these committees act only as party spokesmen. The opposition parties usually decide their positions on issues outside the legislative chambers, and whatever compromises there are on policy issues are arrived at through direct negotiations with the LDP leadership. In most cases, however, authoritative decisions on public policy issues are made by the various ministries (that is, by higher civil servants) either alone or in collaboration with the LDP. Sometimes these decisions are made within the LDP, especially by faction leaders, cabinet ministers, and the Policy Affairs Research Council (in which considerable influence is exerted by the bureaucrats). It should not be forgotten, however, that these party leaders are almost without exception all Diet members and that under certain circumstances genuine, if partial, resolutions of public policy are produced in the Diet itself.

Oversight. Does the Diet serve as a check on the government, namely the cabinet and the bureaucracy? Theoretically, the national bureaucracy is supervised by cabinet ministers who are themselves almost all members of and collectively responsible to the Diet. This theoretical supervision is enforced by the fact that the Diet can pass a motion of nonconfidence in the government. In actuality, however, the government dominates the legislative process in the Diet, and cabinet ministers are incapable of checking the bureaucracy because of their short tenure in office. The Diet does not exercise much direct oversight of government activities, in contrast to the U.S. congressional practice. More often than not the standing committees of the Diet are chaired by men who once held office in the very ministries they are supposed to watch over. Thus, as many Japanese scholars have pointed out, the people who are supposed to be under oversight are doing the overseeing.

Thus far, the most effective check on the government has been by the opposition parties during question periods, particularly those in the Budget Committee. Although the Budget Committee does not supervise the formulation of the national budget (which is done by the Budget Bureau of the Ministry of Finance), it has served well as a forum for questioning cabinet ministers and higher bureaucrats on all matters related to government, and these question periods receive wide press and television news coverage.[6] Other potentially useful means of Diet oversight are reports of the independent Board of Audit, which must be approved by the Diet, and the Diet's power to investigate. In fact, the oversight function of the postwar Diet is derived from this constitutional mandate to investigate. Unfortunately, this power has not been vigorously used by the Diet.

Representation. The last important function of the postwar Diet is its representation function. Diet members, like their counterparts in the United States, spend much of their time representing the interests of their constituents. They not only pressure the national bureaucracy for local pork-barrel projects but also help expedite administrative actions for their constituents and provide other services such as employment contracts and introductions to

schools. Through these efforts, Diet members humanize the relationship between the government and their constituents. These local services are also
necessary for reelection, and Diet members learn that in order to retain the
prestige and power of being part of the national legislature they must be
responsive to the needs and desires of their constituents. Being a successful
"representative" is a must for those who aspire to become political leaders, since
long years of apprenticeship in the Diet are a prerequisite for leadership positions in postwar Japan.

Factors Affecting the Functioning of the Contemporary Diet

The most important factor affecting the functioning of the Diet at present is
Japan's hegemonic party system. The conservative Liberal Democratic party has
controlled both houses of the Diet without interruption since its formation in
1955. As was noted previously, Japanese parties, including the LDP, are well
disciplined in the Diet, and no crossvoting is permitted. Under these circumstances, the LDP has dominated Diet deliberations in both plenary sessions
and committee meetings. Presiding offices of the Diet as well as committee
chairs have become agencies of the governing party rather than of the Diet or
guardians of committee autonomy (though there are some exceptions), as is
often the case in the U.S. Congress. Two additional factors should be noted.
First, the fact that there has been no alteration of power among parties has
meant that the bureaucracy's channel of information has been tied only to the
LDP, and this circumstance has had definite consequences on Diet deliberations. Second, until very recently, all opposition parties have been ideologically
opposed to the major policy stances of the LDP, leaving no room for compromise on issues.

That the relative strength of the parties in the Diet may be the most critical
factor was shown in the late 1970s. By that time, the opposition parties had increased their Diet strength enough that the difference between them and the
LDP was not great; in fact, they came to control some committees. Because of
this development, the LDP was forced to compromise on some legislative and
fiscal measures, thus somewhat approximating an ideal picture of the Diet.
Moreover, with the increased strength of the opposition parties, the Diet as a
whole was able to exert more influence on the national bureaucracy than ever
before. (This point is explored in Chapter 5.) When the LDP made a comeback
in the 1980 elections the old patterns reemerged. The experiences of the late
1970s point up the importance of political party strength and suggest that a
breakdown of the hegemonic party system may bring about a more
autonomous Diet in the future.

Another factor affecting the functioning of the Diet in postwar Japan is the
preeminent role still played by the national bureaucracy in the legislative process. The higher bureaucracy has been the center of political power ever since

Is the generally passive role of the Diet likely to change in the future? Instead of a direct answer to this question, three possible adjustments will be noted that do not require institutional changes but might serve to improve the effectiveness of the Diet. The first of these is to strengthen the Diet's oversight function. It is regrettable that, despite its constitutional preeminence, the postwar Diet has been subordinate to the executive branch of government — that is, the cabinet and the higher bureaucracy. The only way for the Diet to reverse the trend is by beginning to assert its constitutional prerogative of supervising the government. As has been noted, the activities of opposition parties during question periods have been laudable in this regard, but the Diet as a whole, including the LDP members, should do much more. It should make more vigorous use of public hearings by the standing committees as well as by special investigation committees. In particular, the Diet should more closely scrutinize the administrative implementation of the laws it has enacted — a subject to which it has paid very little attention thus far. The Diet should also exercise more "real" fiscal control over government expenditures.

The second improvement is more effective utilization of standing committees. Hans Baerwald does not think much of the grafting of the U.S. system of standing committees onto a British-style parliamentary system, but this innovative postwar arrangement should be used to the fullest extent.[9] In this era, there needs to be some kind of specialization even in a parliamentary system. To achieve this specialization some degree of permanence or institutionalization of committee assignments, continuity of committee membership, and selection of committee chairmen is necessary. These changes should help produce an esprit de corps among committee members. This could be done informally, as in the United States. At any rate, without the accumulation of expertise in the standing committees, and more importantly in committee members themselves, it will be very difficult indeed effectively to oversee the executive branch.[10]

Related to the first and second improvements, and perhaps more important to the future of the Diet, is a third change, namely, in the attitude of Diet members. The most urgent need of postwar Japan is for them to realize that they are, above all else, the people's representatives and legislators with commensurate power over the government, not simply agents of their respective parties or interests. Their orientations need to be reformed to accord with the public image of their office, as was suggested by Benjamin, Cicco, and Ori's study. Unfortunately, considering just the two major parties, a bureaucratic outlook seems to dominate much of the LDP leadership at present, and the Japan Socialist party thinks of itself as representing labor unions more than the general public. If the Diet is truly to function as the supreme organ of state power, as it was described by the 1947 Constitution, members' perceptions of their roles must be changed accordingly.

Notes

1. To cite two other examples of formal constraints on the Diet: treaties and other international agreements were ratified by the emperor with the consent of the privy council, not the Diet; and Diet sessions were limited to three months.

2. *Asahi Shimbun* [Asahi Newspaper], November 23, 1980.

3. For details see Roger Benjamin and Kan Ori, *Tradition and Change in Post-industrial Japan* (New York: Praeger, 1981).

4. For a recent example, see *Asahi Shimbun*, December 3, 1980.

5. For such a view see Hans H. Baerwald, *Japan's Parliament: An Introduction* (London: Cambridge University Press, 1974).

6. Except for the interpellation sessions, Diet activities are perfunctorily covered by the media, since the passage of bills is often a foregone conclusion under the hegemonic party system of postwar Japan. The media are also aware that substantive legislative decisions are made outside the Diet, such as during ministry-LDP negotiations, and these negotiations are well covered by both the press and television.

7. Roger Benjamin, John A. Cicco, Jr., and Kan Ori, "The 'Prestige' Level of the Japanese Higher Civil Service," *Journal of International Studies* 3, no. 2 (July 1980).

8. Baerwald, *Japan's Parliament*, p. 88.

9. Ibid., p. 101.

10. According to Baerwald (ibid., pp. 93–94), many Diet members consider standing-committee assignments as a chore, not as an opportunity to make names for themselves as policy experts, as is frequently the case in the U.S. Congress.

2

Political Parties and the Diet

Hiroshi Yamato

Changes in Relative Party Strength in the Postwar Period

The Beginning of the Two-Party System

In postwar Japanese politics 1955 was a particularly important year. During that year the conservative Liberal and Democratic parties merged to form the present Liberal Democratic party (LDP); and the left and right socialist factions, which had been split over the San Francisco peace treaty and U.S.-Japan security treaty, merged to form the present Japan Socialist party (JSP). With these changes, the continual shifting of alignments among parties that had gone on since the end of the war came to an end, ushering in an era of two-party rivalry.

The era began, however, with a very unbalanced relationship between the two parties, as the ruling LDP held an almost two-to-one majority in both houses of the Diet—299 to 154 in the House of Representatives and 120 to 68 in the House of Councillors. In the quarter century since, the LDP has maintained its practically unchallenged control of the government, and a basic pattern of conservative-progressive confrontation has emerged.

Even before the mid-1950s the Japanese economy had completely recovered its prewar strength and, propelled by waves of technological innovation, had begun modernizing Japan's industrial structure, launching Japan on the path of rapid growth. The government and the LDP took the Western democracies as their model and, with efficient decision making in the Diet made possible by the LDP's wide majority and with the cooperation of the economic sector, fostered rapid modernization of the entire society. By contrast, the opposition parties—the JSP and the Japan Communist party (JCP)—took the socialist countries as their models and criticized the modernization policy on the basis of ideology.

With regard to national security, the government and the LDP supported the expansion of conventional military strength based on the U.S.-Japan security treaty while the opposition parties advocated unarmed neutrality, asserting that Japan must rely on "the justice and faith of the peace-loving peoples of the world" as the preamble of the new Constitution stated. The intervention of U.S. troops in Vietnam aggravated these unproductive ideological debates between the ruling and opposition parties.

In 1960, with the support of the Japan Confederation of Labor (Domei) behind it, the right wing of the JSP split off and formed the Democratic Socialist party (DSP). In 1964, another party, the Clean Government party (CGP), was formed as the political arm of the religious group Soka Gakkai. The initial policies of both these two new opposition parties were anti-LDP and anti-U.S.

The conservatives (the ruling LDP) and the progressives (the opposition parties) generally were divided on the issues of Japan's modernization and national security policy. In the latter half of the 1960s, however, policies for rapid economic growth like the income-doubling plan implemented by the Ikeda cabinet (1960–1964) brought new prosperity to people at every level of society. Japan's GNP rose to surpass even that of West Germany and, in 1968, became second only to that of the United States in the free world. Meanwhile the Soviet Union and the People's Republic of China (PRC), which had both continually attacked the U.S.-Japan security treaty, began to turn toward support of the status quo and frontal attacks on the treaty gradually died down. At the same time, the conflict between the PRC and the Soviet Union, the upheaval in Czechoslovakia, and the Cultural Revolution in the PRC revealed the weaknesses and economic stagnation of the socialist countries. These events tended to undermine the persuasiveness of opposition-party arguments.

The Emergence of New Parties and Ruling Party–Opposition Party Parity

At the outset of the 1970s, previously suppressed undercurrents of change began to surface, which led to major shifts in the Japanese political structure. First were the radical changes that occurred in the international environment, particularly the "Nixon shocks" of 1971 when the United States suddenly changed its policy toward the PRC and devalued the dollar; then came the oil crisis of 1973. The Nixon shocks signified the relative weakening of the hitherto unchallenged economic and military strength of the United States, upon which Japan had grown so dependent. The oil crisis taught the lesson that the era of "unlimited cheap resources" that had made rapid economic growth possible had come to an end.

Second were the major changes that occurred in the Japanese social structure partly as a result of rapid economic growth. In the twenty years between 1955 and 1975, fully one-third of Japan's population — 37 million people — moved from rural areas into the industrial belt along the Pacific seacoast. As a result, the rural communal society that had been the foundation of Japanese conservatism and the basis for the traditional social order began to crumble, and the population that had shifted to the cities suffered from urban problems, such as inadequate public facilities for transportation, housing, and sewage. Along with these changes in the social structure, the substantial wage hikes brought about by the yearly "spring labor offensives," which began in 1955, stimulated a diversification in popular values and strengthened interest in goals beyond the economic sphere.

Thus, although Japan's GNP rose to be second highest in the free world, rapid changes in the international environment and the domestic social structure led to the emergence of new social values and an erosion of the national consensus on the priority of rapid economic growth. The effects of these new values were seen in the results of the House of Councillors elections of 1974 and the general elections of 1976 (the so-called Lockheed elections), which marked the ebbing of LDP power, the appearance of new parties, and closer parity in Diet representation between ruling and opposition parties. The number of independent—that is, uncommitted—voters grew rapidly, and, as part of this process, an offshoot of the LDP called the New Liberal Club was formed in 1976. The United Social Democratic party broke away from the JSP in 1977. Following the House of Councillors elections of 1977 and the House of Representatives elections of 1979, the differences in number of seats between the ruling and opposition parties was reduced to a mere four seats in the upper house and nine seats in the lower house.

LDP Single-Party Rule and Opposition Response

Nevertheless, the relative strength of the parties was such that, although its share of the vote fell below 50 percent for the first time in the 1967 election and dropped to the 40 percent bracket in later years, the LDP still retained an overwhelming plurality of the vote and of seats in the Diet and continued the stable single-party control that had begun in 1955. Then, quite unexpectedly, in the simultaneous elections for both houses of the Diet in 1980, the LDP recovered a margin of seats in both houses roughly equivalent to its most prosperous period of power ten years earlier.

By contrast, the strength of the main opposition party, the JSP, has consistently waned. From a peak 166 seats in the House of Representatives, won in the first election after party unification in 1958, the JSP fell into a period of chronic stagnation and has never since gained more than about half the seats held by the LDP in either house. Meanwhile, the JCP and the CGP, and most recently the DSP, vie furiously for second place among opposition parties, each holding about one-third to one-half as many seats as the JSP. The New Liberal Club and the United Social Democrats, at least in terms of Diet seats, have no appreciable influence.

In the early 1970s none of the opposition parties was strong enough to displace or even challenge LDP control alone, but, as the trend toward parity in

Diet representation gained momentum, each party began to formulate independent plans for "coalition government." These stratagems included the
CGP's "Plan for a Middle-of-the-Road Reform Coalition" and the JCP's
"General Plan for a Democratic Coalition Government" in 1973, and the JSP's
"General Plan for Popular Coalition Government" and the DSP's "Plan for Pro-
gressive Coalition for Democratic Government" in 1974. All of these, however,
were unrealistic proposals formulated within each party. Following the 1979
general elections, which brought the period of parity to its climax, the Clean
Government and Democratic Socialist parties agreed on a bipartisan "Plan for a
Middle-of-the-Road Coalition Government;" and the Socialist and Clean
Government parties in turn concluded an "Agreement on a Plan for Coalition
Government." Both plans tried to combine ideals with concrete policies and
represented somewhat more mature approaches toward coalition government
than earlier attempts. Yet the interparty relationship of the opposition parties
is quite complex: while the JSP envisioned a government of all the opposition
parties, including the JCP and the DSP, the JCP advocated a government
revolving around itself and the JSP alone, and the CGP, DSP, and right-wing
factions of the JSP envisioned a tripartite coalition of these three groups. In the
wake of the LDP's landslide victory in the 1980 elections, however, the debates
on coalition government have largely faded.

The Policy Formation Process and Political Parties

U.S.-Style Parliamentary Process and Party Response

Although the basic law governing the Diet changed after World War II from
the imperial Constitution to the present Constitution, the parliamentary-
cabinet system was maintained. Allied General Headquarters under General
Douglas MacArthur ordered the revision of the Constitution and, while pre-
serving the established nature of the Diet, which had been modeled after the
British Parliament, added constitutional ideas from the United States that gave
the Diet a more prominent position in the government structure.

As a result, the Japanese parliamentary-cabinet system both draws on British
tradition and incorporates the standing-committee system used in the U.S.
Congress. Diet members belong to one, or at most two, standing committees
where they have an opportunity to gain expertise in a specific area of government. These committees in both houses correspond to a specific government
ministry or agency; for example, the Standing Committee on the Cabinet cor-
responds to the Ministry of Posts and Telecommunications. In addition, each
party has a policy affairs research council whose divisions parallel the activities
of the standing committees.

Thus, there is a parallel structure among party committees, Diet committees, and government ministries that facilitates consideration of proposed legislation. For example, a proposed bill from the Ministry of Health and Welfare is first examined and debated (and perhaps modified) by the Social Affairs Division of the LDP's Policy Affairs Research Council (PARC) and then by the PARC Policy Deliberation Commission. If approved, it then goes to the LDP's Executive Council for final approval (or modification) as party policy. If that body approves and decides that it should be introduced as a bill, it is sent to the LDP Diet Policy Committee, which will determine how and when it will be introduced in the Diet. There the bill will usually be entrusted to the House of Representatives Standing Committee on Social and Labor Affairs. Once committee deliberations are complete and full house approval is obtained, it will be sent on to the House of Councillors, where it will go through a similar process and, if passed, become law. In this way, the system of standing committees in the Diet has a powerful impact on party capabilities and organizational structure for policy making. The Diet members who belong to the standing committees have semipermanent membership, and, because they are also members of the appropriate divisions of their parties' political affairs research councils, the system forms a network for deliberation of proposed legislation entirely different from the U.S. standing committee system.

Continued Single-Party Rule and the Bureaucracy

Except for a nine-month period during 1947–1948, Japan's conservatives have held power continuously since the end of World War II. As was already pointed out, the incumbency of the LDP alone, measured from the time when the two major conservative parties merged in 1955, is more than twenty-five years—a period of uninterrupted political control without precedent in other democratic countries.

The political structure established in 1955 based on the LDP's stable majority in the Diet allowed the ruling party to function as a "Diet within the Diet." All proposed legislation, including the budget, was automatically approved by the Diet if it gained the approval of the LDP. The LDP Executive Council is the decision-making body that passes on all new or revised laws, and the LDP Policy Affairs Research Council is the real decision-making body for the national budget.

In formulating policy, it is now general practice for the LDP to make full use of the bureaucracy, which, in turn, voluntarily gives full consideration to majority-party wishes in its actions. In this process, government officials are given ample time to study the political stance of the LDP and consult closely with party officials. Moreover, through ministers and parliamentary vice-ministers, the LDP controls appointments to the highest positions of the bureaucracy. Since criticisms made by opposition parties in the Diet are aimed at the cabinet and the government bureaucracy behind it, the LDP and the bureaucracy support each other through the medium of the cabinet. The bureaucrats' identification with the partisan interests of the ruling party, therefore, is very apparent.

In Japan's parliamentary-cabinet system, in short, the ruling party and the government are virtually the same. Moreover, through its prolonged incumbency the LDP has established increasingly strong ties not only with the bureaucracy but also with various interest groups. Thus the distance between the ruling and opposition parties is quite large. Although the LDP can mobilize the bureaucracy through the cabinet to achieve its policy aims, the other parties usually must be satisfied with opposition for the sake of opposition. Because of this pattern, there are rarely any cases like those found in Great Britain or the United States in which the ruling and opposition parties cooperate to formulate government policy.

In deference to the ruling party, the bureaucracy offers very little information to opposition parties. Practically speaking, all the policy proposals made by government agencies reflect the will of the ruling party, and the opposition only sees bills after they have been debated by the LDP. Even then the bills are accompanied by only limited information. The ruling party skillfully manipulates the bureaucracy through the cabinet, thereby shaping the overall framework of government policy. As long as the LDP maintains its dominant position it will, quite naturally, continue to command the unquestioned loyalty of the bureaucracy.

Policy-making Capabilities and Ex-Bureaucrats as Politicians

Through prior review of all government bills introduced in the Diet and through participation in the budget compilation process, the LDP Policy Affairs Research Council (PARC) now wields considerable influence over policymaking, once the exclusive preserve of the bureaucracy. Party leadership in this realm has gradually grown stronger, in large part because of the contributions of former bureaucrats who are now members of the Diet.

After World War II, occupation authorities purged the vast majority of party politicians from public office as punishment for wartime activities. To fill the vacancies thus created, Prime Minister Yoshida Shigeru brought a large number of young bureaucrats into the political arena. These were men from important ministry and agency positions, and among them were several who later became prime ministers—Ikeda Hayato, Sato Eisaku, Fukuda Takeo, and Ohira Masayoshi. By contrast, the opposition parties drew their political leadership from labor unions.

The technocrats who had gained experience in policy formation in their bureaucracies produced a competent policy-making staff within the LDP and devised organizational mechanisms through which the bureaucracy would reflect the party's wishes. These developments made possible ruling-party deliberation on draft bills, intervention in the budget compilation process (the foundation of all government policy), and leadership in the determination of foreign policy. The LDP PARC, in particular, dominates the formation of policy. The bureaucracy may attempt to promote some policies of its own by utilizing the influence of the ruling party, but this party mechanism has the ultimate power to determine whether the bills pass or die.

Thus, in order to gain passage of a desired measure, a ministry or agency consults with other government offices to line up support for the measure and simultaneously seeks the funds needed for its implementation. To obtain support, it works through Diet members who have influence in such government offices, and to obtain funds it approaches the Ministry of Finance through the LDP PARC. The latter, therefore, particularly in recent years, has acted as a coordinating body among ministries and has provided the organizational channel through which the interests of various pressure groups are brought to the attention of the government.

The Lobbying Role of Political Parties and Diet Members

A characteristic of Japanese politics is the absence of lobbyists, who play such an important role in the legislative process in the United States. Since the U.S. standing-committee system was grafted onto the Japanese parliamentary system, lobbyists might be expected to have become important in Japan too. In fact, however, it is the parties themselves that act as lobbyists in Japan. This situation results from several factors. For one, unlike U.S. parties, Japanese parties are permanent, nationwide organizations that are always available as channels for voters. For another, there are differences in the nature of pressure groups and popular attitudes toward politics. Finally, especially for the LDP, there is the manner of selecting candidates to stand for election in medium-sized constituencies. As the system operates, most LDP members of the lower house must fight the election not so much against candidates from opposing parties as against other Diet members from other factions of the LDP itself. For that reason they must try to outdo their rivals in providing specific services to their constituents, such as obtaining appropriations for local public works projects, offering consultations on taxes, and making other grass-roots-oriented efforts.

Diet members in each party maintain secretaries in their districts whose task is to attend all important ceremonial occasions and to be prepared to deal with the various petitions of constituents. These secretaries note complaints about government policies or actions and relay them to the member and his or her staff in Tokyo. For the LDP, in addition to this kind of individual casework, it is common for various interest groups to enlist the support of the LDP Policy Affairs Research Council, which has such a powerful influence on government decisions. During the years of the LDP's incumbency a number of interest groups have become associated with the LDP social welfare groups, business organizations, agriculture-related organizations, and construction firms. LDP candidates have come to rely on these groups for electoral support, and each group lobbies the party and influential Diet members on taxes, subsidies, and other issues. The LDP organizations that draw on these lobbying groups are the different divisions of the Policy Affairs Research Council. In addition to having the power to examine bills prior to their introduction in the Diet, division committees are directly involved in the compilation of the national budget, so there is a natural tendency for them to act as lobbyists.

The Functioning of the LDP Policy Affairs Research Council

Structure and Operation of PARC

PARC is composed of the chairman, vice-chairmen (six members of the House of Representatives and one of the House of Councillors), members of the Policy Deliberation Commission (a kind of executive committee composed of nineteen members from the House of Representatives and four from the House of Councillors); sixteen divisions (see below), numerous special research committees and special committees, and a secretariat. The chairman of the PARC holds, along with the secretary-general and the chairman of the Executive Council, one of the three top-ranking positions in the party hierarchy under the party president. The position is filled by the president with the approval of the Executive Council, and the vice-chairman and members of the Policy Deliberation Commission are chosen by the chairman and approved by the Executive Council. Recent prime ministers/party presidents Tanaka Kakuei, Miki Takeo, Fukuda Takeo, and Ohira Masayoshi all served as chairman of the PARC at one time or another.

All policy measures adopted by the party, including legislation proposed by the ministries, must go through the Policy Affairs Research Council. As was indicated above, its divisions correspond to ministries and to the standing committees of the Diet. At present, these divisions include cabinet affairs, local government, national defense, foreign affairs, judicial affairs, financial affairs, construction, social and labor affairs, commerce and industry, communication, transportation, agriculture and forestry, fisheries, educational affairs, science and technology, and environmental affairs. All LDP Diet members from both houses belong to either one or two of these divisions. LDP members of standing committees of the Diet are automatically members of the corresponding council division. (For example, members of the standing committees on social and labor affairs of both houses are also members of the Social Affairs Division of PARC.) The bills reviewed and debated in the council divisions are submitted to the Policy Deliberation Commission, where they are again examined.

Whether these bills will be submitted to the Diet is determined by the Executive Council, largely on the basis of its political judgment; if approved, they are sent to the Diet Policy Committee, which arranges for their introduction to the Diet.

Coordination Between Government Agencies and the PARC

There have been many cases in which the divisions of the PARC and its Policy Deliberation Commission or the Executive Council have changed the substance of government bills before their introduction to the Diet or have held them up past a Diet deadline so that they could not be introduced. Therefore, in order to assure a smooth passage through the party review and debate process, senior officials of the ministries bring their bills to the attention of concerned influential Diet members and explain the aims and contents beforehand. This is one of the distinctive techniques of Japanese politics, generally known as *nemawashi*. (This idiom literally means "tying up the roots" [of a plant before transplanting]; it is used in somewhat the same way as the English "tying up loose ends," except that it covers more than just minor details and should be done at the beginning rather than the end of a process.)

Interest groups, no less than the government bureaucracy, are skilled at working through influential LDP Diet members, the divisions of the PARC, its Policy Deliberation Commission, the Executive Council, or other party organs to achieve favorable treatment. They use exactly the same *nemawashi* techniques as the bureaucrats.

When interest groups work through powerful politicians to achieve their policy goals, these politicians will have a bill drafted through their connections with high-ranking officials of the related ministry and will take charge of the deliberation process to gain support from other party leaders and lay the groundwork for a party consensus. Actually, the government bureaucracy and interest groups do not act totally independently; they maintain continuous behind-the-scenes consultations. These involve not only the ruling party but, on occasion, opposition parties to assure a smooth settlement.

Foreign Policy Decision Making and LDP Party Organization

Since its birth in 1955, the LDP has dealt with a succession of important foreign policy issues, including the restoration of diplomatic relations with the Soviet Union, membership in the United Nations, revision of the U.S.-Japan security treaty, the question of Japanese reparations, normalization of Japanese-Korean relations, reversion of the Ryukyu and Ogasawara islands, and normalization of relations between Japan and the People's Republic of China. While supporting Japan's ties to the free world based on close friendship with the United States, the party maintains congenial relations with the Communist world in the so-called omnidirectional diplomacy.

Although foreign relations is properly the preserve of the Ministry of Foreign Affairs, in these important foreign policy decisions the ministry has consistently acted primarily as an information gatherer, leaving the policy-formation role to LDP party leadership and the debating process to the party organization. Although the cabinet is composed of LDP members, for important foreign policy decisions it requires the advice of the Foreign Affairs Division of PARC and the Special Research Committee on Foreign Affairs as well as the approval of the Executive Council.

As global interdependence has grown tighter, particularly in recent years, foreign policy not only has become a concern of national-level politics but has also begun to profoundly influence the prosperity of local industries in individual Diet members' districts. Interest groups, therefore, have started to voice their opinions on foreign policy issues through their Diet member and through government ministries and agencies. There are, for example, about six hundred thousand households of cattle-raising farmers and three hundred forty thousand households of orange growers in Japan. Although these are not large numbers, relatively speaking, the voices of these two interest groups have grown quite strong. When the members who represent them are opposed it is very difficult, for instance, to resolve the question of increased meat or orange imports. The various arms of the Policy Affairs Research Council and the Executive Council play an important role in coordinating views on such matters with delicate foreign policy issues.

The Role of LDP Factions

Although they are not part of the formal structure of the Liberal Democratic party, factions are one of the most salient features of its organization. For all practical purposes, the LDP is a federation or coalition of factions. These factions are, in fact, "parties within the party," for they are formed by groups of Diet members, led by party bosses, and raise their own political funds separately from the regular funds for the party as a whole. Diet members strive to elect members of their own factions at each election level, and, when cabinet ministers and party executives are chosen, each faction exerts pressure to have its own members appointed. The factions sometimes force changes or withdrawal of formal policy decisions made by the government or the party.

The presence of factions, in fact, makes possible a single party representing a wide spectrum of political thought. The factions are in a sense a necessary evil, given the present medium constituency system, which forces the party into intraparty fights within the same electoral district, and given the fact that electoral campaigns are largely carried on by each individual candidate's supporters organization (*koenkai*). Indeed, the factions wield extremely strong power in the election of Diet members and in the election of a party president (who automatically becomes the prime minister).

So strong was the power of factional politics that the method of having only LDP Diet members select the party president led to abuses. This method was replaced in 1975, during the period of the Miki cabinet, by a preliminary election participated in by all party members throughout the country. That election was praised as a progressive step in creating a modern party based on the masses rather than on local bosses. On the other hand, it was also strongly criticized for having simply spread factional politics to the local level, and many have argued that the preliminary election method should be abandoned.

The Roles of the Ruling and Opposition Parties in the Policy-making Process

The Ruling Party and the Policy-making Process

Cabinet policies, new laws, and the budget by which they are implemented are, as discussed above, introduced to the Diet only after review and debate by the ruling party. It is here that the Japanese character of the country's parliamentary-cabinet system is most evident. The LDP conducts prior deliberations on all policy proposals called for by the cabinet, and if that deliberation process is not complete the proposals will not be approved for introduction to the Diet. Thus, behind the government stands the ever-present restraining force of the ruling Liberal Democratic party.

Almost all legislation has a tendency to concern more than one ministry or agency, giving rise to frequent rivalries among government officials and disputes over jurisdiction. The divisions of the LDP Policy Affairs Research Council take the initiative in resolving most of these conflicts. In particular, most cases involving disputes over official jurisdiction among ministries and agencies are ultimately decided by agreement between divisions of PARC.

The ruling party's most important function in this process is to see that bills and budget proposals move smoothly through the Diet. For this purpose, both the LDP and minority parties have established Diet policy committees that focus solely on matters in the Diet. These committees are actually informal organs of the Diet, and it is within them that "political bargaining" takes place among parties concerning proposed legislation and the budget.

Nevertheless, in the twenty-five years that the LDP has held a majority in both houses of the Diet, the enactment of any law has required the formal sponsorship of that party. In some cases, important bills have been threatened by opposition-party delaying tactics, but the LDP has always coped—sometimes by making minimal changes to satisfy its opponents and sometimes, when that technique was not successful, by pushing the bills through by sheer superiority of votes.

Absence of Common Ground for Ruling Party–Opposition Party Cooperation

Because the determination of all government policy has been consistently monopolized by the LDP, no opening has remained through which the opposition parties can exercise any influence. Legislation introduced by the government has consisted entirely of bills already thoroughly reviewed and debated by the ruling party, and, though the other parties might attempt to block their passage, any concessions the opposition succeeds in extracting rarely affect a bill's substance.

Thus, instead of a system in which the opposition, along with the ruling party, functions as monitor and critic of government, the Japanese system has become one dominated by constant criticism of the ruling party by the opposition. This state is not, of course, wholly the fault of the minority parties, but it represents one of the problems inherent in Japan's unique adaptation of the parliamentary-cabinet system. The LDP is the de facto power behind the cabinet. Recognizing that fact, the opposition concentrates on criticizing the majority party in the Diet.

Another reason the opposition must focus on criticizing the ruling party derives from the fact that the relationship of the two leading parties — the LDP and the JSP — is one of ideological confrontation. The LDP supports the principles of liberalism and Western-style parliamentary democracy, and the JSP seeks to achieve a peaceful, democratic socialist revolution through the parliamentary system. Major government policies in such areas as foreign affairs, defense, education, and welfare are easily subject to ideological confrontation along these lines. Largely because of this confrontation, the possibility of agreement on policy between the two major parties is still a long way off.

Thus, the JSP can do little more than simply criticize the LDP, and, because of an obsession among minority parties with the idea that such criticism is the only effective way to appeal to the electorate, all other opposition parties follow suit, creating a solid line between themselves and the ruling party. In this way, the opposition has concentrated its efforts on criticizing the ruling party rather than on monitoring and criticizing the cabinet as well as the ruling party. This is a major characteristic of Japan's political system.

Political Change and Growing Realism
Among Opposition Parties

The party system established in 1955 was characterized by the minority parties' basic strategy of all-out opposition to all major government/LDP policies introduced in the Diet. In the early 1970s, however, as the growing strength of the opposition parties in the Diet ushered in a period of near parity in representation, subtle changes occurred in the established pattern of LDP domination of the policy-making and policy-executing process. The public began to expect that the opposition parties, too, should take direct responsibility for policy decisions, forcing those parties to turn toward more realistic goals.

In particular, the more realistic line adopted by the DSP and then the CGP concerning foreign policy and defense (two areas that have traditionally sharply divided conservatives and progressives) began gradually to change the atmosphere of Diet deliberations. This policy change, stated clearly in the agreement finally concluded by the DSP and CGP in December 1979, called the "Plan for a Middle-of-the-Road Coalition Government" ". . . continuance for the time being of the U.S.-Japan security treaty and maintenance of the Self-Defense Forces with strengthened civilian controls." This political about-face is the first step toward laying a basis for consensus on policy, at least between the moderate opposition DSP and CGP and the ruling LDP.

As a result of the close parity in Diet representation, both the ruling party and the opposition parties have begun to change their earlier strategy of confrontation to one of compromise and adjustment. Frequent meetings have begun to occur among ruling and opposition party leaders in charge of policy to coordinate the presentation of important legislation. This cooperation is unlike the previous stylized maneuvering of the Diet Policy Committee.

Japanese politics have functions almost entirely under the leadership of the LDP and the government bureaucracy, but indications are that the political trends described above will shift the center of power increasingly from the executive to the legislative branch. The bureaucracy must look more than ever before not only to the LDP but to the opposition parties as important sources for forming a consensus. The LDP itself must realize that in addition to its role as the leading party, conditions have changed to require that it act as a coordinator between the government and the opposition parties.

In the simultaneous elections for both houses held in June 1980, the LDP won an overwhelming victory, breaking the near parity in Diet representation. Nevertheless, in the interest of raising the status of the Diet, the posture of dialogue among the parties acquired during the period of Diet parity should be preserved.

The Lessons of Prewar Politics

Political parties are what make parliamentary democracy work. Not only are they indispensable to the functioning of parliamentary politics, they are in a position to determine the fate of democracy itself, as was vividly illustrated by the developments before World War II.

Japan's first political parties emerged out of the struggles surrounding the enactment of the Meiji Constitution in the 1870s and early 1880s, when the new spokesmen for people's rights and freedom fought against the power of the old feudal clan cliques. With the convening of the first imperial Diet in 1890, the parties aligned with the clan-dominated oligarchy, the Great Achievement Society, and the Nationalist Liberal party, and the opposition majority made up of the Constitutional Liberal and the Constitutional Progressive parties, took turns harassing the government. In response the second Ito cabinet discarded its previous "suprapartisan" stand and appointed the head of the Liberal party as home minister in 1896 in an attempt to compromise with the opposition parties. From that point on, party-based political power began to develop within the oligarchical government. In the functioning of the Diet, party power was an indispensable factor.

Conflict and compromise between the forces of the clan cliques and the political parties continued thereafter. In 1898 the first Okuma cabinet took office based on the Constitutional party, and in 1900 the fourth Ito cabinet, based on the Friends of Constitutional Government Association, came to power. With the appointment in 1918 of the "commoner prime minister," Hara Kei, a member of the House of Representatives and president of the Friends of Constitutional Government Association, Japan's first authentic party cabinet was formed. Party-led cabinets were continuous from 1924, when the first Kato cabinet was formed, through the collapse of the Inukai cabinet in 1932 following the May 15 incident in which Inukai was assassinated.

This was the golden age of prewar party politics, but incidents of corruption and mud-slinging among the parties, symbolized by the Ministry of War secret funds scandal (1925), the private railway scandal (1929), and the Tokyo municipal assembly scandal (1928), led to growing distrust of party politics among the public. Popular disillusionment with party politics, coupled with the rise of the army, was a major factor that led the country toward war. The result of the decay of party politics was that the parties dissolved themselves in 1940 under the rise of ultranationalism in order to establish a single "suprapartisan" party called the Imperial Rule Assistance Association. The proletarian parties were also responsible for this trend. The Social Mass party, formed in 1932 as the only proletarian party, won thirty-seven seats in the 1937 lower house elections, yet because of severe internal strife, it too eventually succumbed to the tide of party dissolution. The Communist party, founded in 1921, on the other hand, suffered massive arrests of its members in 1928–1929 and was already on its way to extinction. These developments were entirely unprecedented in the history of Japanese constitutional government, and with the Tojo cabinet in October 1941 there began a period of "collaboration politics" under the Imperial Rule Assistance Association without political parties. Although the Meiji Constitution and the imperial Diet continued, when the parties ceased to exist, parliamentary politics was reduced to a mere shadow.

As we have seen, the lessons of this experience of party politics led to the establishment after the war of strong political institutions based on parliamentary democracy; party independence that would help democracy to function was assured.

Japanese parliamentary democracy has thus far avoided the perilous course taken by prewar politics and has achieved growing maturity and sophistication. Today, however, the most compelling goal of both the ruling and opposition parties is to create modern party organizations with wider grass-roots support.

3

Diet Structure, Organization, and Procedures

Koichi Kishimoto

Introduction

The Japanese political system is based on a division of power among the three branches of government—administrative, legislative, and judicial. Under the present Constitution, promulgated in 1947, the Diet consists of the House of Representatives and the House of Councillors, both popularly elected, and is "the highest organ of state power" and "the sole law-making organ of the State." This is a considerable departure from the prewar Diet defined in the imperial Japanese Constitution (Meiji Constitution) of 1889. Then, the imperial Diet could only "assist" in the legislative process, over which the emperor held supreme authority. Now, under normal circumstances, a bill passed by the two houses becomes law, and the emperor only performs the formality of announcing the law with the advice and approval of the cabinet. The Diet is the sole legislative organ, and its powers are not restricted in the same way that the U.S. Congress is restricted by the veto power of the president. (There are, however, occasions when the Japanese Supreme Court may declare certain Diet decisions unconstitutional.)

The parliamentary-cabinet system of Japanese politics requires the Diet to designate the prime minister from among its members. At the same time, the House of Representatives is empowered to pass a resolution of nonconfidence in the cabinet or reject a confidence resolution. In either case, the cabinet must resign en masse or the House of Representatives must be dissolved within ten days. Unlike the U.S. system, the Japanese bicameral system is dominated by the House of Representatives. Nevertheless, there do exist checks and balances between the legislative and administrative branches in Japan like those between the president and the Congress in the United States. The majority party in the Diet, especially in the House of Representatives, forms a cabinet by selecting the prime minister, but that cabinet may be forced to resign or the House of Representatives be dissolved through a nonconfidence resolution.

According to the postwar Constitution, Diet functions include, among others, the right to propose constitutional amendments, to vote on the budget, to ratify treaties, and to establish an impeachment court. Other powers vested in the Diet are considering petitions, proclaiming a state of emergency, approving the dispatch of self-defense forces for defensive actions, considering the budget for public corporations (such as the Japan Broadcasting System and Japanese National Railways), and approving appointments of members of the National Personnel Authority, the National Public Safety Commission, the Central Elections Administration Committee, and the policy board of the Bank of Japan and appointments of many other civil servants. Beside the general functions of the Diet as a whole, each house is given autonomous powers to select its officers, set its house rules, and conduct investigations into government affairs.

The Bicameral Diet and the Functions of the Two Houses

The Japanese parliament is a bicameral system, consisting of the House of Representatives and the House of Councillors. Both houses are composed of "elected members, representative of all the people."

With the abolition of the former aristocratic hierarchy in 1946, a problem arose as to the nature of the second house. The House of Peers that existed under the Meiji Constitution was to be replaced; therefore, a British-style upper house did not offer a solution. Nor could the U.S. Senate be used as a prototype because Japan is not a federal state like the United States. Nevertheless, the second house, also composed of elected members, needed to be distinguished from the House of Representatives.

In the end, the postwar Constitution differentiated the two by setting the term of office of members of the House of Councillors at six years (with half being elected every three years) and that of members of the House of Representatives at four years, unless terminated earlier by legislation. (In reality most general elections for the House of Representatives have followed a dissolution.) On the other hand, the House of Representatives was given a predominant position over the House of Councillors, being accorded final authority to designate the prime minister and to approve treaties and the budget. When an emergency arises while the House of Representatives is dissolved, the House of Councillors may be convoked in an "emergency session." Thus the upper house can be a stabilizing force since its longer term of office is not threatened by a dissolution, and it can deal with government matters in longer and broader perspective.

Other differences between the two houses include the number and qualification of members and the size of electoral districts — all of which are governed by election laws. Currently, the House of Representatives has 511 members elected from 130 districts, and each district elects 3 to 5 members except for 1 district that elects only 1 member. Candidates must be at least twenty-five years old to qualify for running. At present, the House of Councillors has 252 members, of which 152 are elected from the 47 local constituencies (prefectures), each selecting 2 to 8 members, and 100 are elected from the nation at large. Candidates must be at least thirty years of age. (Japan has universal suffrage for all citizens over twenty years of age.)

During the postwar period the number of seats in the House of Councillors has increased by only 2 to accommodate the reversion of Okinawa to Japanese control, but seats in the House of Representatives have increased by 45. In addition to 5 seats added upon reversion of Okinawa, the lower house was enlarged twice (in 1964 and in 1975) to reflect increases in the voting-age population in urban areas. The imbalance (primarily between urban and rural districts) in the ratio of voters to members elected has always posed a problem in defining electoral districts for the House of Representatives and the local constituencies of the House of Councillors. This is the "weight of one vote" issue.

Aside from a handful of independents, candidates usually center their election campaigns around their political party affiliation, which plays a major role in their being elected to the Diet. Political party strength in the 94th session of the Diet (as of December 1980) is indicated in Table 3.1. The Liberal Democratic party (LDP) holds a majority of the seats in both houses, followed by the Japan Socialist party (JSP), which has less than 40 percent of the LDP seats.

Each house is independently organized and selects its own presiding officers, termed the speaker and vice-speaker in the House of Representatives and the president and vice-president in the House of Councillors. Each house also has a similar structure centered around standing committees, and each has its own secretariat and legislative bureau. In addition, the two houses may jointly establish a Judge Impeachment Court. The National Diet Library serves the needs of both houses and is also used by the administrative and judicial branches and the general public.

The presiding officers of the two houses are elected within each house from among its members. Under the Meiji Constitution, the House of Representatives presented three candidates each for the position of speaker and vice-speaker to the emperor, who made the final choice. In the House of Peers, the emperor made the appointments directly. The current Constitution provides that any member elected by a majority assumes the post of presiding officer.

The function of the presiding officer of each house is to maintain order in the house, fix the order of business, represent the house, and supervise its administration. Presiding officers may also vote on an issue in the case of a tie. The vice-speaker and vice-president act as presiding officers in case of temporary absence or vacancy.

In order to "smoothly and impartially" carry out the functions described above, the neutrality of the speaker and president is considered important.

Table 3.1

Political Party Strength in the 94th Diet
(As of December 1980)

Party	Number of Members House of Representatives	Number of Members House of Councillors
Liberal Democratic party	286	135
Japan Socialist party	106	47
Clean Government party	34	27
Democratic Socialist party	33	11
Japan Communist party	29	12
New Liberal Club	11	--
Shinsei Club	--	7
United Democratic Socialist party	3	--
Niin Club	--	4
Independents	8	6
Vacancy	1	3
TOTAL	511	252

Because of this concern, it has been proposed that the presiding officers be required to give up their party affiliations. In recent years many presiding and deputy presiding officers voluntarily left their parties to become independent after having been elected. Thus the presiding officer is not the leader of the majority party in each house. In exercising their authority, presiding officers are guided by the results of consultations between political parties and the two house management committees, which act as advisory bodies in each house.

When the ruling and opposition parties are in conflict, however, and compromise seems impossible, the speaker or president may act independently. In case of extreme conflict, Diet sessions have sometimes become chaotic and even violent, and there were two occasions when a presiding officer decided to call in police from outside to maintain order. (Ordinarily, order is maintained by regular Diet security guards within each House.) There has been only one instance in each house when the speaker and president actually exercised their power and changed the agenda during a plenary session. Major foreign policy, defense, and security issues (such as revision of the U.S.-Japan security treaty in 1960 and normalization of Japanese-Korean relations in 1965) have tended to fuel the conflict between the ruling and opposition parties. With the recent narrowing of the gap in seats between the parties, however, and the growth of a more realistic approach to consultations, violent disagreements have practically disappeared. Customarily, presiding officers do not vote, even though they are elected members of the Diet; in fact, only once has a presiding officer's vote been needed in order to break a tie. But with the reduced gap between the ruling and opposition parties, they may be required to cast a deciding vote more often.

Other officers in each house are the presidents pro tempore, who serve as acting presiding officers until the speaker/president and vice-speaker/vice-president are elected; the chairmen of standing committees, who are the core of the Diet's legislative activities; and the secretaries general, who head each house's secretariat and also serve as house parliamentarians. Except for the latter, who are not members of the Diet, these officers are elected from the membership of each House during a plenary meeting. Although the leaders of each house are chosen by formal votes at a plenary meeting, the candidates are actually selected beforehand by party leaders. In the case of the LDP and, to a lesser extent, the JSP, the choices are usually subject to intraparty factional struggle.

The House of Representatives has eighteen standing committees and the House of Councillors sixteen (listed in Table 3.2). All of these are governed by the Diet Law. This is the basic law that established the postwar Diet and governs its organization and procedures. It dates from March 1947—even before the postwar Constitution came into effect. In the House of Representatives, the Committee on Science and Technology and the Committee on Environment were newly formed in September 1980 and have no counterparts in the House of Councillors.

Except for the four committees on budget, audit, house management, and discipline, the committees have been established to correspond to the various ministries of the cabinet. For example, the Committee on Foreign Affairs has jurisdiction over activities covered by the Ministry of Foreign Affairs, and the Committee on Commerce and Industry covers the Ministry of International Trade and Industry, the Economic Planning Agency, and the Fair Trade Commission. The Committee on the Cabinet has the widest jurisdiction, covering not only the cabinet Secretariat and the prime minister's office but also several important agencies that do not have ministerial status, such as the Defense Agency, the Administrative Management Agency, the National Personnel Authority, the Imperial Household Agency, and the Hokkaido Development Agency.

Members of standing committees are appointed by the speaker or president as recommended by the parties and apportioned according to each party's representation in the house. Every Diet member must serve on at least one standing committee. The prime minister, ministers, and parliamentary vice-

Table 3.2

Standing Committees of the Diet and Their Sizes

Committee	Number of Members	
	House of Representatives	House of Councillors
Cabinet	30	20
Local Administration	30	20
Justice	30	20
Foreign Affairs	30	20
Finance	40	25
Education	30	20
Social and Labor Affairs	40	21
Agriculture, Forestry, and Fisheries	40	25
Commerce and Industry	40	21
Transport	30	20
Communication	30	20
Construction	30	20
Science and Technology	25	--
Environment	25	--
Budget	50	45
Audit	25	30
House Management	25	25
Discipline	20	10

minister, however, resign from their standing committees when they take those positions. In the House of Representatives, the eighteen standing committees alone require a total of about 570 members so that, in order to fill all these committees and the several special committees as well, some representatives must serve on up to three committees. The same is true with members of the House of Councillors and its committees.

Because of party business, party leaders are too busy to participate in daily committee activities, so most of them belong to the Committee on Discipline, which seldom meets under normal circumstances. Thus, the committee has been nicknamed the "party chiefs committee." It has under its charge maintenance of internal discipline and punishment of members for disorderly conduct, and it considers questions of membership qualifications. The Committee on Budget considers the budget, and the Committee on Audit has jurisdiction over the settlement of accounts and approval of contingency fund disbursements. (A detailed discussion of these two committees can be found in Chapter 5.)

Of those with specialized functions, the committees on house management are by far the busiest. They are basically responsible for the overall management of the business of each house, and they advise the presiding officer. Their most important functions are to decide on the convocation of plenary meetings where the Diet exercises its power as a legislature and to determine the daily order of business. The presiding officers and their deputies usually attend the meetings of the committees when such decisions are to be made. The committees on house management also have jurisdiction over the interpretation of the Diet Law and the house rules governing each house, the budget of each house, and the status and treatment of, and protocol and foreign visits by, Diet members. The number of directors (*aiji*) and proportional party representation on standing committees are also decided by these committees.

In addition to standing committees, each house may appoint special or ad hoc committees to examine issues that are deemed especially important by that house during a Diet session. Normally, seven or eight special committees are appointed, and their jurisdiction and membership are determined at the time of establishment. Members are appointed to special committees by the presiding officer in the same manner as to standing committees, but the chairmen of special committees are elected by committee members from among themselves. Most of the special committees are, in fact, regularly reappointed with every Diet session—for example, the special committees on electoral system reform, Okinawa and the northern islands, or price problems. Recently, in the House of Representatives, one special committee was discontinued—the one that was investigating the Lockheed scandal; and one was established—the Special Committee on Security Issues.

The imperial Diet under the Meiji Constitution had only five standing committees: budget, audit, petitions, discipline, and proposals. A special committee was appointed for each bill being considered. Since there were no committees on house management, the order of business and motions for plenary meetings, as well as protocol affairs and the function of advising the presiding officers, were all discussed at party negotiating conferences. These were held in the presence of the speaker, vice speaker, president, vice-president, and selected Diet members serving as party officers. Whatever decisions were arrived at in these negotiating sessions became guiding principles followed by all.

In the present Diet system, the committees on house management have taken over these functions, but the custom still remains in part: when a newly elected house of representatives first meets and before the standing committees have been appointed, the secretary general and representatives from each party (usually reelected members of the former committee on house management) meet to discuss the management of house affairs in a party negotiating conference. In the House of Councillors, this function is carried out by the half of the House Management Committee not up for election.

The imperial Diet and the present Diet also differ in the locus of the dominant forum of legislative activity — in the Diet as a whole in a plenary meeting, as in the imperial Diet, or in the committees, as at present. This difference is reflected in the organization of the secretaries of each house. The organization and number of people working in the secretariats was vastly augmented when the Diet assumed its current role of highest organ of state power and sole lawmaking body. Besides an independent secretariat under the direction of a secretary general who is an officer of that house (but not a member of the Diet), each house also has its own legislative bureau. The House of Representatives' Secretariat has over sixteen hundred employees in its legislative bureau. Of this staff, each house has approximately seventy qualified specialists (*sennon-in*) assigned to its standing committees.

The secretariats and legislative bureaus assist the presiding officers, chairmen of standing committees, and individual Diet members, but their functions are not given much weight because the cabinet and ruling party are assisted mainly by the vast organization and staff of the government bureaucracy, and most legislative proposals are government initiated. The National Diet Library also has the function of aiding the Diet, but its capacity is limited with a staff of less than nine hundred. Individual Diet members are allowed a meager staff of only two assistants each. All in all, it must be said that the Diet's supporting staff compares unfavorably to that of the U.S. Congress.

Organization of the Two Houses and Political Parties

The basic structure and functions of the two houses were described in the previous section. The organization of the houses is what permits a smooth functioning of the bicameral system. That organization is not specified by law but is a product of custom and has become a prerequisite to initiating Diet activities. The Diet usually decides on its organization upon convocation; the decision is heavily influenced by the political parties. The parties play a large role in the legislative and administrative process because the Japanese political system is a parliamentary one based on political parties.

The Diet is not run on a full-year basis. The Constitution provides for three types of sessions: an annual ordinary session, extraordinary sessions, and special sessions. The annual ordinary session is usually convened in December for a term of 150 days (the length is set by the Diet Law). An extraordinary session may be convened as occasion demands, and in most years, two or three such sessions are held. According to the Constitution, the cabinet may convoke extraordinary sessions as needed and must do so upon the written request of one-fourth or more of the membership of either house. In the postwar period, there have been twenty-four such requests submitted to the cabinet. A special session is the session that must be convened within thirty days of elections for the House of Representatives that follow dissolution of that house.

For any type of session, in practice, the cabinet has the power to decide when to convene the Diet. The Constitution gives the emperor the formal role of convening the Diet "with the advice and approval of the Cabinet." The session will begin on the date designated in the emperor's convocation note, but the length of extraordinary or special sessions and of their extensions is determined by a concurrent vote of both houses. Compared to the Meiji Constitution, which gave the emperor the power to open and close Diet sessions at will, the present Constitution gives more autonomy to the Diet. To illustrate this point, in a plenary meeting on the opening day of a special session, the House of Representatives will conduct the following business relative to the organization of the House: (1) election of the speaker and vice-speaker; (2) seating of all members; (3) determination of the length of the session; (4) election of chairpersons of standing committees; and (5) appointment of special committees.

Since Japan has a parliamentary system, the prime minister is elected at the special session. Constitutionally this procedure has priority over other matters. For that reason, Diet members move to the election of the prime minister following the election of standing-committee chairmen, normally after election of the chairman of the Committee on House Management.

Just as in special sessions, in ordinary and extraordinary sessions the order of business puts priority on filling vacancies in the organization of the Diet. This function may also occur during the middle of a session and whenever a presiding officer or deputy presiding officer has been charged with no confidence or when the chairman of a standing committee is to be replaced.

Leadership positions and the length of a session are normally decided by voting in a plenary meeting, but in fact that vote merely ratifies decisions that have been determined beforehand. Representatives of each party meet together with the secretary general of the house in a party negotiating conference before the session begins. They discuss how each party will be represented in leadership posts, the length of the session, and the seating of members. Paralleling these negotiations, both the ruling and the opposition party leaders select their candidates for Diet leadership positions. Needless to say, selection of a party leader is given top priority if the post is vacant (this was the case in the Liberal Democratic party following the general elections of December 1976 and June 1980).

Party negotiating conferences have set a pattern in the past few years of selecting members of the ruling LDP as presiding officers in each house and members of the second largest party, the Japan Socialist party, as deputy presiding officers. This custom of dividing these two positions between the first and second largest parties was established in the late 1970s when the balance between the LDP and the opposition came close to equilibrium. In the past, however, when the LDP had an absolute majority, both positions were usually filled exclusively by LDP members. This pattern was broken only once when the opposition parties successfully formed a coalition and their candidate won the speakership.

Political party rivalry heavily influences negotiations on the term of Diet sessions as well as on who will assume which Diet post. Except for ordinary sessions, where term is specified by the Diet Law, the length of Diet sessions is determined by a concurrent vote of both houses. Moreover, the term of a session may be extended whenever both houses agree by concurrent vote. An ordinary session may be extended once and extraordinary and special sessions twice. In case the two houses fail to agree on the term of an extension, or if the House of Councillors does not reach a decision, the decision of the House of Representatives prevails. The lower house is given supremacy in this matter because the term of a session is often a source of major dispute between the ruling party, which wants to deliberate on all proposed bills, and opposition parties, which want to prevent most bills from being taken up. In return for this power vested in one house, the number of times a session may be extended has now been limited.

Because the length of a session affects the number of bills that can be deliberated on, debate on the matter has often been quite heated. Before the number of times a session could be extended was limited, the 13th Diet (December 1951–July 1952) experienced a near riot over the length of the session, which ended up with five extensions and a term totaling 235 days. The longest session recorded was the 71st special session (December 1972–September 1973), which was extended twice and lasted 280 days.

In the turmoil over deciding on the term of a session or an extension there have been many cases when the speaker became entangled in interparty competition and was forced to resign. As was mentioned above, neutrality is valued in a presiding officer. The party leadership role is played on the floor by members of the executive councils of each party. In the case of the LDP, the principal party leaders are the party president (who becomes the prime minister), the party secretary general, the chairman of the Executive Council, and the chairman of the Policy Affairs Research Council. For the Japan Socialist party, the Clean Government party, and the Democratic Socialist party, the top party leaders are the party chairmen, the secretaries general, and the chairmen of the policy boards. Party leadership in the Diet is exercised through the chairman of each party's Diet policy committee under the direction of these party leaders.

In most cases, Diet presiding officers are senior members of the ruling LDP, often chosen by the LDP president in consultation with top party leaders.

Presiding officers, therefore, are not entirely independent of LDP influences, although it is now becoming an accepted practice for them to resign from party membership. When a presiding officer does maintain LDP membership and, under party influence, tries to extend a session in favor of the LDP, that officer is considered to have violated the custom of neutrality and may be forced to resign. The selection of presiding officers and the value placed on their neutrality, especially in the House of Representatives, is complicated by the medium-sized electoral district system, which makes continued party affiliation important for reelection. Those speakers who maintain too close ties with the LDP, however, have often proved too weak vis-à-vis the party leader (the prime minister). Some led the House in a clearly pro-LDP direction and, as a result, were forced to resign over issues other than the extension of a session. The LDP candidates are all selected by senior party leaders and do not resign their party membership. They, therefore, maintain close working ties with the party and carry out their roles under the leadership of the chairman of LDP's Diet Policy Committee. The party-based parliamentary system thus encourages LDP Diet members to work for the passage of as many government-proposed bills as possible.

Nevertheless, every chairman of a standing committee is also obliged to consult closely with the directors (*aiji*) of the committee, just as the presiding officer of a house must respect the counsel of the Committee on House Management. The number of directors for each committee is determined by the Committee on House Management after each election. Presently, in the House of Representatives, the committees on budget and house management each have nine directors, and the other committees have five to eight, depending on their size. Directorships are distributed among the parties in rough proportion to their strength in the House. This practice helps to smooth out party differences by giving the opposition parties a greater voice. It does not, however, prevent sharp disputes, especially in those committees where debates are televised—that is, the committees on the budget, foreign affairs, and the cabinet (dealing with defense issues) and the special committees concerned with public utility rates and social security payments.

In the past, profound differences between the LDP and the opposition parties in the special committees considering renewal of the U.S.-Japan security treaty, Japanese-Korean relations, and the return of Okinawa led to frequent motions for dismissal of the chairmen of these committees, along with motions of nonconfidence in the speaker, vice-speaker, and cabinet ministers. In most cases, however, the motions were ignored and the chairmen retained their positions.

Since the Japanese political system is run by political parties, the Diet follows the lead of the parties, however much the Constitution may call it "the highest organ of state power" and a legislative counterpart to the administrative branch. The position of the Diet is further weakened by the parliamentary-cabinet system, which tends to make the Diet subordinate to the cabinet. The majority party leader assumes the premiership and at the same time selects the presiding and deputy presiding officers and chairmen of standing committees. This custom has been at the root of the "strong prime minister" and "weak speaker" characterization of the system. The much larger staff working for the administrative branch (the bureaucracy) than for the legislative branch reinforces the subordinate status of the Diet.

Some changes have occurred, however, in recent years as the balance of power between the LDP and the opposition approached parity. With the LDP influence gradually diminishing, the speaker of the House of Representatives and the president of the House of Councillors have become more independent of the prime minister and have begun to consider the views of the opposition in operating the Diet. Some observers go so far as to say that the LDP leadership is losing its hold on the party and that a new situation characterized by a "strong speaker" and "strong Diet" is gradually emerging. It is clear, however, that the power of the administrative branch, including the bureaucracy, is still far greater than that of the Diet. This is true in the passage of a bill, the budget, or a treaty.

Legislative Procedures
and the Constitutional Amendment Initiative

The Diet is the only legislative body, and, with a few exceptions, laws are enacted upon approval by both houses. Moreover, such laws cannot be vetoed by any other body. In practice, the bureaucracy plays a significant part in the legislative process, and the influence of political parties is also quite extensive.

The first step in the legislative process is submitting a bill. A bill may be introduced by a member of either house (Diet-originated bills) or by the cabinet (government-originated bills). To introduce a bill, a Diet member must secure the support of at least twenty members in the House of Representatives or at least ten members in the House of Councillors. When the bill affects the budget, however, this requirement is increased to fifty or more in the House of Representatives and twenty or more in the House of Councillors. Although the name of the supporting political party does not appear on it, a bill can only be submitted after receiving approval from the executive council of a party and under the guidance of that party's Diet policy committee. No bills are introduced without party involvement, and the names of responsible party leaders are always included in the list of supporters.

Some of the more specialized bills submitted by a standing or special committee are negotiated among political parties through their members on the committee and are jointly endorsed by all the parties involved. Such bills are called "committee bills," are introduced by the chairman of the committee, and require no supporting members. The drafting of bills is assisted by the legislative bureau of each house.

Government bills originate in the ministries and agencies of the administrative branch. They are submitted to the cabinet Legislation Bureau for examination and clearance and then to the cabinet for approval. Upon passing these stages, a bill is presented by the prime minister to the House of Representatives or the House of Councillors, as is deemed appropriate. In considering a bill the cabinet will seek the advice of the LDP Policy Affairs Research Council, obtain the support of the LDP Executive Council, and follow the guidance of the LDP Diet Policy Committee on when and how to introduce the bill in the Diet. Although most bills originate within the bureaucracy, preliminary negotiation and approval by the LDP is a necessary step in the process — so much so that each ministry maintains a liaison office within the Diet Building to keep in touch with the LDP.

Since the Diet is "the sole law-making organ," it would be desirable for Diet members actively to participate in introducing legislation. In fact, twice as many measures are submitted by the government as by Diet members, and the chances of government bills' passage are much higher because they have a reputation of having weight and substance. Table 3.3 lists the number of bills submitted during a five-year period by the government and by members of the House of Representatives and the House of Councillors, and the number that passed. Including budget measures and treaties, which all originate in the cabinet, the government sponsored an average of 104 bills per Diet session, whereas Diet members introduced an average of only 51. An average of 80 percent of the government-sponsored measures passed, but an average of only 18 percent of the member-sponsored bills did.

When a bill has been introduced, the presiding officer refers it to the appropriate committee for examination. For example, a bill concerning defense matters will be referred to the Committee on the Cabinet (whose jurisdiction includes the Defense Agency), and a bill affecting the national pension system will go to the Committee on Social and Labor Affairs. If a bill concerns a subject that does not come under the jurisdiction of any standing committee, a special committee may be appointed for the purpose of examining that bill.

All bills must be considered by the committees assigned. The present Diet Law mandates a committee-centered legislative procedure where examination of bills by committees is an important step. The imperial Diet had a system of three readings. The first reading took place at a plenary meeting where the bill was introduced and explained, examined in a question-and-answer session, and then referred to a special committee. The chairman reported the results of the committee's examination back to the floor, upon which a vote was taken as to whether the bill should be given a second reading. If the vote was positive, each item of the bill was taken up and voted on individually. The third reading considered the bill in its entirety, and a final decision was made.

Even now, when the House Management Committee deems it especially necessary, the house may ask the sponsors of a bill to explain it at a plenary meeting before it is referred to a committee or while it is being examined by the

Table 3.3

Bills Submitted and Passed, 1975-1980 (Excluding Those Carried Over From the Previous Session)

Type of Bill	Diet Session				
	70th Sess. 12/75-5/76	80th Sess. 12/76-6/77	84th Sess. 12/77-6/78	87th Sess. 12/78-6/79	91st Sess. 12/79-5/80
BUDGET MEASURES					
Number submitted	6	9	6	3	6
Number passed	6	9	6	3	6
TREATIES					
Number submitted	12	18	17	16	41
Number passed	10	12	15	3	42
GOVERNMENT-SPONSORED BILLS					
Number submitted	69	76	82	68	92
Number passed	58	65	74	42	66
Percentage passed	84%	86%	90%	62%	72%
Number amended of those passed	12	16	16	3	15
Percentage amended of those passed	21%	25%	22%	7%	23%
MEMBER-SPONSORED BILLS IN THE HOUSE OF REPRESENTATIVES					
Number submitted	24	52	33	36	58
Number passed	10	11	10	7	9
MEMBER-SPONSORED BILLS IN HOUSE OF COUNCILLORS					
Number submitted	20	19	14	11	17
Number passed	0	0	1	0	1

committee. This practice is used for bills of particular importance and is not regarded as interfering with the committee-centered process. The hearing, however, may sometimes be delayed as a way of keeping a controversial bill from being considered.

A committee bill usually skips the process of committee examination. If necessary, each house may call for an interim report from any committee on a pending bill. In case of urgent need, each house may decide to proceed with the deliberation of a bill for which an interim report has not been made, at a plenary meeting, although this prerogative has rarely been exercised.

Committee meetings are closed in principle to all except Diet members. Normally, however, the chair, which controls access, will make an exception for the media and may permit others to attend as well. The committee first invites a sponsor of the bill—a Diet member or minister, depending on the bill's origin—to explain the reasons for its introduction. Then the bill undergoes detailed examination through questioning; some important bills require question-and-answer sessions lasting forty or more hours. In the case of government bills, a bureaucrat from the sponsoring ministry may respond to questions on behalf of the minister. This official would normally be at the bureau director-general or director level. This is yet another way in which government-originated bills are strengthened.

In contrast to the present system, the imperial Diet gave priority to bills submitted by the government, and the cabinet could amend or withdraw a bill without consulting the Diet. Such is no longer the case. Instead, a bill now depends heavily on the support of the LDP and on the results of negotiations between the LDP and the opposition parties. Whereas previously the cabinet could manipulate bills at its will, now the bureaucrats and government representatives must actively engage in spade work (*nemawashi*) to win the support of the Diet policy committees of the various parties as well as of the chairman and directors of house committees. Careful prearrangement of the date and manner of introduction is part of the strategy to secure the passage of a bill. It should be pointed out that members of standing committees and bureaucrats in the corresponding ministries maintain quite close relations.

Public hearings, prohibited during the Meiji era, may be held, as may hearings in local districts. A committee may also hold a joint meeting with other committees to examine a bill. This event epitomizes the committee-centered legislative procedure. For example, a set of bills concerning pollution issues was assigned to a Special Committee on Industrial Pollution in the House of Representatives and was jointly studied by the standing committees on Local Administration, Judicial Affairs, Social and Labor Affairs, Agriculture, Commerce and Industry, Transportation, and Construction.

After the question-and-answer session, a bill may be amended before voting or voted on directly. As indicated in Table 3.3, about 20 percent of the bills that are passed are amended. Most of the amendments, however, are minor adjustments—for example, a change in the date of implementation because of a delay in passing a bill—and do not imply that the Diet is exercising any particular strength.

After committee examination, a bill is reported back to the floor of the house for voting. At least one-third of all the members must be present to constitute a quorum, and a bill requires a majority vote of those present for passage. If the vote is a tie, the presiding officer has the deciding vote. Bills may be either passed, amended and passed, or rejected in voting. Some bills may be carried over to the following session.

During a regular session the House of Representatives convenes at two in the afternoon on Tuesdays, Thursdays, and Fridays and the House of Councillors at ten in the morning on Mondays, Wednesdays, and Fridays. A meeting may not take place on certain designated days; it may be called for a different day, especially toward the end of the session. In the latter case, the Committee on House Management, or, occasionally, the presiding officer, determines the day. The time of convening may also be altered. Quite often a meeting will be called toward evening when an important bill is to be considered. There have been cases when such a meeting lasted the entire night and into the following day.

The order of business for the day is also determined by the Committee on House Management. The order of the day is published in the Official Bulletin of the House of Representatives/House of Councillors, as well as in the Official Gazette, and distributed to all the members. Matters to be discussed are usually published at the same time and are taken up at the meeting in the order in which they appear in the bulletin. A bill concerning the budget or other urgent matters may be brought up and debated immediately following the committee examination with the unanimous consent of those present.

The proceedings at a meeting begin with an announcement by the presiding officer that a bill or measure is up for discussion. The chair of the appropriate committee then reports on the committee's deliberations and their result. Members may then ask questions about the bill, but this step is hardly ever followed. Usually, the bill is put to debate and a vote is taken without questioning. The presiding officer may call for a voice vote with each member declaring his or her preference or a "sitting-standing" vote with those in favor rising from their seats or a vote by ballot.

In Japan, there is no concept of independent voting. All members vote according to the decision of their party, so the outcome is rarely different from that of the committee meeting. In only one instance has the vote of a committee been changed—during the period of near-equal balance between the ruling and opposition parties. A decision made by a committee with weak LDP representation was overturned by the LDP majority on the floor. When a member is strongly opposed to a party's stance, the only recourse is to be absent in order to avoid voting. This practice led to an unexpected result in May 1980 when the factional rivalry within the LDP kept many members away from the meeting and the opposition parties were able to win a vote of nonconfidence in the cabinet; subsequently the House of Representatives was dissolved.

Why the concept of independent voting has not developed in Japan will be discussed in more detail later, but, simply put, political party influence is very strong in the Japanese political system, starting with elections themselves. In fact, the parties are so powerful that the clash between the majority party, pushing to get a bill passed by the Diet, and the opposition, trying to prevent its passage at any cost, has even resulted in physical violence in extreme cases. During the late 1970s, when there was nearly an equal balance of party strength, the two sides became more even-tempered. But in the period immediately following the war, the Diet was often called riotous and violent. In this turmoil, caused by the conflicting interests of different political parties, it was not surprising to find difficulties arising in the legislative process between the LDP-dominated House of Representatives and the House of Councillors, which (during the 1950s) had many independent members, including those belonging to the Green Breeze Society (Ryoufukai), a conservative independents' coalition.

The Constitution gives the House of Representatives the power to override upper house decisions. It states that a bill passed by the lower house upon which the House of Councillors makes a different decision will become law when passed a second time by the lower house with a two-thirds majority of those present. In addition, failure by the House of Councillors to take final action within sixty days after receipt of a lower house–passed bill (time in recess excepted) may be determined by the House of Representatives to constitute a rejection of the bill, thus allowing the lower house to override with a second vote.

These two provisions, however, do not prevent the House of Representatives from calling for a meeting of a joint committee of both houses in order to reach a compromise. (Joint committees are composed of ten members of each house and are appointed at that time.) Such conference committee meetings have been held twenty-eight times so far. The first was called in February 1948 to resolve the conflict between the two houses on the selection of the prime minister. Another was held in August 1953 on the proposal to amend the Public Office Election Law. Bills have been referred back to the House of Representatives to override an upper house decision twenty-eight times, only once due to the failure of the House of Councillors to act within sixty days. Again, the last time this power was exercised was in 1957.

With the merger of the two conservative parties (in 1955) and the two socialist parties (in 1953) to form the LDP and the JSP respectively, the multiparty system began to center around these two large parties, and a similar party configuration appeared in both houses. The LDP gained an absolute majority in the upper as well as the lower house, and thus there were few differences in the decisions made by the two houses. Consequently, conference committee meetings were no longer needed, and bills were no longer referred back to the House of Representatives from the House of Councillors. Moreover, during the recent period of near equilibrium in party strength in the lower house, the LDP's power to override the upper house was considerably weakened.

Before closing this section, a brief note on the process of amending the Constitution is in order. It is an issue of considerable interest at the moment.

The present Constitution was written in 1946 under the influence of the occupation. It replaced the Meiji Constitution in its entirety, but was promulgated in accordance with the provisions of that Constitution (Article 73). The emperor summoned the imperial Diet to a meeting and presented the proposal for the new constitution. After being examined by a special committee, the proposal was brought to the floor and passed in the presence of a quorum of both houses, by an absolute majority of over two-thirds of those present. Yoshida Shigeru was prime minister at the time. The new Constitution was promulgated on November 3, 1946, and came into effect on May 3, 1947.

Although all necessary legal steps were followed in establishing the present Constitution, voices were heard calling for amendments or even a complete rewriting to produce an "independent" constitution as soon as the occupation ended. Former politicians like Hatoyama Ichiro, who had been purged from political office during the occupation, led the movement for constitutional revision. Hatoyama, upon succeeding Yoshida as prime minister in 1954, campaigned in favor of amending the Constitution in both the 1955 general election for the House of Representatives and the 1956 regular election for the House of Councillors. The Diet that was elected, however, did not have the two-thirds majority (in either house) favoring Hatoyama's position that is required for initiating the amendment process. Article 96 of the Constitution states that "amendments . . . shall be initiated by the Diet, through a concurring vote of two-thirds or more of all the members of each House, and shall thereupon be submitted to the people for ratification. . . ."

The clause calling for an "independent Constitution" in the charter of the Liberal Democratic party is a legacy of Hatoyama's ideology, but the movement subsided shortly thereafter. Although the idea of constitutional revision has now been revived with the changing international situation and growing conservatism in domestic politics, the prospects of the Diet's actually taking the initiative are quite slim. Two-thirds of the House of Councillors is 168 members. As can be seen from Table 3.1, the total LDP membership is far below these figures. The other parties have no intention of amending the Constitution, and, moreover, there is no consensus on the issue within the LDP. It is highly unlikely, therefore, that the Constitution will be amended in the foreseeable future.

The Parliamentary-Cabinet System
and Dissolution of the Diet

In Japan, where the parliamentary-cabinet system prevails, the prime minister is selected from among the members of the Diet by vote of the Diet. The Constitution does not limit the selection to members of the lower house, but all postwar prime ministers have come from the House of Representatives.

Upon being elected, the prime minister forms a cabinet by appointing the ministers of state, a majority of whom must be members of the Diet. In practice, almost all have been Diet members—only one or two have had a non-Diet background. Of the twenty-two ministries of state, only two or three of the portfolios are given to members of the upper house; all the rest go to lower house members.

The cabinet is collectively responsible to the Diet in the exercise of executive power. At the same time, the prime minister may remove any minister in order to maintain the unity and integrity of the cabinet. In fact, this power has been exercised only twice: once in 1947 with the removal of the minister of agriculture and forestry in Prime Minister Katayama Tetsu's cabinet, and once in 1953 with the dismissal of another agriculture and forestry minister by Prime Minister Yoshida.

In contrast to the present system, under the Meiji Constitution the prime minister was appointed by the emperor upon consultation with the Elder Statesmen (*genro*), former prime ministers, and personal advisers (the "imperial order"). The prime minister then would select ministers regardless of whether they were Diet members or not; moreover, the army and navy ministers were selected from active-duty officers in the army and navy. Each cabinet minister was directly responsible to the emperor in an individual, not collective, capacity, and no one even thought of the cabinet's being responsible to the imperial Diet. Consequently, nonparty military- or bureaucratic-centered cabinets often emerged under the Meiji Constitution. The present Constitution, therefore, differs considerably from the old one in providing a firm foundation for a balanced parliamentary-cabinet system.

The present Constitution also clearly affirms the supremacy of the House of Representatives in the selection of the prime minister. Article 67 states that if the two houses disagree and no agreement can be reached through a joint committee, "the decision of the House of Representatives shall be the decision of the Diet." The only case of disagreement in designating a prime minister occurred in February 1948 following the resignation of the Katayama cabinet. The House of Representatives chose Ashida Hitoshi for prime minister, while the House of Councillors named Yoshida Shigeru. The two houses failed to agree at the joint committee meeting, so Ashida became prime minister.

The vote of nonconfidence is the other constitutional provision supporting a balanced parliamentary-cabinet system and the supremacy of the House of Representatives in that system. Article 69 states that "if the House of Representatives passes a nonconfidence resolution, or rejects a confidence resolution, the Cabinet shall resign en masse, unless the House of Representatives is dissolved within ten days." This provision functions as a check and balance between the legislative and administrative branches.

A nonconfidence resolution, by its nature, will be proposed by the opposition, and a confidence resolution will be proposed by the government party. A motion for a vote of confidence or nonconfidence must be supported by at least fifty members. About twenty nonconfidence resolutions have been submitted in the House of Representatives so far (there have been no confidence resolutions yet), but only three have passed. The first was against Prime Minister Yoshida's second cabinet in December 1948, the second against his fourth cabinet in March 1953, and the third against Prime Minister Ohira Masayoshi's second cabinet in May 1980. In all three cases, the cabinet did not resign but instead dissolved the House of Representatives, forcing a general election.

If the cabinet decides to dissolve the lower house following a vote of nonconfidence, it will have the emperor issue an official declaration of dissolution in accordance with Article 7. (Article 7 requires the emperor to act in matters of state "with the advice and approval of the Cabinet.") Often, however, the cabinet will decide to dissolve the House of Representatives itself (in order to hold the election at what it considers a politically favorable time). Such cases are called "Article 7 dissolutions" and have occurred ten times in all, starting with Prime Minister Yoshida's third cabinet in August 1952. In fact, of the thirteen general elections for the House of Representatives since 1945, only one has followed completion of the full four-year term of the lower house; the remaining twelve have all taken place after a dissolution. Thus, the actual term of office served by representatives has averaged only two-and-a-half years even though the Constitution mandates up to four years.

The impact of a dissolution on individual house members is quite serious. An order for dissolution is usually wrapped in the traditional purple cloth used for ceremonial purposes and is brought into the House by the chief cabinet secretary in the midst of a plenary meeting. The order is handed to the secretary general of the House, who in turn gives it to the speaker. The speaker rises from his chair, stops the meeting, and reads the order of dissolution. The House is usually in a state of unrest from the moment the chief cabinet secretary appears. After the order is read, the members join in a loud chorus of "banzai" (cheers). The louder one shouts "banzai," it is believed, the better luck one has in getting reelected.

Once dissolution is announced, the members of the lower house lose their seats and must prepare for the succeeding election. The election must follow within forty days of the date of dissolution. The Public Office Election Law limits campaigns to twenty days (twenty-three for the ordinary election for the

House of Councillors), leaving very little time for candidates to prepare and campaign. A special session of the Diet must be convened within thirty days from the date of an election following a dissolution. New and reelected members meet and decide the organization of the House, elect a prime minister, and proceed with deliberations.

When the House of Representatives is dissolved, the House of Councillors goes into a recess at the same time. The cabinet, however, may convene the upper house in emergency session during a time of national emergency. This has occurred in only two instances—once in August 1952 and once in March 1953. Measures passed at such sessions are considered provisional, however, and become void unless confirmed by the lower house within ten days after the opening of the next Diet session; so it can hardly be said that the House of Councillors has any overriding decision-making power.

The Japanese parliamentary system celebrated its ninetieth anniversary on November 29, 1980. It was on July 1, 1890, that the first election was held under the Meiji Constitution, and the imperial Diet, the first parliament in Asia, was established on November 29 of that year. The parliamentary system then went through various transformations, at times being severely criticized for losing power and substance and becoming a mere appendage of the government. Nevertheless, general elections continued to take place, and the system survived. Following World War II, the Constitution was revised, greatly expanding the role of the Diet. The structure, organization, and procedures of the Diet discussed above reflect this change. The next steps forward lie in passing reapportionment laws and realigning electoral districts, improving the role of the House of Councillors as the second house, and overcoming the problems of political party factions and political slush funds. In the legislative process itself, there still remains the problem of the Diet's inadequate staffing in the face of the huge bureaucratic network available to the administrative branch.

Given a positive attitude and patience, the Diet will move in the right direction, accomplishing its tasks step by step within the present framework. After all, the Japanese Diet has just turned ninety, whereas the British Parliament celebrated its seven hundredth anniversary in 1965.

4
Diet Members

Shoichi Izumi

Diet Members Before and After the War

Of the three branches of the Japanese political system, the legislative branch underwent the greatest change at the end of World War II. Granted, the administrative and judicial branches experienced some changes, but their basic structures were not affected as was that of the legislative branch. Rather than an organ controlled by the emperor under the Meiji Constitution, the Diet became "the highest organ of state power" under the postwar Constitution. Commensurate with that definition, the status of Diet members rose to the point where they now exercise the highest power in the Japanese political system.

The prewar House of Representatives was composed largely of local notables, that is, rich landowners, the most successful entrepreneurs, and the like. The House of Peers, which had equal powers, consisted of the nobility and those appointed by the emperor. The prewar Diet can almost be said to have reflected a system of noblesse oblige, whereas postwar Diet members, including even those in the House of Councillors, have the same status as other citizens and are not considered a privileged class. (The recent emergence of second-generation Diet members must be noted, however.)

Several factors have contributed to this popularization of the Diet. First, Japan was democratized politically and socially in the immediate postwar period during the occupation. Moreover, politicians and high-ranking bureaucrats active during and before the war were purged, putting new faces into positions of power. Evidence of this democratization of the political arena is found in the diversity of the social, educational, and occupational backgrounds of the candidates running in the first postwar general election, held in 1946. The phenomenon of new faces, however, did not last long. Little by little, a system of party-nominated candidates began to emerge that gave priority to incumbents running for reelection and made it increasingly difficult for independent newcomers to win. Thus there gradually has developed a tendency toward fixed membership in the Diet.

Another factor contributing to the popularization of the Diet has been the increasing financial burden on candidates running for public office. A candidate needs more than a solid footing in his or her constituency and a name. The voters have shown a growing inclination to support candidates with ample funds. They have placed greater emphasis on the ability to attract money than on the capabilities or personality of the candidate, although at the same time claiming not to be influenced by the power of money. This, of course, does not apply to all candidates—there are many exceptions.

A third factor is the increasing attention paid to Diet members by the mass media. Before the war, names of Diet members (except for a very few influential persons) did not usually appear in newspapers. With their increased status after the war, however, Diet members became newsworthy, and mass media coverage of them was increased. The newspapers and certain periodicals follow the status of members in party factions, relationships between factions, the sources of campaign funds, and numerous other items, leaving nothing unsaid. The press treatment of Diet members is equivalent to that of movie, television, and sports stars, thus helping to popularize their image.

There is a Japanese saying that "a dandy has neither money nor power." The popular image of a Diet member is perhaps just the opposite—that the member has money and power if not elegance. It can almost be said that this image makes people fearful. Government bureaucrats, especially, are careful to avoid disagreements with influential Diet members out of concern for their careers. Usually such officials call Diet members *sensei*, an address of respect. This relationship is a complete about-face from the prewar hierarchy that put high-ranking bureaucrats above Diet members. Now members of the Diet rank just after the heads of the three branches of government in protocol, in seating at a state dinner for example. The same ranking applies to salaries. Article 35 of the Diet Law states that Diet members "shall receive an annual payment of not less than the highest pay for ordinary government officials" (by which is meant administrative vice-ministers).

The present political system has turned serving in the Diet into a profession. The imperial Diet had few bills to deliberate besides those concerning the budget, and its sessions were brief. Moreover, the government tried to convoke the Diet as infrequently as possible. Perhaps because of such limitations, once in session the imperial Diet held heated debates. In contrast, the postwar Diet is required by the Constitution to hold a session once a year, and the session's length has been set at one hundred fifty days by the Diet Law. In addition, there are quite often extra sessions as well as extensions of sessions. Altogether, these sessions require that members remain in the capital nearly year round, just as in the United States. Furthermore, campaigning, now considered vital for public office holders, was once part-time in nature but is increasingly a full-time job. There are still quite a number of Diet members who have outside sources of income, but, like members of Congress in the United States, they are probably not deeply involved in those careers. This is probably true even of members of local assemblies in Japan.

If there is anything that can intimidate a Diet member, it is the mass media. Close contact with the press and broadcasting media is considered so important that some observers go so far as to say that a politician has little chance of getting ahead without a friend in the media. If it becomes known that a particular member is favored by the press corps, that member will most likely catch the attention of party and faction leaders, gaining opportunities for advancement. On the other hand, if a member is alienated from the media, difficulties can be expected when adverse news appears. The mass media are at once the best of friends and the worst of enemies to a politician whose career depends on maintaining good public relations. Cultivating friendships in the media, therefore, is one of the greatest concerns of a Diet member.

One difference stands out when comparing Diet and Congress members. In Japan, a Diet member is rarely considered a legislator. Bills almost never originate with individual members, and members do not propose them. Most of the members themselves do not consider legislation their most important responsibility. Perhaps as a result, the status and prestige of Diet committee chairmen is much lower than that enjoyed by their U.S. counterparts. Although congressional committee chairmen may not be quite as powerful as in the past, they are still considered specialists in their area and frequently hold office nearly permanently. In Japan, the committee chair is considered to require some specialization, but the post is less permanent in nature, often being filled according to the political imperatives of faction and party politics as well as by the seniority system. Compared to committee chairmen, the numerous directors of the Liberal Democratic party's Policy Affairs Research Council enjoy far greater prestige and influence. This difference results from the fact that key officials of the LDP are directly involved in the actual legislative process, intervening and guiding government officials, whereas committee chairmen are often no more than moderators of debates between the LDP and the opposition parties. The lack of legislative initiative reflects the tradition of the Meiji Constitution system and is a habit not easily shed, despite the changes brought about by the introduction of the U.S.-style committee system.

If they are not legislators, what are Japanese Diet members? They are generally considered politicians, although in the case of postwar Diet members they may be better called "interest-intermediary politicians." Here the term "interest" not only applies to the immediate interests of a member's constituents but implies all kinds of other interests. A Diet member may often cooperate with a particular interest group and receive political funds in return. (To be sure, some of the parties do not encourage this close collaboration with interest groups.)

How does interest representation relate to the supposed lack of lobbying in Japan? Each interest group has, in fact, lobbyists in all but name who work closely with members of the Diet to get them to influence political parties and government agencies. In that sense, Diet members themselves act as lobbyists. Since the final decisions on policy affairs, however, are largely determined beforehand by the parties and government authorities, there is no need for lobbying on or near the Diet floor. Thus it is true that U.S.-style lobbying in the Diet itself is absent in Japan.

So far this description has emphasized the differences in the political cultures of the two countries. Needless to say, however, the similarities outnumber the differences, and the fundamental psychology and behavior patterns of parliamentary members in relation to their constituents are no doubt commonly shared by all parliamentarians worldwide.

The Electoral Process

Legal Requirements

The legal requirements to stand for election to the Diet are very simple. Any Japanese citizen over the age of twenty-five may run for election to the House of Representatives, and anyone over age thirty may run for the House of Councillors. The Public Office Election Law excludes those judged legally incompetent, but, otherwise, there is not even a requirement for length of residence in a given electoral district. In this respect the Japanese system resembles the British. Unlike candidates in the United Kingdom, Japanese candidates do always have some connection with their district. It may be their place of birth, residence, or business, but they never declare candidacy in a district where they are totally unknown despite the law's permitting it.

Electoral Districts

Japan is divided into 130 electoral districts for House of Representatives elections and 47 local districts, coterminous with the 47 prefectures, and 1 national district for House of Councillors elections. The House of Representatives currently has 511 members—with one exception, each of the 130 medium-size districts elects 3, 4, or 5 representatives. Of the 252 members currently in the House of Councillors, 152 were elected from the 47 local prefectured districts in proportion to their populations (with each selecting 2 to 8 members), and the remaining 100 are elected from the single nationwide district.[1]

The main source of controversy about the Japanese electoral district system is not the question of adopting small or medium-size districts, but rather the very system or law that allows Diet members themselves to decide how many are to be elected from each district. In the United States, the number of House members from each state is automatically reapportioned, within the given limit of 435 seats, every ten years based on the results of the national census. The legislature of each affected state redistricts or modifies the boundaries of its congressional districts. To be sure, this redefinition of districts is affected by political interests, but whatever dissatisfaction there may be with the results, the U.S. system does not allow those who will be affected by the decision to make the decision. This is one area in which the Japanese Diet can be improved by adopting the U.S. practice.

The Public Office Election Law states that the number of seats in the Diet may be altered according to the results of the national census, conducted every five years. The number was indeed altered to add more members in 1964 and 1975—a total of forty-five in all. In 1964, a proposal by the Electoral System Commission (composed of both Diet members and others) to reduce the number of seats met with fierce opposition from its Diet-elected members, making the issue taboo thereafter.

More recently, in February 1980, the Tokyo District Court ruled that the present electoral districts were apportioned unconstitutionally, noting that the disparity between the largest and smallest districts showed a difference in the ratio of voters per elected member of over two to one. The Supreme Court decision is yet to be announced,[2] but it is clear that the Diet will have to seek a more balanced representation by either (1) increasing the total number of seats, (2) maintaining the present total but making adjustments within that framework, or (3) abandoning the present medium-size districts for a small-district system.

Of these three choices, the first is less than ideal, given demands for administrative reform and decreased government spending. Each Diet member costs the nation approximately ¥40 billion annually, so increasing the number of seats in the lower house would probably be politically infeasible. The second choice, somewhat following the U.S. practice, would most likely be supported by both ruling and opposition parties in principle but would undoubtedly cause a split between them when it came to the actual adjustment. As for the third choice, of small districts, the opposition is so vehemently against the idea that Prime Minister Suzuki will not even propose it. Thus, Japan is sorely in need of a neutral body that can help resolve the present deadlock.

Candidate Selection

An important aspect of candidate selection in Japan is the process by which an aspirant procures an official endorsement from a political party. The usual procedure, common to all parties, is for the candidate to be recommended by the local party representative and to receive official endorsement from central party headquarters. The most difficult step is obtaining the initial recommendation.

All the opposition parties seem to be able to agree on their party-endorsed candidates without heated controversy, but the ruling Liberal Democratic party is not. Two reasons can be given for the relative lack of controversy in the minority parties. First, the opposition parties usually run only one, or at most two, candidates per district, and in most cases the candidates are incumbent Diet members and/or their designated successors. Second, with the exception of the New Liberal Club, the opposition parties put greater emphasis on party platforms than on individuals. However strong their convictions may be, candidates from one of the minority parties must conform to party decisions. (National-level or local-level decisions may have greater weight depending upon the party; national-level decisions prevail in the Clean Government and Japan Communist parties, and local decisions are more important in the Japan Socialist and Democratic Socialist parties.)

The LDP, on the other hand, emphasizes individual candidates as much as the party. Indeed, an official endorsement is not required to win an election if one is backed by sufficient supporters.[3] Recent trends, however, do favor candidates with official LDP endorsement, making it necessary for aspirants to try to win such support. Because of the emphasis placed on individual platforms, all who have something to say seem to want to compete for office, and the LDP headquarters is overwhelmed with requests for special recognition. The present medium-size electoral district system, which permits multiple candidacies in each district, aggravates this intraparty competition. A one-member district would reduce challenges to incumbents or make it easier to predict a candidate's strength and so would eliminate some of the unnecessary competition. As it stands now, a newcomer in an LDP stronghold has just as much chance of winning in the election as a veteran, a fact that encourages competing candidates.

Another factor making candidate selection difficult in the LDP is the division of the party into a number of strong factions, each competing for increased representation in the Diet and expanded local influence. Each faction finds it necessary to have its own candidate(s) running in every district, thus further complicating candidate selection by the party. As a result, the LDP often does not make a decisive selection but gives its official endorsement to all in order to avoid more controversy.

The factional conflicts within the LDP are often attributed to the medium-size electoral district system. Those supporting this view say that it is natural for conflicts to arise when a candidate must run against others from the same party. They argue that without the medium-size district system, factional antagonism would not have developed to its present ferocity. Is a small single-member district, therefore, a viable solution? Would it help eliminate factions? It is true that with only one seat at stake there could only be one LDP candidate, but that restriction would not eliminate the difficult process of boiling down the number of aspirants to that one; there would still be plenty of chances for factions to push their candidates as hard as ever. Competition among incumbent Diet members would be eliminated, but factional divisions originated in the process of selecting the LDP party president, and changing the electoral district system would not erase that rivalry.

Japanese political parties have yet to develop a good system for selecting official party candidates, like the primaries in the United States or the candidate selection committees in the United Kingdom (which screen aspirants). The present process allows little room for input by voters or rank-and-file party members. Before any reform is introduced, whether it is a change to small districts or some kind of proportional representation, the process must be made more accessible to the general public.

Election Campaigns

Once a person decides to run for office, the intention must immediately be publicized in order to gain as many supporters as possible before the official campaign begins. The officially designated campaign period is only the ceremonial conclusion of a much longer process of vote gathering; it is almost a part of the election itself. In the case of a complete newcomer's running from the Liberal Democratic party, preparations must begin approximately a year before the election. The first step is the establishment of a small office in the district. Then, before supporters' groups (*koenkai*) can be organized, the candidate must become known—and must pay courtesy calls on influential party members, as well as on friends and acquaintances from school days to the present, and try to be included in as many circles as possible in order to gain contacts. If successful, these efforts will crystalize in the formation of fund-raising and campaign support groups that can carry the candidate to a victory in the election. The entire process entails a substantial financial sacrifice on the part of the candidate.

The procedure for declaring candidacy is relatively simple. The candidate or a proxy files an official declaration form with the Board of Elections and submits a registration fee to the Ministry of Justice. The fee is ¥1 million for a House of Representatives seat or for a local district seat in the House of Councillors and ¥2 million for running in the national constituency of the House of Councillors. Once registered, the candidate may open a campaign office, and there is a twenty-day official campaign period ending the day before the election.

The smallest details of campaign activity are regulated by the Public Office Election Law, which is often called the "law of don't." For example, civil servants are prohibited from campaigning for candidates; house-to-house canvassing and signature-collecting campaigns are not permitted; a candidate may not provide his or her campaign staff with food or beverages; visitors to campaign offices may be given tea and cookies but may not stay for lunch. Public demonstrations and speeches are also strictly regulated by the law. All such public activity is prohibited unless given prior clearance. A candidate may drive around and use a loudspeaker to announce his or her name to people on the street but may not use it to make a speech from the car. Rosters, leaflets, and other campaign literature are strictly regulated and must be inspected by the Board of Elections, which bans any individual creativity that deviates from official regulations.

Japanese election rules have clearly been established to prevent corruption and financial abuse, but they are so restrictive that they are often not adhered to. Most candidates probably do not even know the maximum amount of campaign funds they may spend (the campaign's financial manager must know because a report on finances must be submitted after the election). For House of Representatives elections, the legal limit is calculated by dividing the total number of registered voters in the district by the number of representatives to be elected from the district, multiplying the result by ¥27 and adding ¥9.7 million. Thus, the total campaign spending of a candidate running in the first electoral district of Tokyo, which elects three members, should not exceed

$$\frac{457,387}{3} \times \yen27 + 9,700,000 = \yen13,816,482$$

(at ¥225 to the dollar, this is approximately $61,400). This is one of the highest figures in Japan because the electoral districts in the Tokyo metropolitan area have high population densities. It should be noted that this limit applies only to spending during the official campaign period and is in addition to the campaign expenses that are publicly financed, especially media costs (explained below). As a result, the legal limit has little impact and, according to postelection financial reports, is often not even reached.[4]

With successive revisions of the Public Office Election Law in 1967, 1971, and 1975, there has been a trend toward increased public financing of election campaigns. Candidates who receive a certain minimum number of votes are now reimbursed for nearly all of their expenses for campaign literature and a considerable portion of their expenses for sound trucks, drivers, etc. All candidates are given free postage for a certain amount of campaign mail and free, if limited, use of the mass media. Each candidate is allotted five-and-a-half minutes of television time to promote his or her candidacy, once on a public TV channel and once on a private channel. As TV attracts the widest of all audiences, there probably has not been a single candidate who has declined the opportunity to appear. The same conditions apply to the use of radio—a time allotment of five-and-a-half minutes, aired twice. Free newspaper space is also made available. Each candidate may place an ad two columns wide by about four inches long in any daily newspaper, which is run five times for candidates for the House of Representatives or local district seats in the House of Councillors and six times for candidates for the national constituency of the House of Councillors. These allowances are free; however, they are also the limits to which candidates may utilize the media—candidates are prohibited from buying any air time or newspaper space. In this respect, the Japanese have shown foresight in regulating media usage by candidates, especially in view of the fact that most campaign funds in the U.S. go for the purchase of radio and television time.

Campaign Financing

Campaign financing in the broadest sense includes all the expenses of developing community support as well as all the other costs of getting elected. It is rare for any candidate, regardless of party, to be able to meet the entire cost solely from personal income. The means of financing the balance, however, differ from one political party to another.

In the case of candidates running from the Clean Government party or the Japan Communist party, funds come from the party treasury and from donations from party members and supporters. The Clean Government party allows its candidates to form some personal support groups, but the JCP apparently does not tolerate any such organizations. The Liberal Democratic party, Democratic Socialist party, and New Liberal Club all make funds available from the party or its factions and encourage personal support groups for each candidate.

There are two types of support groups or support activities. One is a group of voters organized to help the campaign, and the other is formed primarily for the purpose of fund raising. In most parties, these two activities are carried out by a single group structure that combines the two functions. The LDP, however, maintains two separate groups—the campaign support group in the candidate's local district and the fund-raising group, usually in Tokyo. Funds raised by the latter are not necessarily reported to the Ministry of Home Affairs, as is required by the Political Funds Regulation Law. In fact, except for groups formed around the leader of a party faction, often called study groups, most groups do not report the funds they raise. Fund-raising groups organized by individual candidates operate on a membership system in which the fee collected is small. The bulk of political funds for an incumbent LDP Diet member or new candidate comes from the faction to which he or she belongs. The party itself offers only enough financial aid to cover the registration fee for declaring candidacy, and it will provide loans. Under such circumstances, most funds have to come from faction sources.

The LDP receives funds from business and industrial circles through its National Political Association. LDP factions also receive their funds from those sources. The Japan Socialist party relies on party membership fees and income from publications, as well as donations from the General Council of Trade Unions (Sōhyō) at election time. The Democratic Socialist party similarly receives donations from the Confederation of Labor (Domei). The Clean Government and Japan Communist parties have only their party membership fees and publication income, and the New Liberal Club obtains income in the same way as the LDP.

Social Background of Diet Members

Occupational Background

Because membership in the Diet has become a profession in itself, the members' professional or occupational background usually means the positions they held before being elected. The most frequently named category—far outnumbering other professions for members of both the House of Representatives and the House of Councillors—is that of former employee of a business. This category, however, encompasses a wide range of extremes, from those who held executive or managerial positions in large firms to those who belonged to an agricultural cooperative, and the status may often only be nominal. For example, someone who was in fact a member of a prefectural assembly or a secretary to a Diet member may use "president of a company" or "organization executive" as a euphemism for such employment. The next most frequently mentioned occupational background categories are those of former bureaucrat and former labor leader, which are much more specific. Following those is the category of former local politician or secretary to a Diet member. There are few former lawyers, their number having decreased considerably from prewar and immediate postwar times. This phenomenon may be accounted for by the decline in prestige of lawyers in general and the fact that detailed legal knowledge is not a critical qualification or a condition required of a Diet member. It should also be noted that lawyers are not in the best position for collecting votes.

If there is such a thing as an advantageous position or career for gathering votes, it is that of a high-ranking official in a government agency that voters turn to for protection of their interests, or a mayor or other municipal leader who is already a local celebrity, or a leader of a labor union or farm association.

The situation is somewhat different, however, for candidates running in the national constituency of the House of Councillors. There what is needed most of all is a nationally known name. That election format—where as many as one hundred candidates may be competing for fifty upper house seats on a single nationwide ballot—has given rise to what is known as "television personality Diet members." These may be divided into two groups: those who were in TV journalism, such as newscasters and announcers, and those who were TV stars. The former are usually associated with the Democratic Socialist party and the latter generally are in the Liberal Democratic party or are independents.

Television personalities were first brought into the political arena in the early 1960s by the LDP. Their names being well known already among the general public, they were believed to require less financial support to get elected. There had been in the early postwar period an active movement in the House of Councillors, formed by "men of culture," such as writers and scholars, to support their interests in the national constituency. (This group, called the Green

Breeze Society, tended to be politically independent.) As political parties gained influence in the upper house, however, an increasing number of candidates with bureaucratic and labor backgrounds emerged, and the parties began to look for those with well-known names to run in the national constituency election. Eventually the men of culture were replaced by those whose background was in the more popular television medium, and they all affiliated themselves with particular political parties.

Breaking down the Diet by political party, LDP members are mainly former bureaucrats, executives of larger corporations, and leaders of farming, forestry, or fishing organizations. Socialist party members are largely former labor union leaders, including those from the teachers' union. Fewer and fewer are independent professionals such as writers and scholars. At a recent meeting, in November 1980, the JSP decided that it ought to try to appeal more actively to lawyers, academicians, and bureaucrats, but the question remains of how to finance this campaign.[5] Clean Government party Diet members are usually former executives of small and medium-size firms or officials of the party secretariat. Former labor union leaders and executives of small and medium-size firms form the bulk of Democratic Socialist party Diet membership, whereas Japan Communist party members range from party officials to lawyers and writers. The JCP has a larger share of lawyers than do the other parties.

In recent years more members are coming out of local political groups. Japan is at a transitional point at which the politicians who have been active in the thirty-five years since the war are now being replaced by a younger generation. At the same time, there is a growing tendency to replace the ex-bureaucrat Diet members (the so-called "parachuted-down-from-the-bureaucracy" member) with those having a more locally rooted background, such as former members of prefectural assemblies.

Second-Generation Members

Along with the shift to a younger generation, there is an increasing number of second-generation members or hereditary politicians. The results of the fall 1979 election show that 146 Diet members were second-generation politicians. The majority of them belonged to the LDP, of course, but some were elected from every party except the Clean Government and Japan Communist parties. The term "second-generation member" contains a note of criticism as well as an element of envy. The feeling of envy may be directed at candidates who are elected (so it is said) solely because their fathers had been Diet members, but who thus gain the privilege of being called *sensei* and of walking on the red carpet that is laid out for Diet members. The critical note is stronger, however, because these members are seen to have breached socially acceptable bounds and turned a profession into a family business with a hereditary title.

A difference does exist between second-generation Diet members who succeeded fathers that died and those whose fathers retired. In the first case, the support group of the deceased member has an active voice; in the second, the incumbent gives the position to his family member upon retiring. This latter case has brought criticism about making a family business out of Diet membership and has led to questioning the principles of the retiring members. In fact, the problem is rooted in fundamental Diet election practices that need to be reconsidered. That is to say, most campaign activities, especially in the case of the LDP, are centered around individual candidates. Many Diet members consider their support group in their district to be a personal possession and, moreover, one that was acquired only through long hours of hard work and a large investment made jointly with local leaders. It is quite natural for those involved in the support group to want to fill the vacancy caused by death or retirement with the closest relative of the former member; sometimes even the widow is pushed forth when no other relative is available.

The number of second-generation members may or may not grow, but it will certainly never diminish as long as the present electoral process is maintained. Only when a system permitting an open selection of candidates by registered voters becomes established will the number of second-generation members begin to decrease. It should be pointed out, however, that a second-generation candidate has to have some popular appeal and appear capable of handling the job; and many, in fact, are trained for it by serving as Diet members' secretaries.

Academic Background

Most Diet members have a high level of education — on the average, they are college graduates (or the equivalent under the prewar system). In particular, a high percentage of LDP, DSP, and JCP Diet members are graduates of national universities; the percentage is much lower for the JSP and CGP. Among private universities, Waseda graduates are by far the most numerous, and the majority belong to the LDP.

Women Members

At present there are nine women in the House of Representatives; seven are members of the Japan Communist party and two are members of the Japan Socialist party. The House of Councillors has seventeen women; twelve were elected from the national constituency and five from the prefectural constituencies. Six of the women are in the LDP, five in the JCP, two each in the JSP and CGP, and two are independent. With the exception of the first postwar election in 1946, when a record thirty-nine women were elected, the total number of female members has been relatively stable. The changes have come in the disappearance of women members of the LDP, CGP, and DSP in the House of Representatives and in the predominance of the JCP in the seats held by women. In the House of Councillors, five of the six women LDP members were elected from the national constituency, and all but one are "television personality" Diet members.

The reasons for the small number of women members may be the same as in the United States.[6] There is still a strong belief among both sexes that the profession of politician is not suited for women and that, work and family not being compatible, women ought to give priority to the family. However, as the political profession evolves, it is likely that more women will enter politics.

Daily Life of Diet Members

Let us start by looking at a day in the life of a newly elected Diet member.[7] Mr. A, a Liberal Democratic party member, was elected to the House of Representatives from a constituency in the Chubu region[8] in the June 1979 election. A graduate of Keio University, he had been a businessman in a large private firm. The son of a Diet member and thus a second-generation member, he is, at age thirty-three, in name and experience a newly elected representative.

He rises at four in the morning, gets dressed, and takes the New High Speed Line ("Bullet") train to Tokyo. He heads straight for the Diet Building, where he welcomes the 166 members of his district support group who have come up for a tour of the building, joining them for the tour and a souvenir photographic session. At noon, he attends a gathering of the Kochi Club (the Suzuki faction caucus) at the club's headquarters in Akasaka. In the afternoon he is at his office in the Diet office building, where he listens to petitions for holding the Olympics in Nagoya (in his district) and hears an explanation of how the budget situation will affect his prefecture from the prefectural representative stationed in Tokyo. A group of educators from a city in his district arrive in Tokyo with a petition on school reforms, and Representative A accompanies them to the Ministry of Education for a meeting with ministry officials. In the evening he attends a reception given by his support group with his wife and mother at a hotel in Tokyo. After leaving the reception he and members of the executive council of the support group hold a meeting in Roppongi (an area of Tokyo with numerous bars). His day finally ends at a little past eleven o'clock, and he will stay at the Diet housing compound near the Diet Building.

This day does not include any plenary meetings of the Diet or committee meetings (Mr. A belongs to two standing committees); such is the case when the Diet is in recess. When the Diet is in session, meetings are scheduled every Tuesday, Thursday, and Friday for the House of Representatives and every Monday, Wednesday, and Friday for the House of Councillors. A meeting will not be called, however, if there are no bills scheduled for floor debate. The committees meet two or three times a week. Of course, not all committee members attend every meeting, and attendance is low when nothing of importance is under examination or up for vote. Review and debate on bills and oversight of government activities cannot be considered time-consuming, although they are the "main" job of Diet members. Most of a member's time is taken up with services to constituents and attendance at various meetings that lead to obtaining political funds. As election time approaches, the member's life becomes more and more occupied by commuting back and forth between the district and Tokyo; often this is called the Friday-Tuesday shuttle because the Diet member goes back to the district on Friday and returns to Tokyo on Tuesday.

Secretaries or assistants play an important role—supporting, assisting, and even substituting for the member in some cases. (Not, however, at formal Diet plenary meetings or committee meetings, which prohibit proxies.) Secretaries are the Japanese counterpart of a U.S. Congress member's personal staff. Two are provided at government expense for each member. A few influential members also have several others at their own expense. In addition, most members hire privately one or two secretaries to staff their district offices.

A secretary's ability can be crucial to the success of a Diet member; it is not an exaggeration to say that members are appraised according to how their secretaries are appraised. Secretaries are important especially in maintaining good relations with constituents. They are the ones who usually receive constituents' petitions, play the role of intermediary in channeling them to the appropriate government offices, and make sure that the petitioners return to the district satisfied. The secretary usually acts on instruction from the member but at times is required to make independent decisions. The secretary's skill in maintaining connections with government officials and efficiency in handling the job are tested on such occasions. A secretary's ability can thus be regarded as determining the member's ability to serve the interests of the constituency and therefore has an influence on the member's reelection. Secretaries also take the place of members at various meetings, the most important of which are wedding and funeral services in the home district. They may attend party meetings and monitor Diet and party committee meetings that the member is unable to attend. Whatever the role played by each secretary may be, it certainly has great impact; it presents another face of the member in the political arena.

Of the two government-funded secretaries, the salary of the first is equivalent to that of assistant bureau directors in government agencies, and the second receives the same salary as section chiefs. Secretaries are considered temporary civil servants (with special assignments) and are in fact treated as civil servants in terms of health insurance, pensions, and the like. The difference lies in their not having entered government service through national examination, as is customary for regular civil servants. Diet members choose their own secretaries, who may be family members. Often, the position is given to a relative or a person from the member's district. Some political parties, however, assign secretaries; for example, most of the secretaries of Clean Government and Japan Communist party Diet members have been chosen by their party. Some important members of the LDP hire private secretaries at their own expense, maintaining a staff of ten or so in a separate office—a well-known hotel, for instance, near the Diet Building. As mentioned before, most Diet members hire at least one or two private secretaries or assistants to be "locally stationed" in their district offices.

Some secretaries become future Diet members. As was discussed above, a second-generation Diet member may have gained experience in the job as secretary to his or her father or another member. Other aspiring future members may run for a prefectural assembly seat from their secretarial position before running for a seat in the Diet. Having a secretary elected to the prefectural assembly helps to publicize the Diet member employer, so members may encourage people on their staff to run.

In comparing the staff of a member of the Diet and that of a member of Congress, besides the obvious matter of size, one outstanding difference is the almost total absence of legislative assistants in Japan. This is a natural consequence of the Diet member's restricted capability and role in the legislative process; so, in fact, there is little need of legislative assistants. Nevertheless, not all secretaries spend all their time serving the needs of the constituents; some assist and even substitute for Diet members in doing research and studying legislation.

The postwar Japanese Diet was modeled on the U.S. Congress in certain areas, for instance, committee staffs and the research services of the National Diet Library. In both quantity and quality, however, the Japanese counterparts are inferior to the U.S. committee staffs and to the Congressional Research Service of the Library of Congress. The difference is particularly striking in the committee staff system. There are many fewer staff members in Japan even though there are more legislators per committee than in the Congress. In terms of quality, congressional staffs have higher levels of specialization and enjoy a higher social prestige — they have greater mobility and can interchange with staff members in government agencies, research institutions, and universities. Such mobility hardly exists in Japan. Many reasons may be given for this difference, but one is the prevalence of the lifetime employment system in the government just as in the private sector. It is a reflection of the difference in attitude toward and image of the legislative organ in Japan and the United States.

Brief mention should be made of the pay and allowances provided to Diet members. The Diet Law stipulates that members should receive not less than the highest-paid civil servants. These are administrative vice-ministers, so Diet member's salaries in 1980 totaled ¥13.6 million per year. (At an exchange rate of 225 yen to the dollar, this amounts to $60,444.) The salary is paid at a monthly rate of ¥800,000 ($3,556), plus twice-yearly bonuses totaling ¥4 million ($17,778).[9] In addition, each member receives an annual allowance of ¥7.8 million ($34,667) to cover transportation and communication expenses (travel, telephone, postage, etc.) and ¥7.2 million ($32,000) per year for legislative research costs. The latter is paid to the political party that the member is affiliated with and thus serves as a government subsidy to finance party functions. As was already mentioned, two secretaries are on the government payroll; and for Diet members whose constituency is outside Tokyo, overnight lodging facilities are available. There is also a pension system for members. For transportation, all Diet members are provided with a free pass on all lines, and the speaker and vice-speaker of the lower house, the president and vice-president of the upper house, and the chairmen of standing and special committees in both houses are all provided with a private car and chauffeur. Any member in office over twenty-five years is given a special transportation allowance of ¥2.4 million ($10,667) per year.

Future Role of Diet Members

The ability and character required of a politician ranges over a wide spectrum: the perception to foresee the needs of the time; the capacity to understand policies; a desire to serve the people; strength to maintain a democratic outlook; and much else. Since each individual has strengths and weaknesses, it is impossible to find a person endowed with all the ideal capabilities and character traits. At the present time, the most important prerequisite for a politician may well be an ability to effectively lead people. The politician should not be a dictator or a self-complacent leader but rather one who is not afraid of criticism by the people. In other words, a politician who has no strong beliefs and opinions and curries the favor of constituents has no place in the Diet. A Diet member by definition is the representative of a constituency and therefore of its interests; the job requires the member to speak up for the interests of those constituents and reflect their opinions in government affairs. However, this task need not be an obstacle to upholding strong personal convictions and policy opinions, since the two ought not to conflict with one another.

In reality, elections are such a preoccupation for Diet members that not only are members forced to spend most of their time serving their constituents, they may even, albeit in only a few cases, lose interest in being legislators — in studying policy and overseeing government affairs. As the saying goes, voters do not expect a Diet member to aim above their interests, so voters must take some of the blame for keeping members away from their main job. Diet members who are faithful to their principal occupation of legislator may not find enough time to serve their constituents and therefore find themselves out of office in the following election. This dilemma is a reflection of the low level of political maturity of the general public. At the same time, the members themselves are not free of blame for failing to lead in the political education of the people. As long as politicians continue to dismiss the problem of political immaturity among voters, or, to be more blunt, as long as they take advantage of that immaturity, Japan will remain a nation of economic strength and political weakness. What is needed now are competent individual Diet members who are willing to serve with enthusiasm and to take the lead in reforming the Diet system to improve its public image and capacity to function effectively.

Notes

1. Because House of Councillors elections are staggered, with half the members elected every three years, the local (prefectural) districts, in fact, elect only one to four members at each election; but fifty are elected from the nationwide district.

2. The Japanese Supreme Court ruled once before in an apportionment case, in 1975, holding that the House of Representatives electoral districts in existence at the time of the December 1972 general election were unconstitutionally apportioned. This decision eventually resulted in the addition of twenty more seats to the lower house.

3. The LDP makes a distinction between officially endorsed candidates (*konin*) and those who are recommended (*suisen*). The former are eligible for financial and organizational assistance from the party, but the latter are not.

4. Since no campaigning is supposed to take place prior to the official campaign period, the Public Office Election Law assumes that no funds will be spent prior to that time either. But this is just when most spending does occur. As Gerald L. Curtis says, "The various restrictions [of the law] have not made elections inexpensive, they have simply made most expenses illegal" (*Election Campaigning Japanese Style* [New York: Columbia University Press, 1971], p. 219).

5. *Asahi Shimbun* [*Asahi Newspaper*], November 23, 1980, morning ed.

6. See Anita Shieve and John Clemens, "The New Wave of Women Politicians," *New York Times Magazine*, October 9, 1980, p. 30.

7. This account is based on an article in the series "What Is Government," in *Nikkei Shimbun* [*Nikkei Newspaper*], January 5, 1981, morning ed.

8. The central region (i.e., between Tokyo and Kyoto), around the city of Nagoya.

9. Scheduled, semiannual "bonus" payments are common in Japan—they are simply part of one's salary—and Diet members are treated just like other government employees in this regard.

5

The Diet and the Bureaucracy:
The Budget as a Case Study

Koji Kakizawa

The Relationship Between the Diet and the Bureaucracy

Prewar Diet-Bureaucracy Relations

In the relationship between the Diet and the bureaucracy, the latter is often thought to have the greater power and influence. It is clearly stated in the present Constitution that the Diet is the supreme organ of state power and the sole law-making authority; yet the bureaucracy maintains a firm control over the legislative process. To understand how this system works, an understanding of the historical situation from the early Meiji period is necessary.

Japan's modernization, which began with the Meiji Restoration in 1868, took place under the traditional emperor system, guided by a bureaucracy that formulated and implemented policies designed to "enrich the country and strengthen the army." The bureaucracy, which received its authority directly from the emperor, was responsible for both domestic and foreign policy.

By contrast, the Diet was born out of the movement for people's rights, which arose after the Restoration, and was not established until 1890. It was under the control of the emperor and the executive branch of government, which was directly responsible to the throne. Moreover, it was not supreme even·in the legislative area. Imperial edicts, for example, could be proclaimed without Diet approval and had the same force as law. The power to appoint the prime minister was held by the emperor, not the Diet. Naturally, the emperor's prerogative was exercised in practice by the bureaucrats who worked under his direct authority. This practice established the institutional superiority of the imperial bureaucracy, which, except for a short time in the Taishō era (i.e., during the 1920s), maintained control until the end of World War II.

Postwar Diet-Bureaucracy Relations

In the early postwar period, under the new Constitution, a more thorough form of parliamentary democracy was adopted; it was then that the Diet was specified as the highest organ of government. Nevertheless, while the occupation continued, everything was subject to the directives of allied General Headquarters, so that in fact the Diet was still powerless. Moreover, occupation rule was carried out through the existing bureaucratic organizations. Under these circumstances the traditional bureaucracy returned almost unblemished to its former position of power. The occupation was a form of bureaucratic politics, simply substituting General Douglas MacArthur for the emperor as supreme authority.

When the San Francisco peace treaty was concluded in 1951 and Japan's sovereignty was restored, changes in the relationship between the Diet and the executive branch began to emerge for the first time. There was a gradual strengthening of the authority of the Diet, but the movement was far less dynamic than expected, and even today the greatest influence on the political process is not that of the Diet but that of the bureaucracy. Personnel flows between these two branches of government illustrate this situation.

The Bureaucracy as a Source of Political Leadership

The primary influence of the Diet over the executive branch lies in its power to appoint the prime minister, the distinctive characteristic of a parliamentary-cabinet system. The chosen prime minister then appoints the heads of the ministries and the parliamentary vice-ministers. Each minister holds legal authority over appointments to his staff, but in practice, except for two or three cases since the war, most ministers actually have little influence in personnel matters. This lack is especially clear in the top-ranking position in the bureaucratic structure, the post of administrative vice-minister, which is filled by consensus among current senior officials and retired members of each ministry, completely independent of the Diet. Thus, while the political heads of the ministries have formal authority over appointments, their influence in practice is virtually nil.

Moreover, because of the frequent reshuffling of cabinets, the average term of a minister is only 278 days. In such a short time, it is rarely possible for an appointee to gain the knowledge and mastery of his ministry's affairs necessary to effectively control administration and appointments. As for parliamentary vice-ministers, their powers are so limited that the post is often called "the ministry's appendix."

On the other hand, the influence of the bureaucracy on the Diet is great. About 15 percent of the present members of the House of Representatives and about 25 percent of those of the House of Councillors are former bureaucrats. Among parties, the percentages are much the highest for Liberal Democratic party Diet members, 24 percent for the lower house and 41 percent for the upper house. The figures for previous years are generally higher, testifying to the substantial "pipeline" that exists between the bureaucracy and the Diet.

Another important point is that politicians with bureaucratic backgrounds often hold key posts in political parties. A look at the background of Japan's prime ministers, for example, shows that eight of the fourteen postwar prime ministers were former bureaucrats (see Table 5.1). These ex-bureaucrat Diet members are usually members of the Diet committees that supervise the ministries in which they previously served. In most cases they act as channels, mainly to introduce ministry opinion into the Diet rather than to transmit Diet opinion to the ministries. This function creates a give-and-take relationship in which politicians, serving as representatives of each ministry in the Diet, obtain various benefits for their constituencies through influence in the executive branch, which controls effective power.

The Diet and the Bureaucracy in the Legislative Process

The Creation of Bills

A greater number of bills are introduced by the cabinet than by individual Diet members. For example, of 187 bills submitted during the 91st session of the Diet, 102 or 55 percent were introduced by the cabinet and only 85, or 45 percent, by Diet members.

Far more significant is the fact that the numbers and percentages of bills that were finally approved show an even wider gap: during the 91st session, 75 of the bills submitted by the cabinet were passed, a 74 percent success rate, while only 10 Diet member bills were approved, or 12 percent. The low rate of passage of member bills is not solely a phenomenon of the 91st Diet. The figures are little different for earlier sessions, providing a clear indication of the advantage enjoyed by government bills as well as of the bureaucratic leadership characteristic of the legislative process in Japan.

Deliberation on Proposed Bills

One of the peculiarities of Diet proceedings related to the points mentioned above is that ministry officials, not the majority party, assume the task of shepherding bills through the approval process. In this sense, the Diet is not a forum for debate among the different parties. For example, almost all of the committee meetings where bills are actually debated are attended by ministry officials known as government "committee members." In the examination process, it is customary for the substantive and significant interpellations to be supplied by these officials, not by cabinet ministers. The bills drafted by the government are usually supported by the majority party and opposed by the minority parties. Typically, the government "committee members" from the ministries respond to the questions of the opposition parties, and then behind-

Table 5.1

Postwar Prime Ministers

Name	Background (Last government position held)
Shidehara Kijuro (October 1945-May 1946)	Bureaucrat (administrative vice-minister of foreign affairs; ambassador to United States)
Yoshida Shigeru (May 1946-May 1947, October 1948-December 1954)	Bureaucrat (administrative vice-minister of foreign affairs; ambassador to United Kingdom)
Katayama Tetsu (May 1947-March 1948)	Political party leader
Ashida Hitoshi (March 1948-October 1948)	Bureaucrat (Ministry of Foreign Affairs; counsellor, Japanese embassies)
Hatoyama Ichiro (December 1954- December 1956)	Political party leader
Isibashi Tanzan (December 1950- February 1957)	Political party leader
Kishi Nobusuke (February 1957-July 1960)	Bureaucrat (administrative vice-minister of commerce and industry)
Ikeda Hayato (July 1960-November 1964)	Bureaucrat (vice-minister of finance)
Sato Eisaku (November 1964-July 1972)	Bureaucrat (administrative vice-minister of transportation)
Tanaka Kakuei (July 1972-December 1974)	Political party leader
Miki Takeo (December 1974- December 1976)	Political party leader
Fukuda Takeo (December 1976- December 1979)	Bureaucrat (director general of Budget Bureau, Ministry of Finance)
Ohira Masayoshi (December 1979-June 1980)	Bureaucrat (secretary to minister of finance)
Suzuki Zenko (July 1980-present)	Political party leader

the-scenes bargaining takes place between the ruling and opposition parties.

One reason that party representatives do not engage in any real debate derives from the weakness of the Diet Secretariat. Unlike the U.S. Congress, which is served by a large and competent staff, the Diet has a secretariat which is no more than an administrative wing. Moreover, the staffs of individual Diet members are hired primarily to handle various ceremonial functions and casework in their constituencies and rarely provide support for political activities in the Diet.

Under these conditions, it is no wonder that individual members cannot even begin to compete with the overwhelmingly superior organization of the bureaucracy in drawing up bills or debating them. Opposition party members' inability to compete with the bureaucrats in the legislative process naturally lead them to focus their attacks on government failures and blunders in implementing legislation.

Implementation of Legislation

It is no overstatement to say that the main role of the Diet is not so much to make laws as to scrutinize the ways in which laws are implemented by the executive branch. The Diet's concerns tend to focus on the implementation process rather than on the legislative process.

As stipulated by the Constitution, the Diet has the authority to investigate not only the implementation of legislation but the entire management of the Japanese government. There is nothing wrong, therefore, with the Diet's looking into any problems arising out of the way the government administers the law. What is wrong is that the Diet seems to be preoccupied and even content with nit-picking criticism of every government mistake precisely because of its inability to formulate overall national policies.

Another reason that Diet members tend to be preoccupied with specifics instead of addressing themselves to wider issues is their need to serve their constituents. Given today's political conditions, the surest way to get reelected is to be able to produce benefits for the home district. As a result, members of the Diet are more interested in individual or local cases than in broad problems. For example, rather than taking an interest in the improvement of the nation's roads as a whole, members will be more concerned with gaining as large an appropriation as possible for road improvements in their own districts to help ensure success in the next election.

Faced with such a fault-finding Diet, the bureaucrats fall back on defending their obligation to preserve confidentiality as public servants. Civil servants are required by law not to reveal any secrets they acquire in the process of carrying out their duties, and the tugs of war in Diet debates often revolve around the scope of government secrecy.

The Diet and the Bureaucracy
in the Budget Compilation Process

The process of compiling the national budget is mapped out in Figure 5.1. In this section this process will be analyzed through the final deliberations in the Diet in three parts: (1) the process of drafting the Ministry of Finance budget proposal, (2) the process of drafting the government budget proposal, and (3) the process of Diet review and approval.

Drafting the Ministry of Finance Budget Proposal

May-August of previous year. The business of drafting the budget begins in each ministry about May or June of the year preceding the new fiscal year, which in Japan runs from April to March 31. Each ministry calculates its estimated revenues and expenditures for the coming year and formulates an estimated budget proposal. This work is done under the direction of the accounting division in each ministry secretariat, which divides the budget into standard budget and new expense requests and assesses the needs of each bureau and division within the ministry. The standard budget is determined on the basis of the budget of the previous year, adjusted according to expected increases and decreases. It consists of expenses that are required by law and those incurred by government contracts. New expense requests refer to all expenses beyond the standard budget, centering on costs for carrying out new or expanded ministry policies and programs.[1] The latter are subject to revision by the Ministry of Finance (MOF). Following several rounds of negotiations between the accounting division and the bureaus, a final draft of the ministry's estimated budget proposal is drawn up and submitted to a ministerial conference for approval. This proposal must be submitted to MOF by August 31. Meanwhile MOF carries on a parallel process of budget preparation. One of its jobs is to estimate tax revenues for the forthcoming fiscal year. This task is handled by the Tax Bureau within the ministry, which must formulate accurate estimates even as changes occur in tax laws and economic forecasts as the year progresses. Another job is the compilation of reference materials, including standard budgets and estimated budgets needed to assess each ministry's budget proposal. Criteria for standard budgets are provided for each ministry so that MOF and the ministries generally are quite close in their estimates of standard budgets. Estimated budgets are calculated on the basis of economic forecasts, budget scale, policy priorities, and unit prices.

July-August of previous year. About the middle of July, the Ministry of Finance sends a memorandum to each ministry with policy guidelines for drafting estimated budget proposals for the coming fiscal year. The memo indicates, for example, the framework within which requests can be made, especially the rate of increase allowed over the current year's budget. At one time, each ministry was free to request any amount it deemed necessary, and, since the

Figure 5.1
Outline of the Budget Process in Japan

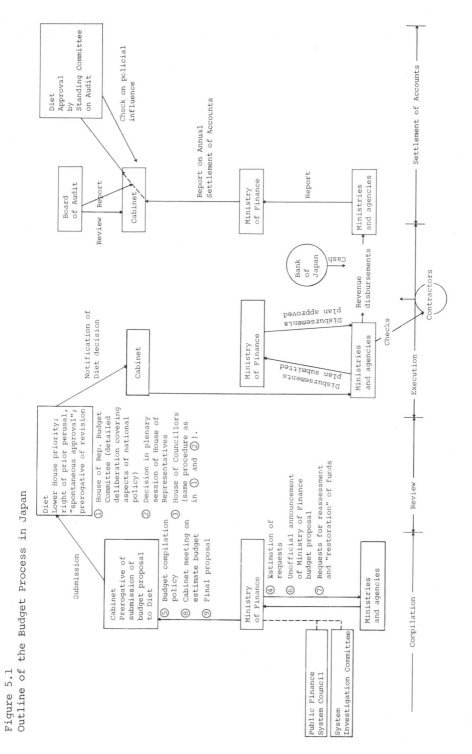

ministries understood that requests would be drastically cut anyway, there was a tendency to submit greatly inflated budgets. However, in order to prevent the wasteful expansion of public finances and to rationalize the assessment procedures, it has been the practice since 1961 for a fixed rate of increase to be established by the cabinet.

During the first part of August, the cabinet is supposed to set policies for drafting the budget for the forthcoming fiscal year. Because of the difficulty of forecasting the economy and the tendency for decisions on other important matters to be delayed, however, the cabinet's final decision is usually made much later—as late as the end of December in a normal year. It is simply extremely difficult to accurately plan ahead because of the complexity of social and economic conditions. Moreover, the chances are that by the time the budget is submitted to the Diet conditions will have changed considerably. Therefore, what is called the Budget Compilation Policy is not actually decided upon in most years until close to the time the Ministry of Finance budget proposal is completed. Consequently, this policy is not actually followed by the line ministries or relied on by MOF in its assessment of ministry proposals. Rather, the cabinet policy has come to be confirmation of policies already established through the budget drafting process in response to changed conditions. Since final budget policy is not provided to the ministries in time to affect the drafting of their estimated budget proposals, the cabinet agrees on a set of guidelines, and these are transmitted, as was indicated above, by MOF in July.[2]

September-December of previous year. The process of assessing the estimated budget requests turned in prior to August 31 begins in the Ministry of Finance Budget Bureau in September. Budget examiners and their subordinates listen to ministry officials explain their requests and question them closely.[3] They may ask for further documentation and/or for a revised budget proposal to be submitted. From mid-October through early December, numerous meetings are held within the Budget Bureau to study and evaluate each revised proposal in detail. Following this process, a succession of Ministry of Finance meetings examines the revised proposals from an overall budget viewpoint in relation to revenues—reports and recommendations become available at that time from the Tax System Investigation Commission on changes in the tax system and from the Public Finance System Council on changes in government bonds policy.[4] An MOF ministerial budget conference then approves a final draft of the Budget Compilation Policy and forwards it to the cabinet, where it is ratified and issued along with economic forecasts for the coming year. Finally, in late December or early January, the ministerial conference approves the now completed MOF budget proposal, which is then reported to the cabinet by the minister of finance.

Influences on the Ministry of Finance budget proposal. Throughout the budget compilation process, MOF officials obviously carry the most weight in decisions. According to the Constitution and provisions of various public finance laws, the person ultimately responsible is the minister of finance; but, in reality, that official has little chance to make a mark on the budget. The prime minister's influence, too, is almost imperceptible at this stage. Most of the discussion is between members of the various ministries submitting budget proposals and Ministry of Finance officials who compile and assess them. It is during the course of the tugs of war between MOF budget officials and the bureau chiefs of the ministries that parts of the budget are really determined.

Although it may appear that political parties and pressure groups are not involved in the compilation of the budget at this stage, that perception is not altogether correct. They are not apparent on the surface, but the demands and priorities of the ruling Liberal Democratic party and of financial circles in other groups that wield great power are in fact reflected in the budget. One channel through which strong demands can be made on the Ministry of Finance is the LDP Policy Affairs Research Council (PARC), whose divisions exert pressure on particular bureaus of the line ministries to increase their budget requests. Another channel is informal influence directly on MOF officials, either through PARC or through the ties maintained by Diet members who came out of the Ministry of Finance. The opposition parties have almost no influence at this stage of the process.

Drafting the Government Budget Proposal

Outline of process. At the same time the Ministry of Finance budget proposal is presented to the cabinet by the finance minister, it is unofficially announced to the ministries. The figures in the MOF proposal, however, are often quite different from the amounts requested by each ministry; in many cases they have been drastically cut. When a ministry feels it cannot accept the amount alloted, it submits a *restoration request*, that is, an appeal that cutbacks made by the MOF be restored. There then ensues a period of about two weeks during which *revival negotiations* take place before the government budget proposal is finally determined. These negotiations are a complicated struggle engaged in not only by the line ministries (represented first by accounting division and bureau directors and then by the administrative viceminister), and the Ministry of Finance (represented first by Budget Bureau examiners and then deputy directors) but also by members of the Liberal Democratic party and a variety of pressure groups. Disputes that are not resolved at the administrative (*jimu*) level are taken to the policy (*seisaku*) level in negotiations between the minister of finance and the heads of each ministry, who try to solve all unsettled issues. Political difficulties that still remain are taken care of in discussions between the minister of finance and the top leadership of the LDP who meet at the prime minister's official residence.[5]

The funds restored in this process rarely represent more than 1 or 2 percent of the entire budget, and the bottom line is hardly affected. The MOF budget proposal provides for this very eventuality by including a pool of funds especially earmarked for adjustment. Each ministry's budget contains unallocated funds. During revival negotiations the Finance Ministry will apportion these funds to programs that line ministry officials insist must be restored and/or for which they can muster political support. Because of this apportionment particular line items in the MOF budget proposal may increase, but totals for each ministry rarely differ from the original allocations.[6]

Immediately following the final political negotiations at the prime minister's residence, a cabinet meeting is held to ratify the agreements just made. At this meeting a rough draft of the government budget proposal, with estimated revenues and expenditures, is approved. After MOF officials make final calculations, a followup cabinet meeting is held (usually the same or the following day) at which the final government budget proposal is confirmed. At that point, the budget compilation process ends; but it is still necessary to draw up the formal Statement of the Budget for presentation to the Diet.

Influences on the government budget proposal. Minor issues among the restoration requests can usually be resolved in the first two or three days of the process during negotiations between Budget Bureau examiners and line ministry accounting division and bureau directors. Larger issues are decided in negotiations between Budget Bureau deputy directors and administrative vice-ministers of the ministries. Important political issues that cannot be settled at that level are referred to the ministerial level negotiations for resolution. These negotiations are held in the finance minister's office between the minister, the vice-ministers, and the Budget Bureau director on one side and the heads of the ministries on the other side. The climax of the budget compilation process is the negotiations at the prime minister's residence between the finance minister and the LDP party leadership.

Most problems are handled at the vice-ministerial level negotiations; at least until recently, the ministerial negotiations were largely a formality. In many ways the process is a kind of drama following an established scenario: the Ministry of Finance and the other ministries follow a script written by the Budget Bureau, and a predetermined plot is played out, ending with a climax in which the ministers themselves appear, all problems are resolved, and everyone "lives happily ever after." This represents one of Japan's unique decision-making patterns; the process is conducted in such a manner that matters are brought to a smooth and dignified resolution without damaging the feelings of any of the parties involved.

As can be seen, the minister of finance and the other ministers are given the main roles in the drama written by their subordinates, but it is not they who take the initiative in compiling the budget, and they do not exercise true leadership at any point in the process. One reason for this is that, as mentioned above, most ministers do not possess the knowledge or administrative skill needed to functionally lead the bureaucracy. Another reason is that in Japan a leader generally leaves the actual work to experienced younger colleagues; in return, however, it is traditionally accepted that the leader will be expected to bear the full responsibility for the final outcome.

It should be noted that, in recent years, the prolonged period of LDP power is gradually changing this established scenario. This change is evident at least in the form of negotiations at the prime minister's residence that bring in top party leaders and have superseded the discussion among ministers. It is also apparent in the pressures brought to bear by the LDP during the revival negotiations. During this process, the budget items of greatest concern to the LDP are brought to the attention of the negotiators by being flagged to indicate their political nature. The Ministry of Finance is made aware that these items are the focus of outside pressure and are where political intervention is most likely. Because of the many years of LDP control of the government, the items flagged are usually approved without much trouble. The difficulty with this practice is that, in terms of content, the budget items do not constitute demands of well-coordinated policy. The vast majority are specific requests for funds, for instance to build a bridge or a road in a district or town, and there is considerable risk that such small items may distort the budget as a whole.

Change is also apparent in the fact that the negotiations at the prime minister's residence shift the scene of action from the Ministry of Finance to a different stage, and it has been there that problems not resolved in the ministerial negotiations have been arbitrated. Nevertheless, these high-level negotiations hardly ever deal with anything more significant than the fate of specific cases like those mentioned above; in other words, they rarely deal with policy matters.

Diet Review and Approval

Outline of process. In most years the budget is formally presented by the cabinet to the Diet in the latter part of January. Ordinary bills may be introduced in the Diet not only by the cabinet but by individual Diet members, but in the case of the budget the cabinet alone holds that prerogative. Moreover, there are special restrictions on bills relating to the budget. For example, they must be introduced at the same time as the budget; if they are being presented by individual members, the cabinet must be consulted beforehand; and unlike ordinary bills, which require only twenty names, budget-related bills require fifty sponsors in the lower house. Following Article 60 of the Constitution, the budget is submitted first to the House of Representatives, whereas ordinary bills may be presented to either house first.

Before the Diet begins actually examining the budget, it is customary for the prime minister to address a plenary session of the Diet and outline basic government policies. This address is followed by a speech by the Minister of Finance concerning the policies followed in compiling the budget. General interpellation is then conducted by the various parties in response. The proposed budget is first sent to the House of Representatives Budget Committee where most of the actual deliberations take place. That committee is composed of fifty members and forms various subcommittees that examine the budget from all angles. Public hearings are held. After review and debate, the budget is put to a vote, and the results are reported by the Budget Committee chairman to a plenary session of the House. Debate continues in the plenary session, and a floor vote is taken. When the budget has been approved by the lower house, it is sent on to the House of Councillors, where it goes through a similar process. In reality, the cabinet presents the same proposal to the upper house just after submitting it to the lower house. Thus, preliminary deliberations can be held simultaneously in both houses, although the House of Representatives always votes on the budget first. After the upper house approves it, usually about the end of March, the budget is finally passed and becomes law.

Diet decisions on the budget are made somewhat differently than those on other bills. Article 60 of the Constitution gives the lower house not only the prerogative of first perusal of the budget but a much stronger voice in its approval than in the case of regular bills. In those cases, when the two houses reach a different decision, a two-thirds majority in the lower house can override the upper house. In voting on the budget, however, if the two houses disagree, a joint committee is convened to try to resolve their differences; but if that effort fails, the original decision of the House of Representatives becomes final. Moreover, in the case of ordinary bills, if the upper house does not decide on a lower house–approved bill within sixty days of receiving it (not counting recesses), the lower house may consider the bill rejected by the upper house and vote to override. For the budget bill, however, the time limit on the upper house is thirty days (not counting recesses), and the lower house decision automatically becomes final. This procedure is known as spontaneous approval. Since government cannot be conducted without funds, the budget is expected to be dealt with and approved promptly. Budget bills are approved more easily than others partly because they are required to provide a financial basis for government within the established legal framework and partly because they are effective for only one year.

It should be noted that although the cabinet has the sole prerogative of introducing budget proposals the Diet is free to revise them. On the other hand, although everyone agrees that the Diet is free to revise the figures downward, many hold that it would infringe on the prerogatives of the cabinet to push them upward. A controversy grew around this very problem during consideration of the fiscal 1978 budget. One side, represented by the opposition parties, held that because the Diet is the highest organ of state power it could legitimately make any increase it wanted in the budget. On the other side were those who argued that increases should not be permitted because they would infringe on the prerogative of the cabinet to initiate budget proposals. Diet rules stipulate that "the Cabinet must be given the opportunity to state its opinion regarding any upward revision of the total amount of the Budget," thus appearing to give the Diet the right to make increases as long as efforts are made to avoid violating cabinet prerogatives. Still, no clear standard exists for determining the extent to which the cabinet's prerogatives are being infringed on, so the issue may continue to arise every year. In the case of the 1978 budget, no final decision was reached on what was the proper interpretation of the Constitution, and the government's realistic response was to incorporate part of the opposition's demands for tax reductions.

Political realities in the Diet review process. During deliberations in the House of Representatives Budget Committee, the budget is subject to general interpellation. Many wonder, however, if any meaningful questioning ever takes place because the questions are usually not pertinent to the budget. In reality, the Budget Committee interpellations have become a forum for debate on foreign affairs, defense, the sundry scandals of politicians — in fact, almost any facet of national government. Diet members take advantage of the fact that interpellations are not restricted to the issue at hand in committee meetings and that the Budget Committee is generally attended by all members of the cabinet and draws more public attention than any other committee. Members, therefore, often bring up a controversial topic having popular appeal and use the occasion to gain publicity for themselves. For this reason, many members of the Budget Committee have not read so much as the first page of the budget statement that lies before them.

When the general interpellations have concluded, more detailed deliberations on the budgets of each ministry begin in subcommittees. But even here there is little genuine discussion of overall policy or examination of the budget from that perspective. Most of the interpellations consist of appeals by Diet members lobbying for benefits for their constituencies. A member who previously worked for the Japanese National Railway Corporation, for example, may argue for increased appropriations for his former organization.

As for political party activity, the general pattern has been for the Liberal Democratic party to try to get the budget passed and for the opposition parties to attempt to prevent its passage. With the 1976 general elections, however, the progressive parties achieved near parity with the LDP in the Diet, and, from the time of the 1977 budget onward, the opposition parties have had a substantially greater voice in the process. This period is discussed in more detail in the next section; suffice it here to say that the opposition has not yet gained the strength needed to bring about a complete rewriting of the budget.

The unproductive nature of Budget Committee interpellations and the virtual suspension of government caused by the attendance in the Diet of all cabinet members and high-ranking ministry officials has created problems on several occasions. While the committee is in session, the staff of the ministries, from the ministers on down, can accomplish little of its routine work. Budget Committee meetings require that many government "committee members" be available solely to answer trivial and unconstructive questions.[7] In this connection, Ministry of Finance officials find it necessary to prepare answers to lists of questions that may be asked of cabinet ministers and government committee members. They must do so because if the questioners do not get immediate answers, opposition party members will usually insist that the deliberations be suspended until they do. To avoid any delays, the ministries devote tremendous amounts of time to preparing for all possible questions.

The unproductive struggles between the Diet and the ministries, as seen in the classic example of the Budget Committee, present one of the greatest problems for efforts to reform the government.

Recent Changes and Prospects

As was mentioned at the outset, the Diet has gradually expanded its power vis-à-vis the bureaucracy since the present Constitution took effect. Its strengthened position in relation to the budget process is charted in Figure 5.2. During the Allied occupation the process was completely dominated by the Ministry of Finance. After 1955, a bipolar structure emerged with the Ministry of Finance on one side and a coalition of the other ministries, politicians, and pressure groups on the other side. The decade beginning in 1965 saw a tripolar structure growing out of the prolonged ascendency of the LDP with conservative politicians now forming a separate power center along with the Ministry of Finance and the other ministries. Then, between the general elections of December 1976 and June 1980, there existed a quadripolar structure encompassing the opposition parties as well.

This section will focus on recent changes in the relationship between the Diet and the bureaucracy that occurred during this last period, analyzing the period in terms of (1) changes in the legislative process, (2) changes in the budget compilation process, and (3) prospects for further changes.

Changes in the Legislative Process

Following the 1976 general elections there began a period of near parity in Diet seats between the LDP and opposition parties. Although the LDP brought as many conservative independents to its cause as possible, it barely managed to retain its upper hand in the Diet, and in some committees opposition members gained sufficient strength to overturn the ruling party's control. The 80th Diet session marked the beginning of this period. The growth of opposition party power can be observed by comparing the number of cabinet-proposed bills passed during the ordinary sessions of the Diet from 1965 to 1976 with the number passed since the general elections of 1976. The average for the former period was 108 bills; for the latter it was 67 bills. The average proportion of cabinet-proposed bills revised by the Diet was 33 percent for the former period and 27 percent for the latter. These figures show that the growth of opposition-party strength in the Diet made the approval of bills submitted by the cabinet

Figure 5.2
Changing Structural Dimensions of the Budget Process

LATE 1940s TO EARLY 1950s: ONE-DIMENSIONAL STRUCTURE

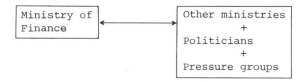

LATE 1950s TO EARLY 1960s: TWO-DIMENSIONAL STRUCTURE

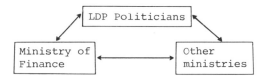

LATE 1960s TO EARLY 1970s: THREE-DIMENSIONAL STRUCTURE

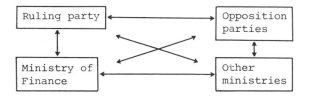

LATE 1970s: FOUR-DIMENSIONAL STRUCTURE

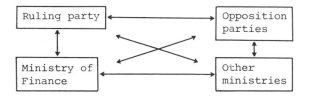

more difficult to gain and that the proportion of bills that the Diet revised declined because of informal prior consultations between the parties, which lay the groundwork for their passage.

As an example of this change, let us look at how two laws, the Revised Social Security Law and the Revised Health Insurance Law, were finally approved during the first extraordinary session of the Diet following the 1980 general elections. Concerning social security, the government, faced with a rapidly aging population and the fact that pension funds would be exhausted in about twenty years under the current law, drew up a bill designed to defer the age at which pension payments would begin from sixty to sixty-five, with the deferment to be phased in over twenty years. The bill also included provisions increasing monthly social security payments as well as improving the kinds of benefits available. The bill became the focus of controversy between the ruling and opposition parties in the 91st Diet when there was near parity in Diet seats between the two sides. It became apparent that a compromise would have to be made incorporating the ideas of the opposition parties. The bill was tabled with the abrupt dissolution of the 91st Diet but was finally passed during the 93rd extraordinary session by limiting the increases in benefit payments and eliminating the age deferral clause.

The bill to revise the Health Insurance Law was also aimed at dealing with the worsening financial plight of a government-managed social welfare program. The original law provided for 100 percent coverage for the persons insured and 70 percent coverage for their families; the revision called for 100 percent coverage for both the insured and their families but required patients to pay half their drug costs. This revision was submitted to the Diet in May 1978 but was not acted on. In April 1980, however, a revised bill was introduced that finally achieved a consensus. The bill called for, among other things, 100 percent coverage for the insured and 90 percent for his or her dependents in the case of hospitalization, and 90 percent coverage for the insured and 80 percent for dependents for out-patient treatment. Like the social security bill, the health insurance bill was not approved until the 93rd extraordinary session.

In these two examples, consensus between the ruling and opposition parties actually consisted of what is commonly called a four-party consensus, that is, one between the Liberal Democratic, Japan Socialist, Clean Government, and Democratic Socialist parties, excluding the Japan Communist party. In this case, the parties treated the two bills as a package to achieve a consensus. That a controversy between the ruling and opposition parties over measures that would have great impact on national life was ultimately resolved and the bills passed by compromise on both sides demonstrates the expansion of minority-party influence in the Diet and of Diet influence on the executive branch.

Changes in the Budget Compilation Process

With one exception, from the time the conservative parties merged to form the LDP in 1955 until fiscal year 1977, the Diet made no revisions in the government's budget. The one exception, involving the 1972 budget, was essentially a technical revision, calling for the deletion of advanced appropriations for aircraft purchases. Thus, no substantive revisions in the content of the budget had been made since 1955, meaning that budget decisions were very much under the control of the executive branch.

Although budget compilation had always been an executive branch prerogative, it was centered around the bureaucracy until about 1965, but since then it has been increasingly under the influence of the Liberal Democratic party. Many reasons have been cited for this gradual shift in leadership, but perhaps the most fundamental is the accumulated skill and know-how within the LDP about the budget drafting process. This growth in knowledge was a logical outcome of the fact that the influence of the Ministry of Finance Budget Bureau was not based on its institutional position but on its monopoly of information. The Budget Bureau could not maintain a perpetual monopoly, however, and so its unchallenged authority gradually began to erode. That erosion became inevitable with the growth of the organizational abilities of the LDP Policy Affairs Research Council that developed through the stabilization of political power following the 1955 merger.

The LDP's stronger position ran into difficulty, however, when the ruling party suffered severe losses in the 1976 general election and the opposition parties gained relative parity in the Diet. Under these conditions, the Budget Committee became a kind of reversal committee, in which the majority were members of the opposition who could force the government to revise the budget. At the same time, the opposition never had the strength to force substantive changes.

In the June 1980 general election, the LDP regained the seats it needed to give it a clear majority on all lower house committees and to put its members at the head of those committees. How the budget compilation process will work as a result of this change merits close attention. Below is a brief summary of Diet revision of recent budgets from fiscal 1977 through fiscal 1980.

Fiscal 1977 budget. This was the first budget brought up after control of the Budget Committee passed to opposition-party members. Their demand to the government and the LDP for a trillion-yen tax cut resulted in heated discussion between the two sides. Ultimately, without altering the size of the budget itself, the government accepted a separate bill calling for a ¥300 billion cut and, at the same time, a supplementary appropriation mainly for social security funds. In the end, the change amounted to a reshuffling of only ¥63.4 million. In other words, on the one hand the government accepted the demands of the opposition, but on the other it refused to revise the budget on the grounds that the revenues quoted there were simply estimates. Nevertheless, except for the technical revision of 1972, this was the first time since 1955 that the government's budget had been touched.

Fiscal 1978 budget. As in 1977, the five opposition parties united in demanding revisions that called for considerable concessions on the part of the government and the LDP. A tenacious LDP strategy of divide and destroy, however, revealed divisions among the opposition. Eventually the New Liberal Club came out in favor of the budget, which was then approved with no more revision than in the previous year.

Fiscal 1979 budget. Negotiations on this budget were moving toward revision, but in the end the LDP refused to accede, creating considerable tension. As a result, the budget was voted down in the Budget Committee but passed by a plenary session of the Diet, the first such reversal of a committee in thirty-one years. Some revisions, totaling ¥11 billion, were made in the budget, however, including the use of contingency funds for certain purposes. This situation seems to indicate the emergence of effective intervention by the legislative branch, made possible by the considerably stronger voice of the opposition parties. Paradoxically, it also shows the LDP's return to a position of strength.

Fiscal 1980 budget. Like that of the previous year, this budget was turned down in the Budget Committee but approved by a plenary session of the Diet. Revisions took the form of changes, totaling ¥14 billion, such as raising social security payments for the elderly, establishing a framework for price controls, and reducing administrative costs.

Toward Constructive Diet-Bureaucracy Relations

It is still not clear how the management of the Diet will change in the wake of the LDP's return to a working majority. From past experience it seems likely that, as a result of the LDP's stable control of the government, opposition influence will gradually subside and Diet budget deliberations will again become a formality. It also is probable that the influence of the LDP on the process of compiling both the Ministry of Finance and the government budget proposals will continue to grow as a result of that party's steady accumulation of knowledge and skill. This change represents a step forward in the maturation of Japan's parliamentary democracy.

On the other hand, considering the direction in which ruling-party influence is moving, there are problems. Politics is intended to provide an important source of leadership and direction for the entire government. The accumulation of political power described in this chapter seems to be aimed less toward accomplishing this fundamental duty than aiding individual politicians' efforts to enhance their power by pursuing the interests of their supporters. Amid the growing complexity and diversity of modern society, legislators must ask whether they can afford to limit the power of the bureaucracy by following the classical division of legislative versus executive branch.

Because of its superior position, the executive branch of government in Japan serves an important role in formulating long-range, coordinated policies that avoid the all too tempting tendency of the Diet to indulge in well-accepted splurges of excessive populism. Rather than seeking merely to limit the power of the executive branch, politicians must bring to the Diet the essence of public will as expressed in the electoral process and, by debate on fundamental problems of government, must strive to guide it in the right direction.

Taking the budget compilation process as an example, the Diet debate on the basic revenue policy for the following year's budget should be conducted around the end of August, as the New Liberal Club has suggested for some time. That would determine the overall framework for the entire budget process, but that process should never be interrupted by government pressure for appropriations for such items as highways and bridges for individual districts.

Notes

1. In Japanese budgeting practice, increases beyond the current year budget, which is essentially not reviewed, are divided into two categories, "naturally increased expenditures" and "policy expenditures." The former may be thought of as fixed and the latter as discretionary spending, in American terminology. In recent years, just as in the United States, fixed obligations have expanded more rapidly than discretionary spending and have outpaced revenue growth. See John Preighton Campbell, *Contemporary Japanese Budget Politics* (Berkeley and Los Angeles: University of California Press, 1977), pp. 84–86.

2. Very recently the cabinet guidelines for the rate of increase allowed to each ministry have been issued as early as April.

3. Japanese budget examiners are considerably senior to those bearing the same title in the U.S. Office of Management and Budget (OMB). There are only eleven in all, compared to dozens in OMB. Campbell states that they are "equal in rank to a division director" (*Contemporary Japanese Budget*, p. 51) and have from three to five principal assistants, each of whom, in turn, supervises a chief clerk and several clerks. (These are all professional, not secretarial, positions.)

4. These are both public advisory bodies to the ministry; their members are appointed by the finance minister and they generally support ministry policies. See Campbell, *Contemporary Japanese Budget*, pp. 24–25 and 238.

5. The party is represented by the "big three" or the "big four" top leaders—the secretary general, the chairman of the Executive Council, and the chairman of the Policy Affairs Research Council, plus the party vice-president when there is one. The party president (that is, the prime minister) does not participate, but the chief cabinet secretary, who is usually his closest political confidant, does.

6. For a complete description of the process of revival negotiations see Campbell, *Contemporary Japanese Budget*, Chap. 7.

7. Government committee members are ministry officials; see above.

6

The Role of the Diet
in Foreign Policy and Defense

Shuzo Kimura

The Diet and Treaties

Diet Ratification of Treaties

Under the Meiji Constitution, the conclusion of treaties was an imperial prerogative reserved to the emperor, and the imperial Diet had no part in the process. The postwar Constitution, however, provides that while the cabinet shall "manage foreign affairs" and "conclude treaties," for treaties it shall also "obtain prior or, depending on the circumstances, subsequent approval of the Diet" (Article 73). But how does this constitutional provision operate in actual practice?

It should be noted first that the requirement of Diet approval is not limited to those international agreements that contain the term *treaty* in their titles. Whether they are called treaties (*joyaku*), agreements (*kyotei*), protocols (*giteisho*), exchanges of notes (*kokan kobun*), or arrangements (*yakujo*), any international pacts meeting the criteria set by the government are considered to fall under the constitutional provision, and Diet approval is sought. The criteria set by the government include three categories: first are international pacts that affect the legislative powers of the Diet by requiring new legislation or the extension of existing laws (international pacts containing legislative provisions); second are pacts that require a disbursement of funds beyond the level already budgeted or permitted by law (international pacts containing financial provisions); and third are pacts that are conditional upon ratification because they contain politically significant international commitments for Japan (international pacts of political importance). Any international agreement falling within these three categories is considered a treaty under the Constitution.

Research by this author has revealed that, from the first postwar session of the Diet through the most recent session (the 92nd, ending July 26, 1980), the government has received Diet approval for 537 treaties, of which 265 were bilateral and 272 multilateral. The Diet has thus approved slightly over 15 treaties per year. Of these 537 treaties, 369 (156 bilateral and 213 multilateral) were approved unanimously, and 168 (109 bilateral and 59 multilateral) were approved over minority dissent. In other words, about 60 percent of the bilateral and about 80 percent of the multilateral treaties were approved with no opposition whatever. Although strong objections raised by opposition parties or even by members of the ruling party have occasionally caused deliberations on a particular treaty to be carried over to a subsequent session, all such treaties were eventually approved. Thus, the Diet has in fact approved every single treaty submitted to it.

The Proliferation of Administrative Agreements

International pacts not falling under the three criteria described above are considered administrative agreements and are concluded without the formal participation of the Diet. Some of these agreements (e.g., an exchange of notes concerning the extension of a yen loan) are concluded independently in their own right; others (e.g., an exchange of notes agreeing to a common interpretation of a treaty to prevent double taxation) are annexes to treaties already approved by the Diet; and still others (e.g., an exchange of notes altering a table appended to an aviation agreement) are negotiated by the executive branch under authority explicitly delegated to it in a treaty approved by the Diet. Though the last two categories may not be politically important, the first includes quite a few pacts of considerable political significance. It contains, in particular, nearly all of the bilateral agreements governing Japanese economic assistance to other nations, including in each case the amount of aid, how it is to be provided, and the projects on which it is to be spent. Most Japanese economic assistance is implemented through such bilateral agreements rather than through international organizations. The agreements to furnish substantial yen loans to Indonesia and the Republic of Korea, for example, are in this form.

As mentioned, one of the government's criteria for needing Diet approval is that the treaty require a disbursement of funds in excess of the amount already budgeted or permitted by law. The other side of this condition is that international agreements that call for disbursing funds within the level budgeted or permitted by law may be concluded by the executive branch on its own. To be sure, administrative agreements on economic assistance stipulate that funds will be provided in accordance with relevant Japanese laws and regulations and within budgetary limits. And the amount to be made available for economic assistance is, in fact, part of the budget submitted to the Diet each year. However, the budget contains only the gross figures, and there is usually no breakdown by country or project. As a result, the Diet lacks the means of controlling the specific forms of economic assistance for which the funds will be used.

Over the last decade, the government concluded an average of about 90 administrative agreements per year from 1970 to 1976, 160 in 1977, 190 in 1978, and 210 in 1979. The trend is clearly up. In 1979, administrative agreements outnumbered Diet-approved treaties by more than ten to one. Though it may be natural for many important international pacts to be entered into on the sole authority of the executive branch, this predominance is one factor diminishing the role of the Diet in setting foreign policy.

The Primacy of the House of Representatives

In the United States, the "advice and consent" power over the ratification of treaties rests with the Senate. In Japan, primacy in such matters is given to the House of Representatives. Normally, a treaty must be approved by both houses of the Diet, but when the two reach different decisions and the difference cannot be resolved by a joint committee or the House of Councillors fails to take final action within thirty days of a decision made by the House of Representatives, the lower house prevails (Article 61).

There have as yet been no cases in which the two houses came to different decisions, so there have been no joint committee conferences. There have been, however, thirteen cases in which the House of Councillors failed to take final action within the thirty-day limit, thus in effect acquiescing to the lower house's decision—a process commonly referred to as automatic passage. Such cases can be divided into two general categories. First are those cases in which the ruling and opposition parties differed so sharply on the proposed treaty that normal deliberations were impossible. Classic examples are the 1960 Japan-U.S. security treaty and the 1977 Japan–Republic of Korea continental shelf agreement. Second are cases in which there was no disagreement over the treaty itself but the treaty could not be voted on because the upper house was in disorder over some other piece of legislation. This type includes, for example, the 1966 Brussels tariff nomenclature treaty and the 1974 convention between Japan and the Soviet Union for the protection of migratory and endangered birds and their habitats.

Diet Deliberations

Given the primacy of the House of Representatives, it is customary to submit treaties of political importance to that house first. In actual practive, the decision on order of submission to the two houses is made by the board of directors (*rijikai*) of the House of Representatives Committee on House Management after that body hears the views of the board of the Committee on Foreign Affairs. The government follows the lead of these decisions.

Once submitted to either house, a treaty is usually referred to the Committee on Foreign Affairs, where the substantive review and debate takes place. In some cases, treaties of particular importance have been referred to special committees established in each house expressly to handle them. The Japan-U.S. security treaty, the treaty on basic relations between Japan and the Republic of

Korea (Japan-ROK treaty), and the agreement between Japan and the United States concerning the Ryukyu and Daito islands (the Okinawa reversion agreement) are cases in point. In either the Standing Committee on Foreign Affairs or a special committee, the debate primarily takes the form of the opposition party's questioning of cabinet members and ruling party committee members. Should the committee deem it necessary, outside experts may also be called to testify or a public hearing may be held.

In this process, Diet approval is sought for the "conclusion" of a treaty, which the government interprets as referring to the entire sequence of events by which Japan commits itself to becoming a party to the treaty: the negotiations, the signing, the ratification, and the exchange or deposit of the instruments of ratification. Therefore, a treaty that requires ratification to take effect and is submitted to the Diet after its signing but before ratification is considered by the government to have been submitted for prior approval. By this standard, only 10 of the 537 treaties approved by the Diet were submitted for subsequent approval, 4 of which went into force with their signing. The only treaties submitted before being signed were 3 that took effect on the date of signing or the following day. Therefore, 527 treaties were submitted after being signed but before ratification, all of which are considered to have been submitted for prior approval.

The question of whether the Diet can partially approve or request alterations in a treaty submitted to it has been frequently debated. The government has taken the negative position regarding both points, and that position has been supported by majority opinion in the Diet. Thus in both interpretation and actual practice, the Diet can only approve or reject a treaty in toto; it lacks the power to make changes.

After the Foreign Affairs Committee has completed its questioning and voted for approval, a treaty goes to the house floor. The committee chairman makes an oral report in which the treaty is outlined briefly and the committee's deliberations are summarized. In most cases, the treaty is then voted on immediately without debate. Floor debate takes place only for the most important treaties and even so is likely to be a formality. After these procedures have concluded in the house to which the treaty was first submitted, the other house goes through exactly the same process.

The Limited Role of the Diet

The Diet's clearest opportunity to speak out plainly on foreign policy comes when it grants or withholds approval of a treaty. In theory, the Diet can substantially tie the government's hands by denying or delaying approval. By its treaty deliberations it can question or seek changes in the government's plans and actions. Since the war, the ruling and opposition parties have frequently been so sharply at odds over questions of foreign policy that Diet proceedings have been disrupted. This was the case, for example, during deliberations on the Japan-U.S. security treaty, the Japan-ROK treaty, and the Okinawa reversion agreement.

As already noted, however, a treaty is not submitted to the Diet until agreement has been reached with the other country or countries and the text of the treaty is settled. The Diet can only approve or reject an already written treaty; it cannot formally participate during the earlier drafting or negotiation process, nor can it make any alterations in the treaty when its formal participation is finally sought.

The Diet in Foreign and Defense Policy

Factors Limiting the Diet's Role

The previous section discussed treaty approval as one aspect of the Diet's formal participation in foreign affairs. This section examines the Diet's part in shaping foreign and defense policy in a general sense.

The first point to note is that the Diet's role in this area is severely limited by Japanese political tradition and the prevailing political situation. Because Japan has a parliamentary form of government, the cabinet is assumed to enjoy the support of a majority of the Diet (for if this support is lost, either the cabinet resigns or the Diet is dissolved). In this form of government, the opposition parties constantly find fault with the government's policies, and the ruling party constantly defends them. There may be numerous differences of opinion within the government party over specific issues, but these differences rarely surface during the formal Diet deliberations. Instead, important policies are decided through informal agreements made within the ruling party or between it and the bureaucracy. The role of the ruling party in the Diet is thus mainly to defend these policies from attack by opposition members.

The LDP has never once lost its majority in either house of the Diet. There have been several changes of government, but they reflected shifts in the power structure within the LDP, not any shift of power to another party. The LDP's decisive victory in the simultaneous election for both houses in June 1980 ended the conservative-progressive power convergence. The conservative party has a firm majority, and, as noted above, even the considerable differences that may exist between the various factions do not surface on the floor of the Diet. All members are regulated in both word and deed by their party, and Diet deliberations are therefore exchanges of stock arguments.

Another major factor that has limited the role of the Diet has been the nearly unreconcilable differences between the ruling and main opposition parties' views on Japanese foreign and defense policy. It was this ideological confrontation between the ruling party and opposition parties over basic Japanese foreign policy that caused disruptions during the Diet's deliberations on the Japan-U.S. security treaty, the Japan-ROK treaty, and the Okinawa reversion agreement and on other occasions. In the area of defense policy, the debate has been especially acrimonious because the government and ruling party seek acknowledgment of the Self-Defense Forces' present status and want to increase their strength, but some of the opposition parties adamantly maintain that their very existence is unconstitutional. Accordingly, the LDP usually tries to get the government's bills through the Diet as quickly as possible, while the opposition parties do their best to block them. There is little chance that Diet deliberations will formulate constructive counterproposals to replace the government's proposals.

Enacting Laws

Given these restraints, what precisely does the Diet do? The Constitution designates the Diet as the only state law-making body, and the Diet can pass any laws consistent with the Constitution. Thus the Diet ought to be able to exercise substantial control over foreign and defense policy by enacting laws in this area. Yet, despite the Diet's constitutional role, most important legislation is initiated by the cabinet, and the proportion of legislation proposed by Diet members has fallen considerably.

In the area of foreign policy, three types of bills are submitted by the cabinet: (1) those related to the reorganization of the diplomatic structure, such as bills revising the Law for the Establishment of the Ministry of Foreign Affairs or the Law for Determining Names and Locations of Diplomatic and Consular Offices Abroad; (2) bills to enact or revise laws required by the conclusion of treaties; and (3) bills such as the Japan Foundation Act and the Japan International Cooperation Agency Law that are themselves of major political significance. The Diet has never made substantial changes in any bills in any of these three categories. Also, as far as this author can discover, there has been only one Diet-initiated bill ever passed that had even the slightest bearing on foreign policy, and this was for a more or less technical revision of the Japan Immigration Service Law exempting foreign emigrants from the repayment of JIS loans for passage abroad. Of the cabinet-initiated bills, those aimed at ratifying controversial treaties may get caught up in disputes, but others usually pass through the Diet with relatively little trouble.

Not so the legislation concerning defense policy. The adamant resistance of the opposition parties frequently causes consideration of defense-related bills to be suspended or carried over to the next session. Like foreign policy legislation, such bills are almost never sponsored by Diet members but are virtually always initiated by the cabinet. There are two types of bills: (1) those aimed at revising the Defense Agency Establishment Law, which defines the organization and size of the Defense Agency, and (2) those designed to revise the Self-

Defense Forces Law, which defines the organization and duties of the various units of the Self-Defense Forces. Debate on these two types of bills is mostly conducted by the standing committees on the cabinet of each house, with the opposition parties frequently trying to prevent passage of the bills by delaying tactics or physical resistance and the ruling party resorting to closure and forced votes.

Thus, rather than actively participating in the shaping of foreign and defense policy through legislative means, the Diet has usually engaged in contests between the ruling and opposition parties, with one side doing its best to get bills through and the other doing its best to prevent them. In contrast to the U.S. Congress's enactment of foreign aid bills and the War Powers Act, the Japanese Diet has never originated any legislation that had any impact at all on foreign or defense policy.

Budget Deliberations

Since the implementation of major foreign policy and defense measures often requires financial support, it is possible for the Diet to play a substantial role in shaping policies by exercising its constitutional power to administer the nation's finances. This possibility has remained largely theoretical, however, for the Diet has almost never made any significant changes in the budgets submitted to it by the government. On only nine occasions has the budget been modified after going to the Diet, and on six of these it was changed by the government and not the Diet. The three occasions on which the Diet itself modified the budget all occurred before the party realignment of 1955.

In the section on administrative agreements above, it was mentioned that the government budget reserves a total amount for foreign economic assistance but does not allocate specific amounts for particular countries or projects. As a result, no close inquiry is made into the actual nature of Japanese economic assistance even though the Diet reviews and debates the budget. As was pointed out in Chapter 5, the Diet concentrates on questioning the government policy in various domestic affairs, unearthing contradictions, and hounding the government on an abstract level. When the opposition turns up some discrepancy or when the government's responses are not consistent, the opposition parties frequently halt the proceedings of the Budget Committee by boycotting them, after which a political compromise must be found to restore the norm.

For example, the fourth defense buildup plan was to begin in 1972, but because of the sudden policy shifts sprung by the Nixon administration in the summer of 1971 (the devaluation of the dollar and Kissinger's visit to China), it was not officially adopted by the National Defense Council and the cabinet as scheduled. Nevertheless, the fiscal 1972 budget submitted to the Diet in January 1972 included funding and concomitant treasury liability for the procurement of three types of aircraft called for under the plan. The opposition attacked the government sharply on this point, arguing that it was inadmissible for the budget of the plan to be passed before the plan itself had been adopted. The proceedings of the Budget Committee were interrupted for nearly three weeks as a result. The matter was finally resolved by a proposal offered by the speaker of the House of Representatives by which the government would resubmit the budget, minus the aircraft procurement funds, and the treasury's liability would be held in abeyance until the defense plan had been adopted and its adoption confirmed by the speaker. All parties accepted this proposal, and normal proceedings were resumed.

In another instance, the fiscal 1979 budget, submitted to the Diet on January 25 of that year, contained funds and treasury liability for the purchase of the E-2C patrol plane. A report by the U.S. Securities and Exchange Commission (SEC), however, noted illegal payments in connection with aircraft exports by the Grumman and McDonnell Douglas corporations. The opposition maintained that the E-2C, manufactured by McDonnell Douglas, should not be purchased until all suspicions were cleared up. Once again, Diet proceedings were interrupted. This time, they were resumed through a compromise between the ruling and opposition parties under which those parts of the budget related to the E-2C were frozen until such time as was deemed proper by the speaker of the lower house and the president of the upper house.

In both of these cases, part of the defense budget was temporarily frozen in a political compromise after a confrontation between the ruling and opposition parties in the Budget Committee. In both cases, however, the funds were later released, and the Diet's actions did not lead to any real change in policy.

Adoption of Resolutions

The adoption of resolutions is another means by which the Diet can give expression to its views on foreign policy and defense matters. Resolutions formally expressing Diet views are binding on the government. Diet resolutions, however, that state the opinion of only one of the two houses have only political or moral rather than legal force.

Table 6.1, based only upon this author's research, summarizes the draft resolutions submitted to the two houses over the past fifteen years, from the opening of the 51st session in December 1965 to the close of the 93rd session in November 1980. As can be seen, forty-six draft resolutions were submitted to the House of Representatives and thirty-seven to the House of Councillors, but less than one-third were actually adopted by either house, the others being withdrawn or shelved. Since the LDP held a majority in both houses throughout this period, any draft resolutions it did not approve were defeated; and it has shown a strong tendency to oppose resolutions that would significantly restrict the government's freedom of action, even though this restriction would be only political and moral.

Table 6.1

Draft Resolutions Concerning Foreign Policy and Defense Issues Submitted December 1965–November 1980

Issue	House of Representatives				House of Councillors			
	Submitted	Adopted	Withdrawn	Shelved	Submitted	Adopted	Withdrawn	Shelved
Japanese nuclear policy	8	1	2	5	6	0	3	3
Calls for disarmament and a halt to nuclear testing	5	4	0	1	11	4	5	2
Okinawa and Northern Territories	12	4	0	8	8	4	1	3
Japan-U.S. security treaty and military bases	7	0	2	5	2	0	0	2
Japan-People's Republic of China relations	6	1	1	4	7	1	0	6
Japan-Republic of Korea relations	3	0	0	3	0	0	0	0
Other issues	5	3	1	1	3	2	0	1
TOTAL	46	13	6	27	37	11	9	17

Note: The period covered in this table is from the 51st through the 93rd sessions of the Diet.

Limitations on the Diet's Investigative Role
in Foreign Policy and Defense Issues

The Increasing Importance
of the Investigative Function

As was discussed above, the Diet has a very limited role in shaping foreign and defense policy through legislative action by ratifying treaties, enacting laws, passing the budget, and adopting resolutions. Of course, even outside Japan, there is said to be a worldwide tendency for legislative branches to shift from actual legislating to disclosing information, raising issues, and overseeing the executive branch. Rather than being central and active participants in policy decisions, legislatures are becoming more peripheral organs influencing these decisions obliquely, overseeing the administration of policy, and bringing government information and issues into the open. This description is particularly true of the Japanese Diet's participation in foreign policy and defense. The constitutional mandate that underlies these Diet functions is its power to "conduct investigations in relation to government" (Article 62).

Treaties, bills, budgets, and resolutions are actual legislative measures and are therefore conceptually different from the investigative function. As was explained above, however, these measures are usually passed by the Diet without any modification, so the results of the Diet's work are less significant than the process the Diet goes through, by means of which issues are brought to light and the government's intentions are clarified. Thus, despite the conceptual distinction, the Diet's deliberations are coming more and more to serve the function of investigation into government.

Committees Responsible
for Foreign Policy and Defense

The Diet, like the Congress, entrusts its investigative functions to both standing and special committees. The standing committees of the Diet for foreign policy are the committees on foreign affairs in each house and for defense policy are the committees on the cabinet in each house. The House of Representatives' committees are composed of thirty members each; those in the House of Councillors have twenty members each.

The committees' jurisdictions vary depending upon the house. In the lower house, the Foreign Affairs Committee is charged with overseeing "matters under the jurisdiction of the Ministry of Foreign Affairs," and the Cabinet Committee is charged with "matters under the jurisdiction of the Defense Agency," besides overseeing the cabinet secretariat, National Personnel Authority, Imperial Household Agency, and other agencies that come under the cabinet. In the upper house, the Foreign Affairs Committee is responsible for matters concerning diplomacy, treaties, international conferences and organizations, overseas commerce, Japanese nationals abroad, travel abroad, migration, and other international affairs. The upper house's Cabinet Committee has jurisdiction over "matters concerning national defense," as well as the Imperial Household, national administrative organization, public officials, and more. Thus, the House of Representatives determines jurisdiction by ministry and agency and the House of Councillors does so by subject, but the result for oversight and investigative purposes is really the same in both cases.

Since the two cabinet committees deal with a wide range of matters other than defense, voices are often heard calling for the establishment of standing committees concerned solely with defense affairs. The LDP in particular adopted this platform because debate on the Self-Defense Forces and the Defense Agency establishment laws were often held up in the cabinet committees by deliberations on other issues. The opposition parties, however, especially the Japan Socialist and Japan Communist parties, strongly resisted the establishment of such committees. A compromise was reached in April 1980 with the creation of a twenty-five member Special Committee on Security in the House of Representatives that was restricted from debating any bills and maintaining the jurisdiction of the cabinet committee over the Defense Agency and Self-Defense Forces. In July 1980 a similar compromise was worked out in the House of Councillors; its Special Committee on Okinawa and Northern Problems was reconstituted as the Special Committee on Security, Okinawa, and Northern Problems. As a result, security and defense questions may now be investigated by both the standing committees on the cabinet and the special committees on security in both houses.

In addition to these committees, the standing committees on the budget in each house give considerable time to the examination of foreign policy and defense issues during the course of their deliberations on the budget, as do the two houses' audit committees. Foreign trade issues are dealt with mainly by the standing committees on commerce and industry in each house.

The Rusty Investigative Function

Although these several committees investigate foreign policy and defense issues, the investigative function doesn't work very well. In fact, Professor Matsushita Keiichi, a political scientist at Hosei University, considers that it has "rusted fast." Three reasons for this failure have already been given. First, the same party remains (semi-) permanently in power and constantly defends the government's interests in the Diet, making it difficult for the Diet to conduct any thorough investigations. Second, the government party and opposition parties are in sharp and largely ideological disagreement over the basic direction of foreign and defense policy. Third, party discipline is so strict as to inhibit Diet members from speaking freely and going beyond formal party doctrine.

A fourth reason is the lack of continuity in leadership on the Diet committees. The chairs of all these committees in both houses have been monopolized by the LDP, which tends to spread them around, just like the ministerial and vice-ministerial posts, to maintain a balance among party factions. Thus, changes of chairman are frequent. From the first postwar Diet session in 1947 through the end of 1980, thirty-eight different people have chaired the lower house's Committee on Foreign Affairs, and, since four of these officiated for two nonconsecutive terms, the position has actually changed hands forty-two times. This same pattern can be seen in the other committees. It is repeated almost exactly in the upper house's Committee on Foreign Affairs, where the chair has been held by thirty-six different people and has changed hands forty-one times since the first postwar Diet session. The average term of incumbency for a chairman is less than a year. Since that is not nearly enough time for a person to gain any special expertise or experience on the issues under a committee's jurisdiction, chairmen rarely take the lead in oversight or investigation of the government. Rather, accepting the views of the ruling party and allied executive branch agencies, they concentrate on getting bills passed and treaties approved as quickly as possible.

A fifth reason for the Diet's ineffectiveness in investigation is the lack of staff support. Standing committees in both houses have their own investigative staffs consisting of six or seven specialists headed by a chief of staff. Special committees have similar specialist staffs working for them. In addition, the National Diet Library has a Research and Legislative Reference Department of nearly two hundred professionals, but only seven or eight of these are specialists in foreign affairs or defense. Thus, the total number of foreign affairs and defense specialists on the staffs of all the standing and special committees and the National Diet Library is fewer than fifty. This number does not begin to compare with the huge staffs of the Ministry of Foreign Affairs and the Defense Agency. Individual Diet members are allowed to hire only two people at government expense, which hardly permits a private policy staff. This weakness in staff resources means that the various committees are inherently limited in their oversight and investigative activities.

The Style of Committee Debate

As noted above, there are almost irreconcilable differences in views between the ruling and opposition parties on basic foreign and defense policies. As a result, committee deliberations in this area tend to be directed not toward forging common policies but toward harping on the other side's shortcomings and logical inconsistencies. When questioned by a committee, government officials volunteer information, explicate the truth, and seek a public judgment rather than trying to fabricate plausible and consistent explanations. In *The Analysis of International Relations*, Karl W. Deutsch defines debate in the strict sense as a form of confrontation between two opposing sides in which both parties' motives, value systems, and perceptions of reality are open to change. It is difficult to discern any debate in this sense in the deliberations of the Diet on foreign policy and defense issues.

As Professor Kinhide Mushakoji has pointed out, government officials, answering questions of the opposition parties, offer neither objective information that might furnish the basis for debate nor concrete policies that respond to opposition criticism. Instead, they evade the issues and try to escape legislative oversight behind a smokescreen of ambiguity. Thus, democratic control over foreign and defense policy is lost in an issue-clouding style of debate. Until something is done to enhance the Diet's investigative function, that body will continue to have little role in foreign policy and defense issues.

Part 2

The U.S. Congress

7
Congress in the U.S. Political System

James L. Sundquist

When the Constitutional Convention that created the United States of America met in 1787, the fifty-five delegates were dominated by the fear of tyranny. They had known the rule of George III of England before the Revolution, and in the dozen years after the war they had suffered arbitrary threats to the rights of property from the legislatures of the thirteen independent states that had been formed out of the colonies. To guard against the despotism of either a single tyrant or a group of tyrants, they scattered the powers of government among a variety of institutions. First, they divided these powers between the national (federal) government and the states. Then they split the national powers among three branches of government—legislative, executive, and judicial. Finally, they divided the legislative share of that power between a senate and a house of representatives.

Thus came into being the American system of checks and balances. In the two centuries since, it has served superbly well the purpose of shielding the nation against tyranny; never has despotism been an imminent danger. But it has also created a continuing problem in the functioning of government, for powers that are scattered in order to prevent their falling into the hands of potential despots are also difficult to assemble for effective use by democratic leaders for entirely good and worthy purposes. In particular, three independently elected institutions that share in both legislative and administrative power—the president, the Senate, and the House—have to be brought into some reasonable degree of harmony for government to function constructively and decisively.

The web that has bound these three power centers is an institution not mentioned in the Constitution—the political party. When the president and the majorities of both houses are of the same party sharing a common set of political and government goals and with leadership that is both strong and accepted, the checks and balances can be overcome, and innovative policies can be enacted and carried out. When the three power centers are controlled by opposing parties or when the harmony among them is disturbed for whatever reason, the checks and balances prevail. The system then tends toward sluggishness and deadlock, and the policy output tends to be biased in favor of the status quo.

How the Checks and Balances Have Evolved

The checks and balances remain today as they were written in 1787. Nevertheless, interpretation of constitutional language can change, and so can institutional behavior. How the principal checks and balances have evolved can be set forth briefly.

The Federal-State Balance

The national government is, in theory, one of "enumerated" powers. The Constitution contains eighteen clauses defining the subjects on which the Congress may legislate, then reserves all other legislative power to the states. Yet the language of these basic enumerated powers is broad and general, and the Congress has steadily expanded the scope of its legislation. Moreover, when it uses the device of grants in aid—that is, providing federal funds to state and local governments—to enter fields that the Constitution's authors may have meant to reserve for the states—education, health, welfare, and municipal public works, for example—it has been able to do so without restraint. The judiciary has held that nobody is injured by grants in aid, making it difficult for an opponent to obtain the standing to challenge the constitutionality of this device in the courts. And since few people in fact have felt injured, political resistance to federal expansionism by this method has been slow to develop.

A constitutional crisis exploded during the Great Depression in the 1930s, when the collapse of the national economy brought forth President Franklin Roosevelt's New Deal. With powerful support in Congress, the New Deal resulted in a revolutionary expansion of the role of the national government in U.S. society for the purposes of relieving unemployment and hunger, reviving the economy, and reforming the economic system. At the same time, however, the cry of federal usurpation of states' rights arose. The Supreme Court of that time, declaring that some of the major New Deal laws exceeded the Congress's enumerated powers, found those laws unconstitutional. This judicial check on the Congress had to be and was overcome (as discussed in the next section). Then the Supreme Court redefined the legislative powers of the national government, and the New Deal was largely sustained. Since the 1930s, only one minor national law has been held invalid as an invasion of states' rights, and that term has virtually disappeared from the national vocabulary. As a practical matter, the only restraint on the national government vis-à-vis the states now is self-restraint, and the federal-state balance is wrought by political forces rather than by constitutional interpretation.

In the political arena, the Democratic party has generally been the party of federal activism, the Republican the party of restraint; this has been the principal issue that divides and defines the parties. When Republican presidents are elected, they do their best to check the expansion of the national government—or even to reduce the federal role. President Eisenhower was held to a stalemate by the Democratic Congress, but Nixon and Ford—backed by the public opinion of their time—succeeded to some degree. Democratic presidents Kennedy and Johnson, on the other hand, behaved in the Roosevelt tradition, launching their New Frontier and Great Society to rival his New Deal, thrusting the federal government into a vast range of activities (civil rights, medical care for the elderly, environmental protection, grants in aid for many new purposes, and so on). However, President Carter, a Democrat, responding to the public antispending mood in the 1970s, proposed little that was new or bold. President Reagan, in his turn, has gone far beyond his Republican predecessors in initiating a drastic curtailment of federal activities.

The Judicial Check on Congress

At an early date, the Supreme Court asserted its power to interpret the Constitution and so to declare actions of the other branches invalid when they contravened its interpretation of that document. Since then, at various times, it has asserted this power in order to limit the expansion of the national government, to protect corporations against governmental regulation, and to protect the civil rights and liberties of individuals. When President Truman acted to take over the management of the country's private steel plants to keep them operating during a strike, for instance, the Court demanded that he give them back to private control—and he, of course, complied.

When the Court renders decisions interpreting the Constitution's guarantees of individual rights, opponents of those decisions sometimes accuse the judges of usurping the functions of legislature and making law. Attacks on "judge-made law" followed especially in the wake of decisions in the 1950s and 1960s outlawing school desegregation, forcing reapportionment of state legislatures to make constituencies of roughly equal size, and forbidding public authorities to prescribe prayers in public schools.

Since federal judges, including Supreme Court justices, serve for life, they may appear to be beyond a countervailing check. Yet such is not the case. Over time, the executive can remold the Court, because the president nominates the justices, subject to Senate confirmation. The Congress also has the power to reorganize the judiciary and can even regulate by legislation the appellate power of the Supreme Court.

The vulnerability of the Court, in the above and other respects, should it outrage the other branches, inhibits its ambition. When the Court in the 1930s, as discussed above, declared a series of New Deal laws unconstitutional, President Roosevelt proposed legislation to enlarge—or "pack"—the Court. He lost the legislative battle but won the war: the threat and the public outcry against the Court, together with his replacement of retiring justices with his own selections, brought about a shift in the Court's position. As noted, the limits of expansion of the national government were in effect erased. On other kinds of questions, however, the Court still checks the other branches in this process — as, for instance, in *Buckley* v. *Valeo*, when it declared invalid certain limits the Congress tried to place on presidential campaign expenditures on the grounds that they violated the constitutional guarantee of free speech.

Executive Checks on the Congress

The president checks — at times, controls — the Congress by two means. The first is informal and unrecognized by the Constitution: the granting or withholding of favors. Presidents can win support among members of Congress, for example, by appointing the members' political allies to executive or judicial posts. Presidents can include projects the members desire in the executive budget or exclude those projects. They can support or oppose legislation that members sponsor. Popular presidents can aid members in their campaigns. The second check is the president's great constitutional power over the Congress, the veto. A president can reject any measure passed by the Congress, and a two-thirds vote of both houses is required to override the veto. That is such an abnormal majority that the threat of veto is often adequate to persuade the Congress to compromise enough to win the president's approval of a disputed bill.

When it is well-organized and determined, the Congress can resort to a countermeasure to the veto. It may, for example, attach the bill as a rider to another bill that the president supports. Thus, bills to appropriate funds, or to raise the ceiling on the national debt, that have to be passed to permit the government to function at all frequently carry unwanted riders. At various times, presidents have tried to induce Congress to permit an item veto — that is, the power to disapprove individual provisions in a bill — but the Congress has never been willing even to consider giving the president any such tactical advantage.

Legislative Checks on the Executive

Although the president can check the Congress at any time on any legislation, through the veto, the Congress has no such control over the president. The constant frustration of the legislative branch is that its checks on the executive branch come either before the fact — before the executive acts — or after the fact, never during the action. Once a law is passed, the Congress has no constitutional right to participate in any way in the execution of the law or even the right to be consulted.

Before the fact, the Congress can check and control the executive by writing into law precise provisions as to how the executive shall carry out the law. The

Administrative Procedures Act, for instance, governs the processes by which executive agencies make and enforce regulations. On many occasions, however, it is obviously impossible for the Congress to anticipate all the circumstances that will arise; therefore, the executive must still be granted considerable discretion in administration of the laws.

Also before the fact is the constitutional requirement that principal officers of the executive branch be confirmed by the Senate before taking office. During confirmation hearings, Senate committees can extract promises from prospective appointees as to how they will carry out their duties, and informal understandings can be reached on future consultation. But confirmation is also a limited check. Clearly, senators cannot know in advance which administration officials might subsequently ignore their commitments or abuse their powers. Nor can they anticipate what circumstances will arise in which they might wish they had received advance commitments. As for informal understandings, in any severe conflict between the branches they can be forgotten or denied, and there is little that senators can do about it.

So once the laws are passed and the officials confirmed in office, as a practical matter, Congress loses control. Constitutionally, it cannot intervene in administration, although attempts to do so are made; it must wait for things to happen, and then if it is not satisfied with the outcome it can try to legislate corrective action after the fact—after the damage has been done—or attempt reprisals in unrelated ways.

The processes by which the Congress tries to keep informed of administrative activity, so that it can act if necessary, are known collectively as *congressional oversight*. These include formal processes undertaken by committees, such as oversight hearings, evaluation studies, and occasional large-scale investigations, and a steady flow of inquiries and communications initiated by committee staffs or individual members or their staffs. Assisting the committees, in addition to their own staffs, are four agencies available to the whole Congress and composed of highly qualified professions—the General Accounting Office, the Congressional Research Service of the Library of Congress, the Office of Technology Assessment, and the Congressional Budget Office. Administrative officials complain constantly of the burden of congressional oversight—the time spent in compiling information and preparing reports and in testifying at hearings, and the harassment that they sometimes feel—yet they acknowledge its importance in keeping them sensitive to the public, whose views the members of Congress reflect. Oversight is sometimes friendly, too, carried on by sympathetic committees trying to build support for agencies. And it is far from intensive for most agencies; members find oversight activities to be tedious, time-consuming, and—except in the case of scandal—not likely to produce publicity and hence possible political reward. Although there has been a great growth in oversight during the past decade, much of the executive's activity remains out of sight and unreviewed.

When the legislators find what they believe to be violation of the congressional intent, or waste or malfeasance, they can react through the regular legislative processes; they can enact corrective or clarifying legislation (subject to presidential veto, of course) or they can reduce or raise appropriations. In extreme cases, they can also act outside those processes: they can expose executive officials to adverse publicity, through hearings and investigations, and members singly or in groups can denounce the officials. The threat of such action — and of legislative or appropriation action as well — can often bring administrators to change their ways. These threats can also, of course, cause administrators to "bend the law" or act illegally; the line between constructive oversight and improper interference is easily and often overstepped.

The Long Decline of the Congress

In the nineteenth century, the United States saw periods of executive dominance, when strong presidents had their way with the Congress, and periods of congressional supremacy, when weak presidents yielded to aggressive congressional leaders. With Theodore Roosevelt (1901–1909), Woodrow Wilson (1913–1921), and especially Franklin Roosevelt (1933–1945), the office of the president caught the public imagination and acquired some of the aura that in other countries is reserved for royalty. Since Franklin Roosevelt's time, at least, the country has expected strong presidential leadership, the media has demanded it, every candidate has promised it, and every president has tried to supply it — even those who, temporarily, might prefer a more passive role.

Moreover, the strong presidency has been institutionalized. Over and over again, in this century, the Congress has assigned new powers to the president and provided the institutional machinery — now assembled in the Executive Office of the president — to execute them. It has organized itself to respond and react, to check and even advise presidential leadership, but not itself to assume the responsibility of being a nation's leader. The shift in power from the Congress to the president can be summarized under four headings.

The President as General Manager

In the Budget and Accounting Act of 1921, the Congress directed the president to present each year a program and budget for the entire executive branch. Before that time, departments and agencies took their requests directly to the Congress, and the legislators exerted the discipline and assembled the budget. After 1921, the president was the channel of control. Subsequently, many acts reinforced the position of the chief executive as manager in the model of the head of a giant corporation, at the apex of a hierarchy of departments and agencies subject to presidential direction. Recently, as will be seen in a later chapter, Congress has sought to reinvolve itself more fundamentally in the budgetary process.

The President as Chief Economic Stabilizer

In the Employment Act of 1946, the Congress made the president responsible for having, at all times, an economic program, aimed at ensuring "maximum production, employment and purchasing power." Before that time, presidents were not legally obliged to take responsibility for the state of the economy, and until Franklin Roosevelt none did. Now they must set forth their economic programs annually. The Congress, of course, may accept, reject, or modify the presidential program, just as it may approve or alter the president's budget. But it is significant that in both these cases the Congress considered locating the staff assistance (the Bureau of the Budget and the Council of Economic Advisers, respectively) in the legislative branch and taking the responsibility for program formulation itself, but in both cases it dismissed the idea in favor of building up the presidency as the point of leadership. Congress did, however, establish the Joint Economic Committee to consider the president's program, prepare recommendations on it, and initiate economic studies on its own.

The President as Foreign Policy Leader

In foreign and military affairs, unlike in domestic matters, the president has always had powers independent of Congress—of uncertain scope—derived directly from the Constitution, in addition to those authorized by statutory law. The president's constitutional authority includes that of recognizing foreign governments and receiving and dispatching ambassadors, which by extension has come to mean the power to conduct diplomacy and to negotiate with other governments. The Constitution also makes the president commander in chief of the armed forces, in charge of troop and ship movements anywhere on the globe. The power to declare war is reserved for the Congress, but in Korea and Vietnam, for instance, war was not formally declared and the president acted under his own authority. After World War I, the Congress attempted by law to enforce a policy of neutrality, to prevent presidents from making commitments or deploying military forces in such a way as to involve the United States in any future war. When war broke out in Europe in 1939, this policy was abandoned as a failure, and for the next three decades the Congress generally left foreign policy and military strategy to the president. It created the National Security Council—again, responsible to the president—to coordinate foreign and military policies, and in a series of resolutions in the postwar period gave the president virtually a free hand—in the executive branch's interpretation, at least—to intervene to any extent and in any manner in designated troubled areas of the globe. The last of these resolutions, in 1964, covered Southeast Asia. President Johnson cited that resolution, along with his constitutional powers, as the basis for carrying on the Vietnam War without reference to the Congress. Congress had to appropriate funds to conduct the war, but it had little alternative to providing the necessary money once U.S. forces were involved in the fighting, although many members took the view that they had not authorized the military actions.

The President as Chief Legislator

In the nineteenth century and even into the twentieth, the Congress was so jealous of its legislative independence that bills drafted in the executive branch had to be transmitted surreptitiously to legislators for introduction and their origin had to be kept hidden to avoid outright rejection as a matter of principle. But in the crisis of the Great Depression, attitudes changed, as the Congress as well as the public turned desperately to the president for leadership. In the legendary hundred days that followed Franklin Roosevelt's first inaugural, bills were not only drafted in the executive branch but were sometimes passed before they were printed or even thoroughly read. By now, congressional attitudes have come to be almost the direct opposite of those of a century ago. Many members expect major bills to be sent to them from the president and his department heads; members demand the bills, complain if they do not arrive on time, and wait until they do arrive before beginning the legislative process.

Every president now sends to the Congress at each session a comprehensive legislative program, contained in the State of the Union Message, the budget, the economic report, and innumerable special messages on particular topics. The president thus sets the agenda for the Congress. More than that, he meets regularly with his party leaders in the Congress to work out the legislative schedule, set forth priorities, and plot tactics, and he often takes more responsibility than do the legislative leaders themselves for mobilizing support for his bills within the Congress. Where once the president's role was limited to approving or vetoing congressional initiatives, the executive branch is now the source of more initiatives than is the legislature, and the president is in that sense the chief legislator as well as the chief executive.

The Recent Resurgence of the Congress

The flow of power from the Congress to the president occurred during a period when both branches were normally controlled by the same party. Party loyalties in the electorate were firm enough that most citizens voted straight tickets—that is, supported their party for all offices on the ballot. Thus, in the seventy years before 1956, the president always had congressional majorities of his own party during the first half of his four-year term, and usually in the second half as well. When the Congress saw the need to center responsibility somewhere—as for preparing a coordinated budget, or an economic program, or a comprehensive global strategy—it was natural to repose it in the president not only as chief executive and head of state but as leader of the political party to which the majority of the members of Congress belonged.

In the last three decades, however, a phenomenon of immense importance in the United States has been the disintegration of political party organizations and the accompanying rise in the number of independent voters and in the extent of split ticket voting. The Democratic party has remained the majority party ever since the 1930s, and in the voting for the less prominent offices of senator and representative, where party attachment is more significant, the Democrats have regularly prevailed; except for 1947–1948, 1953–1954, and (in the case of the Senate only) 1981–1982, they have controlled both houses for fifty years. But in the highly dramatized presidential elections, the voters now tend to choose between candidates on the basis of individual appeal rather than of the party labels they wear. As might be expected, the Republicans have produced the more appealing individual half the time. So, half the time in the past quarter century, the country has had "divided government," with the Republicans controlling the executive branch and the Democrats the legislative or, in 1981–1982, one of the two houses. Under such circumstances, the opposition legislators are to some degree compelled by the dynamics of party competition to reject the president's leadership and even to attempt to discredit him. Conflict is inevitable. At best, when the personalities are compatible, a kind of tenuous coalition government results. At worst, the conflict degenerates into rancor, recrimination, and bitterness, with each branch seeking to gain political advantage by defeating the initiatives of the other.

In the winter of 1972–1973, just before and after the landslide reelection of President Nixon, the interbranch, interparty warfare reached the scale of a constitutional crisis. Aggressive by temperament, Nixon pushed the powers of the presidency far beyond what any of his predecessors had attempted and, in so doing, "aroused a snoozing Congress and made it mad," as one journalist put it. Nixon impounded billions of dollars in appropriated funds, a step that amounted to unilateral repeal of laws that the Congress, with presidential approval, had enacted. He suddenly intensified the war in Vietnam while the Congress was in adjournment. He claimed unlimited power to withhold information from the Congress solely at his own discretion. And he put into effect a government reorganization plan requiring some cabinet members to report to him through other members, along the lines of a proposal Congress had explicitly rejected.

When the legislators met in 1973, they were in an angry mood, many Republicans as well as Democrats. Over the next few weeks, they reached an extraordinary collective resolve to "restore the Congress to its proper constitutional status as a coequal branch of government," in a phrase that was often repeated. Out of that period came a series of legislative measures and a transformation of attitude that has substantially altered the executive-legislative balance in favor of the latter. (Changes in the organization and distribution of power within the Congress, already underway, were accelerated also, as discussed in Chapter 9.) The most important of these developments are described below.

The Congressional Budget and Impoundment Control Act

This measure outlawed the practice of impounding appropriated funds for policy reasons, which earlier presidents had begun on a limited scale but Nixon carried to the extreme. Now the president can only recommend impoundments, with final decision in the Congress. The act also established a complex set of procedures for producing a comprehensive and integrated budget within the legislative branch, geared to a considered fiscal policy, in order to remove the charge of congressional "irresponsibility" that was Nixon's basis for claiming that presidential impoundment was a necessary practice. (These procedures are described in full in Chapter 11.)

The War Powers Resolution

This resolution, passed over the president's veto, was an attempt to reclaim the war-making power — or at least a role in declaring war — for the legislative branch. Under its terms, the president must consult with the Congress to the maximum feasible extent before engaging U.S. forces in hostilities or putting them in a place where involvement might be threatened. When the president does so deploy them, he must report within forty-eight hours. If the Congress does not approve his action within sixty days, he must cease the involvement. The procedures of the act have been followed in some minor incidents but have not been tested in a major conflict. Both President Ford and President Carter accepted the requirements voluntarily, without conceding their constitutionality. (See Chapter 12 for details on the War Powers Resolution.)

Intensification of Oversight

The new assertiveness of the Congress in the 1970s has been reflected in an increase in the number of oversight hearings and in a considerable expansion of staff assigned to monitor the administration of programs, working directly for senators and representatives, for committees and subcommittees, or for one or another of the support agencies, one of which, the Congressional Budget Office, was created in 1974. More and more programs have been subjected to annual reauthorization, which means an annual review, and others to two-year or three-year terms. Support has grown for "sunset" legislation, which would require every program authorized by law to expire and be reauthorized after a designated period, probably ten years. Some laws contain what are known as "report and wait" provisions, requiring administrative agencies to notify the Congress of contemplated actions a specified number of days before the actions are taken. Congressional committees can then hold hearings and express their views formally or informally or can even initiate legislation to block an action they oppose. Such a procedure brings the legislative branch close to the goal of involving itself during the course of administration rather than afterward.

The Legislative Veto

Beyond ordinary oversight procedures lies the procedure of the legislative veto. This device, which was invented in the 1930s but used sparingly until the 1970s, requires by statute the submission of certain contemplated interpretations of law and other actions of the executive departments—arms sales to foreign countries, for example—to the Congress for review and possible disapproval. Some statutes require both houses to disapprove in order to invalidate the action, but others authorize invalidation by action of only a single chamber (or even by a committee, but such provisions are now rare). Presidents from Franklin Roosevelt to Jimmy Carter have steadfastly asserted that legislative vetoes are unconstitutional, on the ground that once a law is passed its execution is the sole prerogative of the executive branch until the law is changed—which cannot be accomplished even by both houses except through the normal legislative processes. Nevertheless, presidents have been forced to accept veto provisions on occasion as the price of getting any law at all. Whether the legislative veto procedure is indeed unconstitutional is a matter ripe for judicial determination, and the Carter administration seized on a case involving the deportation of an alien to start the issue on its way to the Supreme Court. Although President Reagan has endorsed the concept of the legislative veto during his campaign, he authorized his own attorney general to pursue the litigation that the previous administration had begun. Even if this particular legislative veto provision were outlawed, however, that decision would not necessarily render invalid all the other statutory clauses, for the courts may be able to distinguish among various kinds of veto provisions.

Assertiveness in Foreign Affairs

In the clash between the Congress and President Nixon, the thirty years of congressional passivity in the field of foreign affairs came to an end. In a series of events in the next few years the Congress took important decisions in defiance of the president, for the first time since before World War II. The Congress legislated an end to the Vietnam War. It upset President Ford's policy in the Cyprus dispute, siding with Greece and alienating Turkey. It ended the Ford administration's hope for a trade agreement with the Soviet Union by attaching an amendment requiring an expansion of Jewish emigration from that country, which caused the Soviets to cut off negotiations. And it barred U.S. involvement in Angola when the administration sought to channel aid to one of the guerrilla factions. When the White House passed into Democratic hands, the Democratic Congress became somewhat less assertive. Nevertheless, it delayed for a critically long period the assistance the Carter administration wished to send to the revolutionary government in Nicaragua, and it put obstacles in the way of arms sales to Arab countries. It took an inordinately long time in responding to the calls by presidents Ford and Carter for a comprehensive response to the world energy crisis. More than in the preceding decades, the government speaks with multiple voices, most importantly in world affairs, and foreign countries can no longer be reasonably sure that assurance received from the president and his ambassadors will be supported.

The balance between the president and the Congress in the U.S. system has never been static, and shifts will occur in the future as in the past. Some of the institutional changes of the 1970s put the Congress in a far stronger position than before on any occasion when it chooses to challenge and confront the president. The congressional budget process, the War Powers Resolution, and the expansion of legislative staff all make it possible for ambitious members of Congress or aggressive committees to assert a greater and more authoritative role in national policy. Meanwhile, other institutional developments—notably the weakening of political party organizations and the accompanying loss of party discipline—make it more likely that legislators will be, in fact, more assertive in opposition to presidential leadership. The decline of parties also means that periods of divided government—with one or both houses of Congress under control of the party opposed to the president—will continue to characterize the U.S. system. Nonetheless, the resurgence of the Congress may be at or near its crest. Except among the advocates of the legislative veto, there is little demand now for further major accretions of power from the executive; the legislative branch has won its battles on the specific points on which, in 1973, it felt that President Nixon had overstepped the line between the branches, and it may now be about as "coequal" as it wants to be. With unified party control, one might expect trust in the president as party leader to be at least partially restored, and the balance might begin to swing back once more in the direction of the executive.

At least through 1982, however, divided party control will continue. If and when President Reagan's public popularity begins to slide—as any new president's standing tends to do after the initial "honeymoon" period—House Democrats can be expected to become more assertive, as they were during the Nixon and Ford administrations. The result will be some degree of interparty, interbranch conflict. The possibility that such conflict can reach a high level of intensity, leading to stalemate and deadlock in policy making, cannot be dismissed, given the unique American structure of separated powers. Yet at some times of divided government—perhaps most notably during the middle years of the Eisenhower administration—leaders of the two branches have assumed a posture of mutual restraint and respect and have managed to find a basis for collaboration on crucial questions.

8

The U.S. Congress: Structure, Party Organization, and Leadership

Robert L. Peabody

Congressional party leadership in the 96th congress (1979–1980) was as strong and as stable as it had been for several decades. The House and Senate Democratic majorities and Republican minorities were led by experienced politicians. The cumulative seniority of the nine principal leaders in the Congress—the Speaker, floor leaders, and whips—amounted to 186 years of congressional service by 1980. These House and Senate leaders were, in the main, praised and respected by the media and their colleagues. Yet, in seeming paradox, not only that congress but the several preceding congresses, and especially the House of Representatives in those congresses, have been characterized by greater independence, ferment, and challenges to seniority among younger members than at almost any other time in U.S. history.

This chapter will explore the apparent paradox between the drive toward autonomy on the part of the more junior members and the apparent stability of congressional leadership. First, however, it will briefly examine the history of party organization in Congress and then describe the contemporary House and Senate, their structures, party organizations, and leadership.

The Structures of the House and Senate

It is useful to review the basic structures of the two bodies as set forth in the U.S. Constitution. In 1789, the founders were in general agreement on a number of assumptions. Chief among these were a commitment to (1) constitutionalism, that is, specific limitations on government; (2) separation of powers, as expressed in the division among three branches of government—legislative, executive, and judicial; (3) a system of checks and balances among these three main branches; and (4) federalism, or a division of power between the national government and the states.[1]

As the Declaration of Independence and other Revolutionary War pronouncements reveal, the American revolutionaries were apprehensive about all concentrations of power, but especially about power concentrated in the executive branch. Relying on their experiences with colonial government, they were more comfortable with a strong legislature. Significantly, Article I of the U.S. Constitution treats of the powers of the legislative branch. It begins with a broad grant of power: "All legislative Powers herein granted shall be vested in a Congress of the United States, which shall consist of a Senate and House of Representatives."[2] But even these legislative powers are limited to expressed, carefully delineated functions such as the raising of revenue and the appropriating of funds for governmental activities.

Members of the House of Representatives are elected for two-year terms. Senators serve for six years, but their terms are staggered so that one-third of the total is elected every two years. Representatives are apportioned among the various states based upon population. Two senators represent each state, regardless of its size.

The first Congress met in New York City in 1789. It consisted of 65 representatives and 26 senators. As the population increased, the membership of the House gradually increased until following the 1910 census it was stabilized at its present size—435 members.

As more states were added to the original thirteen, the size of the Senate also expanded. With the addition of Hawaii and Alaska in the late 1950s, the Senate reached its present size of one hundred members. Originally, senators were selected by state legislatures. However, with the ratification of the XVII Amendment to the Constitution in 1913, senators, like House members, came to be directly elected by the people.[3]

A member of the House typically represents a constituency of about half a million people. A senator's constituency ranges from less than half a million (for example, Alaska or Wyoming) to more than 20 million (New York and California). Members of Congress, regardless of the size of their constituency, place great emphasis on serving and responding to the needs of the people they represent. Over the years constituency case work has led to expanded personal staffs, ranging in size from fifteen to eighteen in the House to more than forty to fifty persons in a typical Senate office.[4]

Although the House and Senate share most legislative powers, their differing sizes and lengths of tenure and the nature of their ties to their constituents have resulted in significant differences in leader-follower relationships, party and committee organization, and scheduling operations in each body.

The Place of Political Parties
in the Congressional System

Neither the colonial experience, the formal language of the Constitution, nor the initial rules of the House and Senate provided a role for parties in the legislative process. Gradually, however, "factions" began to coalesce around major personalities in the first legislatures and administrations. Men like Secretary of Treasury Alexander Hamilton, Secretary of State (later President) Thomas Jefferson, and Representative (also later President) James Madison attracted others to their causes.

The formation of parties was also encouraged by the constitutional provision requiring the House to choose a Speaker at the beginning of each new congress. By the early 1800s members were taking sides for or against recognized party candidates for Speaker—Republican or Federalist and later Democrat or Whig. As the powers of Speakers emerged in practice, they began to solidify their positions by appointing loyal followers to the chair of key committees. Party-identified chairmen began to guide committee deliberations and to manage legislation on the floor.

Party activity and formal leadership patterns were slower to develop in the Senate than in the House. The vice-president was also designated as president of the Senate by another provision of the Constitution. That document also called for the selection of a member of the Senate as president pro tempore in the vice-president's absence. But neither position ever became one of much Senate influence, in part because the vice-president, as a member of the executive branch, was viewed with suspicion. The vice-president does, however, have the power to vote to break a tie in the Senate. Party floor leaders did not emerge as consistent legislative participants until about World War I.[5] Over the next several decades the formal party machinery of both Democrats and Republicans evolved into their present structure. In the contemporary Senate, both parties are led by floor leaders, majority and minority, who in turn are supported by assistant floor leaders or whips and other, lesser officers.

The Contemporary Role of Parties in Congress

Political parties are the single most important factor in explaining voting patterns in both the contemporary House and the Senate. That is to say, if one were restricted to a single piece of information about a given member's propensity to vote yes or no on a legislative issue, the member's party identification—Democrat or Republican—would indicate, generally speaking, the most. Nevertheless, as compared with its importance in Japan, party is a weak signal in identifying each member's voting pattern. Aside from the opening vote on the election of the Speaker and a few other procedural votes, few roll calls will find all Democrats on one side and all Republicans on the other side. A wide range of influences other than party enter into voting—a member's personality, ethnicity and ideology; district and state forces that affect him or her; presidential and interest group pressures—in addition to the advice of the party leadership or that of other trusted senators and representatives.

U.S. congressional parties remain fragmented and decentralized for several basic reasons. In the first place, unlike candidates in parliamentary party systems, such as those of the United Kingdom, France, or Japan, congressional candidates are nominated at the local level, usually through direct primaries. Their campaign organizations come from local followings. National parties play a limited role in congressional elections even in terms of campaign finance assistance. The principal sources of campaign funds are usually local contributors and, increasingly, political action committees (PACs). Thus, members come to Congress with their strongest and most pervasive loyalties to their districts and only secondary loyalty for the president of their own party or the national party leadership. Conflicts between constituency interests and a presidential or national party position are more likely than not to be resolved in favor of the local perspective.

The organizational character of the House and Senate also reflects its membership, a diverse set of politicians who are expected to pass legislation that is attuned to the interests of the districts and states they represent. These members are brought together not only to initiate, legislate, and oversee national governmental policy but also to look after the unique constituent interests. The variations among competing interests—national, state, and local—can often be extreme. But representatives and senators, if they wish to remain in office, have become adept at reconciling the interests.

Leadership Positions in the House and the Senate

With the exception of the Speaker, the major party leadership positions in the House of Representatives are of relatively recent origins, dating back in most cases to the nineteenth century. The Speaker's position and initial responsibilities were clarified in the first several congresses. Not until 1883, however, did it become commonplace for the losing candidate for Speaker to assume the role of minority floor leader. By 1899, the office of majority floor leader, typically the chairman of the Ways and Means Committee, took on a separate and continuous identity. Party whips, responsible for evaluating and helping to align forthcoming votes, began working closely with the Speaker and floor leaders early in the twentieth century.[6] Although both parties made use of caucus or conference chairmen, these positions would seldom involve major responsibilities until the late 1960s.

The Speaker

This constitutionally designated office is at the apex of the formal hierarchy of the House. The office has a number of important responsibilities. The Speaker presides over the business of the House; the Speaker is the principal leader of his party, the chief administrative officer of the House and chief ceremonial officer. In addition, the Speaker serves as a member of the House, elected every two years and with the same obligations to represent a district as any of the other 434 members.

Every Speaker has been preoccupied with efforts to reconcile his responsibilities as the impartial chief presiding officer with those of his role as the partisan leader of the majority. Often his party is trying to pass legislation that the opposing party is trying to delay by dilatory tactics on the floor. Then the question becomes: Should he use a "quick gavel" to expedite passage of the legislation, or should he hear out the concerns of the minority party? As presiding officer, he has a responsibility to protect the rights of all members, majority and minority. But as the leader of the majority, the Speaker also tries to advance his party's legislative objectives, which will affect his party's ability to continue to control the Congress.

Especially in modern times the Speaker and other party leaders have turned to a cadre of professional staff assistants to help them carry out their leadership responsibilities. In addition, the Speaker can expect the support of such House officials as the clerk, the sergeant at arms, and the parliamentarian. The latter officer is available not only to advise the Speaker on rules, floor procedures, and parliamentary precedents but also to advise other members from both sides of the aisle.

Floor Leaders

The primary responsibility of floor leaders—majority and minority—is to organize their party's forces to develop winning coalitions on key votes. The majority leader is the Speaker's principal assistant; the minority leader heads the opposition. If the president is of the same party as the majority party in Congress, the administration's program becomes the floor leader's major responsibility. The majority leader, working closely with staff aides, also has responsibility for preparing the weekly schedule of legislation coming to the floor. Finally, the majority leader builds support for the time when there will be a vacancy in the Speakership. Traditionally, the majority leader is the candidate most likely to succeed the Speaker when the latter retires or leaves office.

The minority leader plays a complementary role to that of the majority leader. At the beginning of each new Congress, he is nominated by his party conference for the Speakership; but it is a contest he will inevitably lose on a strict party-line vote in the House of Representatives. Thereafter, he generally works closely with his Senate counterpart in efforts to modify or defeat the proposals of the majority party. Or conversely, if the minority party in Congress has one of its own persuasion in the White House, it will try to implement his programs. Thus, Republican leaders, although a minority in Congress, generally cooperated with Republican presidents Nixon (1969–1974) and Ford (1974–1976), but they usually opposed Democratic President Carter's legislative objectives in the 95th and 96th congresses.

All floor leaders, Democratic and Republican, majority or minority, are involved in five broad areas of activity: (1) monitoring internal party organization, especially maintaining relationships with committee and other party leaders; (2) formulating and implementing legislative agendas; (3) keeping in touch with other House members, especially from their own state delegations, regions, and party; and (4) overseeing the activities of key staff.

Moreover, party leaders are engaged in a wide range of external relationships, especially with the White House, executive branch officials, interest group spokesmen, and media representatives. Presidents have held informal meetings with key members of Congress from the beginning, but from World War I on, presidents and their staff began to meet once a week for breakfast with the House and Senate leaders of their own party. Often committee leaders involved in specific legislation will also be included. About once a month presidents will meet with congressional leaders from both parties.

A party leader, almost by definition, is at the center of communications in Congress. Thus, he or she becomes a special source of information for members, lobbyists, and journalists who wish to stay informed and who wish to report back to their constituents or clientele or the broader public. A skillful leader makes as much or more use of interest group spokesmen and reporters as they do of him or her. The relationships are inherently two-way, involving give and take on both sides.

The range and intensity of these activities will necessarily shift from day to day and from one legislative session to another, but party leaders become more frenetic as the biennial elections approach. Their activities shift to include intense campaigning for their incumbent colleagues and for promising challengers to the opposite party's members. Every two years, the minority has the possibility, but rarely the probability, of winning enough seats to become the majority. All four congressional parties have created campaign committees to help provide technical assistance to members, raise funds, and distribute them to incumbents and promising beginning candidates.

Party Whips

The whip is generally viewed as the third-ranking leader in the House majority party and the second-ranking official in the minority party. By tradition, the leaders of the Democratic party appoint their whips. The whip is usually the Speaker's choice, but floor leaders may, from time to time, have a strong input in the selection. Republicans, in contrast, elect their whip, usually at their biannual party conferences. Both House parties have elaborate whip systems composed of three or four regional whips and from ten to twenty assistant or zone whips.

The task of whips, regardless of party, is essentially twofold: (1) to maintain a nearly constant communication with their party colleagues—on the floor, in the corridors, by telephone, and through whip notices and background advisories; and (2) to help their leaders obtain the most up-to-date and sensitive information about how their colleagues feel about forthcoming legislation, especially key floor amendments.

Other Party Offices

Democrats and Republicans have also created other party offices; the most important are the chairmen of their respective party caucuses and policy committees. In past congresses, meetings of the two major party members were generally confined to an opening-day caucus designed to select nominees for the Speakership. But from the mid-1960s on, the two parties began to hold almost monthly meetings in order to discuss party and committee reforms and other legislative matters. As a consequence, the chairman of the Democratic Caucus and the Republican Conference began to emerge as important party leaders who no longer served as mere routine functionaries.

Both parties have also reactivated policy committees in recent decades for the purpose of discussing and taking party positions on major legislation as well as other matters. Republicans have made consistent use of this party mechanism for about two decades; Democrats only since about 1974. As long as the Democrats continue in the majority, their Speaker also presides over their Steering and Policy Committee. In addition to evaluating party positions, this party committee makes assignments of Democratic members to committees of the House. Republicans assign committee positions through a separate committee, called the Committee on Committees. The Republican committee is controlled by the heads of large state delegations through a weighted voting system (one vote for each Republican member in the state delegation).[7]

Party leadership is rather limited in its impact on members in the House. It has even less of an impact in the Senate. Partly, this has been a function of relative size; a senator in a body of one hundred members enjoys a greater sense of autonomy than his or her more numerous House counterparts. A senator's six-year term in office also contributes to his or her sense of independence. He or she is not constantly concerned about running for reelection. The media, especially television, have also contributed to a senator's sense of status by providing a degree of attention that is often criticized by House members.

Whereas the Speakership gradually became the focal point of party leadership in the House, as has been noted, neither of the principal formal offices of the Senate — the presidency of the Senate (held by the vice-president of the United States) and the presidency pro tempore — ever evolved into a position of major leadership. Instead, power has gravitated to the floor leaders, whips, and other party officers.

Floor Leadership

The two Senate parties continue to be characterized by similar formal structures, but as Donald R. Matthews, Ralph K. Huitt, and other observers have noted, in practice they operate quite differently.

The Democratic floor leader has greater potential for centralized leadership because the office also holds with it, simultaneously, the chairs of the other critical decision-making bodies in the Senate Democratic party organization, namely, the Policy Committee, the Steering Committee (which handles committee assignments), and the conference (or caucus). Only the positions of party whip and secretary of the conference and the chair of the senatorial campaign committee remain in the hands of other senators. Moreover, a strong leader can usually affect the choice of the senators who hold each of these positions.

In contrast to Senate Democrats, Republicans have a multiplicity of lesser officers from which to select a candidate for floor leader. A Republican leader must usually share formal power with six or seven colleagues.

Contemporary Senate majority and minority leaders are responsible for five somewhat overlapping primary tasks: (1) managing party organizational machinery, (2) supervising the scheduling of legislation, (3) implementing the flow of the Senate's business, (4) contributing to policy innovation, and (5) enhancing the electoral opportunities of their colleagues in order to achieve or maintain control of the Senate.[8]

Managing the party organizational machinery. The principal difference between Democratic leaders of the Senate and their Republican counterparts has already been stressed, namely, the potential for greater centralization of power under the former. As floor leader and chairman of the conference, policy committee, and steering committee, the Democratic leader has a positional base that can lead to maximizing influence over the party. Of course, even the strongest of floor leaders is constrained by the power of committee chairmen and the autonomy that individual senators enjoy.

The Senate, like the House of Representatives, is organized by standing committees. In the 96th congress (1979–1980) there were fifteen Senate and twenty-two House committees as well as over two hundred subcommittees. The major Senate committees were closely parallel to those in the House — for example, Appropriations, Finance (Ways and Means), and Budget. The Senate committees such as Foreign Relations and Judiciary are also highly esteemed, in part because of their constitutionally derived involvement in treaty making and the confirmation of judges.

Committee and subcommittee chairmen play major roles not only in initiating legislation but also in managing legislation on the floor. As Ralph K. Huitt has observed, "The chairman of the major standing committee in the Senate is an influential and an important man indeed. He usually is in virtual control of his committee."[9] And, of course, the more the chairman dominates the committee, the more independent he can be, if desired from the floor leader.

In general, however, floor leaders work closely with committee chairmen and ranking majority members across a wide range of legislative matters, but especially in scheduling decisions.

Scheduling legislation. A primary responsibility of the majority leader, working with the minority leader, is to oversee the scheduling of legislation for the floor. The assistance or the acquiesence of the minority is essential to the orderly operations of the Senate. The minority generally cooperates with the majority on most procedural questions not just because it has a stake in the integrity of the institution but also because it expects and receives accommodation with regard to its own legislative interests.

To the maximum degree possible, legislative proposals, especially major bills, are scheduled so as to facilitate their orderly discussion, allow consideration of amendments, and reduce time and scheduling conflicts. The combined leadership, in short, tries to accommodate all senators, not only as a courtesy but as the better part of political wisdom.

External events sometimes take over and frustrate the most rigorously developed plans of the floor leaders. Thus, senates of the late 1960s and early 1970s were deadlocked for days at a time over civil rights and Indochina policy. In the 96th congress, an arduous effort to bring up SALT II, the strategic arms limitation treaty, had to be abandoned because of the crisis in Iran and the Soviet invasion of Afghanistan.

Implementing the flow of business. By tradition the majority leader is the first to seek and receive recognition from the presiding officer when the Senate convenes each day. The majority leader's right of first recognition is one of his most important leadership prerogatives. Once recognized, the leader may engage in an exchange with the minority leader as to the schedule or yield time to other Democratic senators. Through first recognition and other procedures, the majority leader generally is able to guide the flow of legislation, unless there is fierce and sustained opposition (especially a *filibuster*, a tactic by which a few senators prolong discussion of a bill) or a breakdown in the majority party's support on a particular measure. In order to circumvent a filibuster, a *cloture* petition must be filed. Three-fifths (sixty votes) of the Senate must vote affirmatively if debate on the measure is to go forward.

Contributing to policy innovations. How involved in the substance of any particular piece of legislation should a majority leader become? The question has been answered in different ways by different leaders. At a minimum, leaders can be expected to take an active part in legislation coming out of the major committees of which they are members and any significant legislation affecting their states. Unlike the Speaker or the House majority leader, Senate leaders do keep their committee assignments even after they are elected to top party positions. Former Majority Leader Mike Mansfield, for example, was a member of the Foreign Relations Committee. Throughout his years in the Senate, he rarely missed involvement in questions of foreign policy.

Robert C. Byrd, the Democratic leader since 1977, has concentrated on energy policy, a specialty greatly facilitated by his chairmanship of the Subcommittee on Interior of the Appropriations Committee. As a direct result of his ties to West Virginia, Byrd has a strong and continuing interest in all matters relating to coal, including the protection of miners from black lung disease.

Supporting the election of colleagues. Members of both parties look for and welcome leadership assistance in their reelection campaigns. Floor leaders are expected to campaign on behalf of their colleagues, and they generally do. But senators also can and do call upon other colleagues, including nationally known committee chairmen and former candidates who have won presidential nominations of their party in the past. Moreover, there will be more than two hundred House members but seldom more than about twenty Democratic senators running for reelection in any one year. Hence, the activities of Senate majority leaders in assisting their colleagues in elections do not reach the frenetic pace characteristic of their counterparts in the House of Representatives.

An incumbent senator enjoys better than two-to-one odds that he or she will be returned to office, even with heavy spending by the opposition. In 1978, in contests not involving incumbents, however, the candidate who spent the most money won in twelve of thirteen cases. In that same election year, $65.5 million was spent by party nominees and independents in the thirty-five contested Senate elections.[10]

Party leadership and organization has never been as complex or intense in the Senate as it is in the House of Representatives. Mainly, this difference stems from the differential in membership. Moreover, with enhanced visibility, extended tenure, and more numerous committee assignments, the average senator has almost always been more autonomous and powerful than all but the top echelons of party and committee leaders in the House. For example, almost without exception, all senators gain one or more subcommittee chairs or ranking committee posts as soon as they enter the Senate. In contrast, in the House, it will usually take three to four terms (six to eight years) before a Democrat inherits a subcommittee chair. Typically, a senator also serves on two or three committees; a House member usually serves on one exclusive committee (Appropriations, Ways and Means, or Rules) or, at most, two of more modest importance (for example, Judiciary and House Administration).[11]

Ultimately, the relative power of House and Senate members comes back to the power of the individual vote. The two chambers are roughly equivalent in constitutional power; 100 senators, more or less, possess one-half of the power of the legislative branch, and 435 members on the House side have the other half. Under the circumstances differences in influence and authority are much more evident in the House, which has had to organize itself more hierarchically in order to function effectively. Still, in recent years, both bodies have undergone a process of democratizing and decentralizing, especially since the elections of 1958.

The process of decentralization is of particular concern to the newer, younger members in Congress. And as their numbers have increased, so, proportionately, has their power.

Every incoming member of the Congress is immediately confronted with gradations of power and influence within and across the two institutions. Some of these differences flow from formal status, the prerequisites of a leadership position, or a position as committee chair. These, in turn, reflect accrued experience, especially seniority on several committees in the House or Senate or both. But gradations of influence can also derive from an individual's superior grasp of issues, more driving ambition, or other personal attributes, such as intelligence. In Congress, as in other organizations, some people rise to the top and others settle into a comfortable lower niche.

Nevertheless, equality of voting power, ultimately, is the great equalizer among all members, from the House freshman to the most prestigious committee chairman in the Senate. Each member has one and only one vote. The day when one Senator or House member could "deliver" the votes of other members has all but disappeared. Occasionally a strategically placed junior member in the House can hold up the pet project or bill of even the most powerful senator, admittedly at some peril and perhaps only for a time. But in the Congress, as with other legislative institutions, with seniority comes increasing power and influence.

Changing Expectations

As noted, the dominant trend of the past three decades has been an increased leveling or democratization in both the House and the Senate. With the benefit of historical perspective it is possible to date these developments roughly from the late 1950s.

In 1957–1958, an economic recession was instrumental in bringing into the House and Senate a large body of new members, mostly Democrats bent on change. Gains were especially heavy in the Senate, with a net benefit of seventeen Democratic seats.

Another large wave of younger, reform-oriented Democrats was swept into the House as a result of President Johnson's landslide margins in 1964. House Republicans also began initiating a series of party reforms in the mid-1960s, following Gerald R. Ford's defeat of Charles Halleck in a contest for minority leader.[12]

Again, in 1974, following Watergate, more than seventy new Democratic freshmen entered the House of Representatives. Many were committed to promoting change in the party structure in Congress. The Democratic Steering and Policy Committee was given new responsibilities, including the power to make committee assignments. This power was formerly exercised by the Speaker and the Democratic members of the House Ways and Means Committee. In an almost unprecedented move, three elderly committee chairmen—Hebert of Louisiana, Patman and Poage of Texas—were deprived of their positions at a pre–94th congress Democratic conference in December 1974. These changes, in turn, created a receptive climate for more demands from younger members among those aspiring to committee or House leadership. Senior members, more than ever before, had to take into account the increasing strength of the junior classes in the overall decision-making processes of the House. Parallel, if less dramatic, changes were taking place among House Republicans.

Over a comparable time span, changes in the Senate have been less dramatic, more gradual, but no less important. Both the Democratic and Republican conferences adopted provisions for the election of committee leaders by secret ballot. As subcommittees proliferated, junior members of both parties became involved more quickly and gained access to added staff. The norm of apprenticeship—that junior members should be seen but not heard—has been all but abandoned.[13]

These trends partly were brought on by and partly reflect the changing patterns of leadership in both houses. The centralized floor leadership characteristic of Johnson and Dirksen gave way to a more decentralized and shared leadership of Mansfield and Scott. Restoration of power in the hands of the formal party leadership has gradually returned under new incumbent floor leaders, Byrd and Baker.

Two additional trends—increasingly higher rates of voluntary retirement in the House and greater electoral insecurity in the Senate—have both contributed to the centrifugal forces affecting both chambers. All through the 1970s voluntary departures from the House steadily rose to a high of forty-nine members in the 95th congress (1977–1978). (Eighteen ran for other offices; thirty-one decided to step down without a contest.)[14]

Senate voluntary retirements also reached a post–World War II high of ten in 1978. But the number of departures has fluctuated more over the years in the Senate than in the House (the previous high of nine was in 1946; the low, two, was in 1964).[15]

Whereas about nine out of ten House incumbents who decide to run for reelection are successful, incumbent senators have faced increasingly unfavorable electoral odds. According to a recent study of the seventeen biennial elections since World War II, incumbent senators seeking reelection prevailed only 68 percent of the time, as compared to a 91 percent success rate for House incumbents. The disparity between the houses reached a high point in 1978, when nearly 94 percent of House incumbents who ran were reelected but only 60 percent of the twenty-five senators who ran were returned to office.[16]

House members and senators in the recently concluded 96th congress were a younger, less senior aggregate than those in any congress in the last three decades. The average House member, at age 49, was more than two years younger than the average member who served in 1949. In the Senate, with the election in 1978 of eight new senators still in their thirties, the average age dropped to 52.7 years, nearly 6 years younger than the average senator in 1949.[17]

The consequences of these democratizing and age-lowering trends have greatly complicated the tasks of House and Senate leadership. Party alignments are more difficult to obtain. The members of the Congress in the 1970s have become less willing to accept leadership commands at face value, more prone to leave the party harnesses. From Senate Majority Leader Byrd's perspective: "The members are younger now; they tend to be more independent; we are living in different times."[18] And as House Speaker O'Neill has observed: "There's no way I can impose party discipline. There is no party discipline in America today. In this day and age, it is completely different from the Rayburn days. . . ."[19]

In the 95th and 96th congresses (1977–1980), however, there seems to have been a swing of the pendulum back toward increased party responsibility and more centralization on the part of leaders. Some of this has occurred as maverick junior members have inherited subcommittee chairs and thus found themselves more satisfied, if not dependent on their leadership for support on legislation of interest to them. Also, as Republicans increased their membership in 1978, party alignments tended to reassert themselves. Every congressional election can have far-reaching effects, not least in terms of furthering or inhibiting individual careers. Nevertheless, the congressional elections of 1980 may be viewed as critical not only to the relative strengths of the two parties in the House and Senate and to the possibility of challenges to existing leadership, but also to longer-range trends toward further centralization or decentralization in leader-follower relationships.

Notes

1. James Madison, Alexander Hamilton, and John Jay, *The Federalist Papers* (New York: Modern Library, 1938); James Madison, Alexander Hamilton, and John Jay, *Origins and Development of Congress* (Washington: Congressional Quarterly, Inc., 1976).

2. *United States Constitution*, Art. 1, Sect. 1.

3. Alvin Josephy, *History of the Congress of the United States* (New York: American Heritage Foundation, 1975).

4. Harrison W. Fox, Jr., and Susan Webb Hammond, *Congressional Staffs* (New York: Free Press, 1977).

5. Floyd M. Riddick, "Majority and Minority Leaders of the Senate: History and Development of the Offices of Floor Leaders," Senate Doc. 92–42, 92nd Cong., 1st sess. (Washington: U.S. Government Printing Office, 1971).

6. Randall B. Ripley, *Party Leaders in the House of Representatives* (Washington: Brookings Institution, 1967), pp. 24–27.

7. This material is adopted in part from Robert L. Peabody, *Leadership in Congress* (Boston: Little, Brown, 1976), pp. 29–31 and 31–38.

8. Adapted from Robert L. Peabody, "Senate Party Leadership: From the 1950s to the 1980s," paper delivered at the Dirksen Center Seminar on Congressional Leadership, Washington, D.C., July 10–11, 1980, pp. 32–53.

9. Ralph K. Huitt, "The Internal Distribution of Influence in the Senate," in *The Congress and America's Future*, ed. by David B. Truman (Englewood Cliffs, N.J.: Prentice-Hall, 1965), p. 89.

10. *Congressional Quarterly Weekly Report* 37 (September 29, 1979):2153.

11. For a comparative analysis of committee organization and activity in the House and Senate see Richard F. Fenno, Jr., *Congressmen in Committees* (Boston: Little, Brown, 1974).

12. Peabody, *Leadership in Congress*, chap. 4.

13. Donald R. Matthews, *U.S. Senators and Their World* (Chapel Hill: University of North Carolina Press, 1960), pp. 92–94; David W. Rohde, Norman J. Ornstein, and Robert L. Peabody, "Political Change and Legislative Norms in the United States Senate," revised version of a paper delivered at the 1974 annual meeting of the American Political Science Association, Chicago, September 1974.

14. *Congressional Quarterly Weekly Report* 38 (January 13, 1980): 79–82.

15. Ibid., p. 79.

16. *Congressional Quarterly Weekly Report* 38 (April 5, 1980): 905–909.

17. *Congressional Quarterly Weekly Report* 38 (January 13, 1980): 79.

18. Interview with Senator Robert C. Byrd, July 13, 1979.

19. Thomas P. O'Neill, remarks at American Heritage Foundation dinner, February 10, 1977. Sam Rayburn (D-Tex.) served as Speaker from 1940 to 1961, except during the 80th (1947–1948) and 83rd (1953–1954) congresses.

9

The Making of a Law:
The U.S. Legislative Process

Ralph D. Nurnberger

In July 1979 President Carter announced the three major components of his energy program; a "windfall profits tax" to tax the oil companies part of their expected higher profits from a decontrol of prices, with the money to be used to finance conservation and development of domestic energy resources; a major synfuels program; and an Energy Mobilization Board to coordinate and expedite actions by federal, state, and local agencies that dealt with nonnuclear energy projects, with the goal of speeding production and cutting red tape. Despite the rhetoric that "urgent actions were required to meet the emergency conditions," it took Congress one year to act upon the three measures.

After the windfall profits tax was introduced in Congress, public hearings were held in Senate and House committees and subcommittees on the proposal. The major oil firms, represented by the American Petroleum Institute, asserted at the hearings that only the large companies could explore for big new oil fields in the most promising frontier territories, such as Alaska and on the Outer Continental Shelf. They claimed that high taxes would reduce their ability to spend on exploratory drilling, resulting in a decreased supply of oil. Experts from the Department of Energy argued the administration's case, claiming that decontrol would raise prices sufficiently to allow additional drilling. In addition, they claimed that the tax revenues would be used to support the synfuels program, and thus the companies would be compensated in the long run. In determining their votes on complicated, technical issues of this kind, members of Congress were forced to sort out for themselves how much additional domestic oil production might be encouraged by decontrol and how much might be lost through the imposition of new taxes. Throughout their decision-making process, they were barraged with advice from oil companies, environmental groups, and labor unions, in addition to the views of their constituents.

After lengthy, often technical arguments in committee and on the House and Senate floor, the House passed a windfall profits tax that was expected to raise $277 billion through 1990, and the Senate passed a version of the bill that was projected to raise $178 billion by 1990. Members of the House and Senate met in a conference committee to reconcile the differences between the two branches of Congress. They agreed to split differences and rewrote the bill to achieve a midpoint figure of $227 billion. The new measure was resubmitted to both houses. The tax measure passed on March 27, 1980, and was later signed into law by the president.

The synfuels measure has a more complicated legislative history. In the House, synfuels legislation normally would have been handled by the Energy and Power Subcommittee of the Interstate and Foreign Commerce Committee. The chairman of this subcommittee, although a member of the president's party, opposed the bill. By means of a parliamentary maneuver, the Democratic majority leader was able to send the legislation to the Economic Stabilization Subcommittee of the Banking, Finance, and Urban Affairs Committee. Although not normally concerned with this type of energy legislation, the subcommittee was expected to attach synfuels to a bill to extend the Defense Production Act. The latter was a Korean War–era measure that authorizes government contracting for national security purposes. More important in this instance, the Banking Subcommittee chairman favored the bill, arguing that it should be passed for reasons of national security.

In the Senate, the Energy Committee chairman, Henry M. Jackson of Washington, packaged synfuel development with programs for solar energy, conservation, gasohol, and other energy measures. It was a compromise solution to help the passage of the bill. Supporters of conservation and solar energy realized that their proposals might never pass if detached from synfuels, and the synfuels supporters needed their votes. The Senate Banking, Housing, and Urban Affairs Committee, which also held hearings on synfuels, reported a much more restricted version of the bill but lost to the Energy Commission version in a fight on the Senate floor. In total, three Senate committees and four House committees researched synfuels issues and held hearings.

At the conference committee, called to reconcile the differences between the House and Senate bills, representatives from the House Banking, Commerce, Agriculture, and Science and Technology committees were selected to represent the House; the Senate conferees came from the Energy Committee as well as the Banking Committee. The bills that they sought to combine were so unwieldy that members and staff aides were forced to specialize in particular sections and almost no one was able to grasp the entire bill. So many compromises were made during the conference committee stage that one of the conferees, Senator J. Bennett Johnson, conceded, "There's something there for the left and for the right." He compared the bill to a cookie jar, with something for everyone.

The final measure established a synthetic fuels corporation that could spend $20 billion to promote the production by private industry of synthetic fuels. This amount could increase by another $68 billion by 1984. It also included subsidies of $1.45 billion for alcohol fuels and $3.25 billion for a solar and conservation bank. Finally, it required the president to resume filling the Strategic Petroleum Reserve.

Although this bill was different from the original measure sent to Congress by the president, Carter decided that he could support the congressional changes in his proposals. On June 30, 1980, nearly one year after he had requested a synfuels program from Congress, President Carter signed into law the new multibillion-dollar package.

The third leg of the Carter proposal, the Energy Mobilization Board, was soundly defeated in Congress. Liberal members of his own party joined with House Republicans to defeat, by a margin of 232 to 131, the establishment of the board. In so doing, they were reacting to effective lobbying by a coalition of environmental groups and those supporting states' rights. The Sierra Club, the Audubon Society, and other environmental groups were concerned that the proposed board would threaten clean air and water regulations, and the National Governor's Association, the National League of Cities, and other state and local associations were concerned that the board might waive state and local laws in an effort to encourage energy production by speeding projects. Together these organizations were able to gain more support against the bill than the oil companies and the administration were able to obtain for its passage. Carter called the defeat of the board "a serious disappointment."

This brief overview of the legislative history of the Carter administration's energy program is representative of the political jousting that is part of the daily operations of Congress. It reflects the impact of public opinion, the role of interest groups, the role of personalities, the relations between the executive and legislative branches, and the extreme complexity of the U.S. system. In sum, it points out that the politicians in Congress must be adept at the art of compromise and conciliation if the deliberative nature of the legislature is to be maintained. It is also important to note that throughout the entire process all participants, the administration, Congress, and interest groups vie for media attention. All seek to gain public exposure in an effort to affect public opinion, which is at the heart of representative democracy.

The Makeup of Congress

Like the Japanese Diet, the U.S. Congress is the national legislative body. Article I, section 1, of the Constitution states that "all legislative powers . . . shall be vested in a Congress . . . , which shall consist of a Senate and a House of Representatives." Thus, Congress serves as the focal point for all divergent interests in the United States' pluralistic society. In the example of the energy legislation, environmentalists, oil companies, energy users, and energy producers all went to Congress in an effort to influence the formulation of national policies. For Congress to fulfill its mandates, divergent groups must all have some form of access.

U.S. representatives are elected for terms of two years; Japanese representatives are elected for four-year terms. Since the United States does not have a parliamentary form of government, Congress is never subject to no-confidence votes. Congress was not dissolved, for example, nor was President Carter subject to a new election after he lost the major vote on the Energy Mobilization Board. Although in both countries electoral districts are determined by population, each of the 435 members of the House of Representatives represents one electoral district with an average population of 450,000. This situation contrasts with the Japanese system, in which each constituency has three to five representatives.

Like members of the Japanese House of Councillors, U.S. Senators are elected for six-year terms; however, their constituencies are different. The Japanese House of Councillors has some members chosen by the nation at large and others selected by localities, but U.S. senators are elected on the basis of two per state, regardless of population. Thus sparsely populated or small states like Alaska, Wyoming, and Rhode Island have the same number of senators as larger states such as New York, California, and Texas.

With the exception that only the House may initiate revenue bills and that the Senate has unique powers over treaties and nominations, both houses have equal legislative powers and functions. The terms "upper house" and "lower house" are not appropriate in the U.S. system.

Scope of Legislation

The complexity of issues and the volume of work confronting Congress is astounding. Nearly 20,000 bills are introduced during an average two-year session. Approximately 5 percent of these are ultimately passed, a fact that serves to illustrate the difficulty of overcoming the various institutional roadblocks in the legislative process.

After introduction, a bill is referred to one or more of the twenty-two committees in the House and their 148 subcommittees or to the Senate's 15 committees and 90 subcommittees. It will be scrutinized and analyzed by congressional staff, a virtual army of assistants whose size, powers, and functions have grown constantly for many years. In addition to a member's personal staff and the committee staffs, Congress is served by the Library of Congress's Congressional Research Service, the General Accounting Office, the Congressional Budget Office, and the Office of Technology Assessment, all of which have also expanded greatly in size. Congressional staff size has almost doubled from 11,700 in 1968 to nearly 20,000 today. Of these, approximately 7,000 staff members serve the 100 senators; over 3,500 work for congressional committees.

The increased staff size has been both a function of and a contributing factor to increased congressional workload. Since the scope of the subjects Congress handles has expanded, the need for staff expertise has grown. Conversely, increased staff often creates work when zealous staff look for areas that need congressional actions. The number of committee hearings nearly doubled from 2,607 in the 84th congress (1955–1956) to 4,067 in the 93rd (1973–1975); in the House they rose from 3,210 in the 84th to 5,888 in the 93rd.

Sources of Legislation

In theory, Congress is the sole legislative branch of the government. In practice, however, it shares legislative responsibility with the executive branch, to some degree paralleling the relationship of the Diet and cabinet. The major distinction is that although the U.S. president is considered the nominal leader of his party, he is not the leader of the political majority in the legislature even when that majority is of the same party. Unlike the prime minister's, the president's legislative agenda is neither binding on his own party members nor susceptible to votes of no confidence. Still, as in Japan, most major bills enacted into law tend to originate in the executive branch although these measures are subject, of course, to delay, defeat, or drastic amendment by either house of Congress.

In the 95th congress (1977–1978), 625 of the total 22,314 measures introduced were submitted to Congress at the request of the administration. Of these, 230 received committee hearing and 44 eventually were passed into law—a higher percentage of success than that for measures introduced by individual members of committees. But the statistics alone do not give an accurate account of the relative importance of the measures. The administration's legislative proposals cover all facets of national policy, including finance, foreign policy, education, transportation, agriculture, and energy. On these major legislative items, largely measures essential to the regular operation of the executive departments, Congress merely responds to presidential initiatives. This practice prevails even if the president and the majority in Congress are of different parties.

Congressional action in the areas of energy, foreign policy, and finance all provide examples of congressional responses to presidential directives. In the case discussed at the beginning of this chapter, Congress felt the need to develop energy programs but was unable to devise a unified national focus. Synfuel bills and tax proposals had already been introduced in Congress before President Carter made his July 1979 announcements. The Carter plans brought together congressional initiatives and proposals from the executive branch. They also helped shape the congressional focus upon specific, coordinated items. Congress responded by passing two of the proposals in modified terms and rejecting the third.

In the foreign policy field, although it is a function of Congress to consider an annual foreign assistance program, work on these items does not even begin until after the State Department has prepared an initial outline of the administration's proposals. Congress may then accept, reject, or modify these suggestions, but only rarely does Congress propose major new foreign aid programs.

Even though the Constitution mandates that tax legislation must originate in the House of Representatives, in practice the budget process actually begins in the executive branch. Though Congress almost always makes some adjustments in this program, most of the president's budget is usually passed. The 1974 Budget Act, which created new budget committees in Congress, has mainly enabled the legislature to react in a more understanding and integrated way rather than to develop many new budget initiatives.

Of the total number of bills each year, the majority are originated by individual members of Congress. The legislation introduced by a representative or senator may stem from his or her political philosophy, campaign promises, or requests from constituents, or from the pressures of interest groups. A member often will introduce a bill even if there is no hope of its passage in order to fulfill a political debt, to satisfy a constituent, or to serve as a bargaining tool to enable negotiation with colleagues or the administration.

Like those of the Japanese Diet, congressional committees may also engage in investigations. These investigations frequently provide the impetus for legislative proposals. Like their Japanese counterparts, U.S. committees, subcommittees, or specially constituted select investigatory committees may investigate the activities of other branches of government and can subpoena witnesses and records to that end.

Every period in U.S. history has had congressional investigations, beginning with a 1792 inquiry into the failure of an army mission against Indian tribes. Investigations may focus on specific acts of government officials, such as the dismissal of General MacArthur by President Truman in the fifties, Watergate and related wrongdoings of the Nixon administration, or the conduct of President Carter's brother Billy Carter. Other investigations may attack specific problems, including organized crime, the possibility of an internal communist threat, racketeering in labor unions, or bribery by U.S. firms overseas.

On the other hand, as part of Congress's oversight responsibilities, investigations are routinely conducted to examine federal programs and how funds are spent. Others are undertaken to fulfill specific legislative mandates.

Congressional investigations range widely in size and media exposure. Most are small and do not receive much publicity. However, the Senate Watergate Committee had a staff of sixty-nine, including seventeen attorneys; the House Judiciary Committee impeachment staff reached nearly one hundred members, with forty-three attorneys.

Regardless of the size or the publicity received by investigations, they must still be viewed as part of the congressional process; they are instruments through which Congress seeks information in order to regulate relations with the executive branch, formulate legislation, or enlighten the public.

Types of Legislation

Regardless of its original source, after a bill has been drafted and phrased in correct legal form, it may be introduced either in the Senate or in the House. The only exceptions are revenue bills, which always must originate in the House. This practice is based on the British custom that taxes must be levied and spent by the house most directly responsible to the people.

Members may introduce either public bills, private bills, or resolutions. Public bills apply to the nation as a whole and become public law if approved by Congress and signed by the president. Private bills relate only to an individual, private matters, or claims against the government. They deal largely with such matters as individual immigration and naturalization cases or land titles. They are usually introduced by a member at the request of the individual involved. If approved and signed, they become private laws, affecting only the parties mentioned.

Bills are given numbers in the house in which they are introduced according to the order in which they are received. House bills are labeled, e.g., "H.R. 7511," and Senate bills are referred to as "S."

There are three types of resolutions: joint, concurrent, and simple. Joint resolutions may originate in either house. They are similar to bills and are subject to the same procedures for passage, requiring the approval of both houses and the president's signature. Joint resolutions are usually used to deal with more specific matters, such as a single appropriation for a certain purpose. They are designated "H.J. Res." or "S.J. Res.," depending upon their house of origin. Joint resolutions are also used to propose amendments to the Constitution. These do not require presidential signature but become part of the Constitution when passed by two-thirds of each house and ratified in three-fourths of the states.

A concurrent resolution, designated "H. Con. Res." or "S. Con. Res.," must be passed by both houses, but since this type of resolution does not require a presidential signature, it does not have the force of law. These resolutions are issued to express the sentiment of both houses, such as, for example, on setting dates for adjournments.

A simple resolution, designated "H. Res." or "S. Res.," involves the prerogatives of only one house. It does not require passage by the other house or presidential action. Simple resolutions are used to deal with the rules of one house, to give "advice" to the administration on matters such as foreign policy, or to express the views of that chamber on any matter—sometimes even the virtues of a baseball team. They do not have the force of law.

Introduction of Bills

Any member may introduce legislation. In the House, bills are introduced by simply placing them in the *hopper*, a basket at the side of the clerk's desk in the House chamber. In the Senate, at the time reserved for the purpose of bill introduction, a senator who wishes to propose a measure formally rises to introduce it. If there is an objection, the introduction is postponed one day. After the bill is formally introduced, its title and number are printed in the *Congressional Record*, often with explanatory remarks by its sponsor.

Frequently bills are cosponsored by several members. This practice enables members to explain their positions early during the legislative process and also to inform their constituents of the legislation they have actively supported. Since the interplay of personalities is often critical to the operation of Congress, the number and reputation of a bill's cosponsors are sometimes a signal of its potential success or failure.

The Committee Process

After a bill is introduced, the Speaker of the House or the president of the Senate refers it to the appropriate committee or committees according to jurisdictions established over subjects by the rules of each house. Both the Speaker and the Senate president normally rely on the advice of the parliamentarians for guidance. Committee referral and actions have been regarded as the most important phase of the congressional procedure.

Each committee has jurisdiction over specified subjects; since members generally remain on the same committee, they gain specialized knowledge in an area. This practice increases the potential for members, particularly the committee chairs, to gain power over legislation that falls within their expertise. Committee recommendations are critical to the success of a bill, since other members of Congress tend to support measures passed in committee. For example, of the 13,230 bills and resolutions introduced in the 96th congress (1979–1980), 1,741 were reported favorably by a House or Senate committee. Of these, only a handful were subsequently defeated.

The committees provide the setting for the most intensive study of legislative proposals; they also are a major avenue for public access to the process. At hearings on legislation, witnesses usually include technical experts, government officials, and spokesmen representing all sides of the issue. Most committee hearings are open to the public, although the committee may also hold closed "executive" sessions.

In addition to hearings, committee members may go on fact-finding trips, sponsor staff investigations, and receive comments from experts in other ways. It is interesting to note that some committee meetings may be held outside of Washington. These meetings usually are scheduled in the areas most affected by a piece of legislation, sometimes in the home district or state of a committee member. In the latter case, the hearing may have a public relations spinoff.

Special interest groups, lobbyists, and others play an active role during the time of committee investigation of a bill. Generally, the investigations and hearings are carried out by subcommittees of the standing committees. Representatives of interest groups may testify at committee or subcommittee hearings. In addition, they may seek to develop personal contacts with the committee members and their staff. They also work toward their goals by organizing public opinion, often with the intent of encouraging a mass mailing campaign in favor of or against the legislative proposals. Thus, the committee system allows special interests a major source of access to the legislative process, with the opportunity to work for or against bills or for their modification.

After a committee has completed its study of a measure, it will usually *mark up* the bill. This means that the bill will be reviewed, section by section, with members making revisions, changing the language, adding parts, or deleting sections to reflect the committee's findings. If the bill has been extensively revised or amended during the committee review stages, it may be rewritten as a "clean bill" and introduced as a separate bill with a new number.

The committee may report a bill favorably; amend, revise or rewrite it completely; or table it. Bills that are tabled in committee are effectively killed, unless they are forced to the floor by a majority vote of the House members (discharge petition) or a special resolution in the Senate, both rare procedural practices.

If the committee votes to report a bill favorably (or report unfavorably, a committee action that rarely occurs because the committee can table a bill it does not wish to support), the bill is returned to the full House or Senate, accompanied by a committee report describing the purpose and scope of the bill and reasons for its recommendations.

Generally, the committee report contains a section-by-section analysis explaining in detail what each part of the legislation is intended to accomplish. Committee reports are often used by courts, executive departments and agencies, and the public as a source of information regarding the purpose and meaning of the law.

Floor Action

After a bill is reported to the House or the Senate by the committee, it must be placed on the appropriate calendar, which is a list of bills to be considered for floor action. In the House, the union calendar is used for all bills raising revenue, general appropriations bills, and bills of a public character directly or indirectly appropriating money or property. The house calendar is used for all other public bills. Private bills are placed on the private calendar.

The Senate prints one calendar for all legislation except treaties and nominations, which are placed on the separate executive calendar. Uncontroversial bills may be considered under what is called the consent calendar; private bills are referred to as being on the private calendar.

More bills are passed by committees and placed on calendars than either the Senate or the House can effectively handle; therefore, both houses have devised means of establishing priorities.

In the Senate, the majority leader determines when a bill will be considered on the floor, often with the advice and concurrence of the minority leader. The Senate can bypass the calendar order and take up any bill by unanimous consent or by a majority vote.

Unlike the House, the Senate has no time limits on debate. Generally, members may speak as long as they wish, and their comments need not be germane to the bill. A relatively small group of senators, therefore, can continue the discussion of a bill almost indefinitely. If this use of discussion is deliberately prolonged, it is called a filibuster, which is a delaying tactic used by a minority to prevent the Senate from reaching a decisive vote. Filibusters may be stopped by a provision of the rules called cloture. Cloture requires support by three-fifths of the entire membership of the Senate. Thus, if sixty senators agree, the Senate may begin to bring a halt to discussion and move toward a vote.

In the House, the majority leader works with the Speaker to determine the order of consideration of bills, which often bears little relation to the calendar order.

The House Rules Committee determines separately the floor procedures to be followed for each bill, including the time alloted for debate. These procedures are printed in a house resolution or rule, which must be debated and passed by the House before it is in order to call up the bill to which it applies. For example, a modified closed rule may allow the offering of only three or four specific amendments to the bill as reported by committee, or it may permit only amendments to certain sections of the bill. By contrast, an open rule allows all members to offer amendments.

The House conducts much of its business while sitting as the *committee of the whole*, a parliamentary procedure that allows it to save time by reducing quorum requirements from 218 to 100. Any 100 members are sufficient to form the committee of the whole. The Rules Committee reports a special resolution or rule to allow for immediate consideration of measures in the committee of the whole. This rule also stipulates a time limit for debate of the issue, granting the majority and minority predetermined equal time for general debate. Members seeking to speak on this issue usually arrange the timing of their remarks in advance. During this period of general debate, amendments may not be offered.

When the time for general debate has ended, the House considers the bill under the five-minute rule. At this time the amendments may be offered, and each member may speak for five minutes. Often members ask for unanimous consent to speak longer. This request is rarely denied. In addition, members may have further comments printed in the *Congressional Record* section "Extension of Remarks."

Upon completion of the debate and amendment phase, the committee of the whole reports the bill, as amended, back to the full House. At this point there can be no further debate, although any member has the right to demand a separate vote by the House on any amendment that passed in the committee of the whole. Otherwise, it is routine for all the amendments that passed in the committee of the whole to be put to the House, en bloc, and passed by voice vote. The final action by the House is to vote for the passage or rejection of the bill.

Numerous factors affect a member's voting patterns. Unlike Japan, the United States does not have a strong centralized party system. This lack of party strength, coupled with the fact that representatives are elected from single-member districts and senators from specific states, allows members to place greater emphasis upon their efforts to satisfy constituent desires.

One result of the recent overwhelming trend toward recorded votes has been that members have become more concerned about constituent views than in the past. For example, in the 90th congress (1967–1968), there were 595 recorded votes in the Senate and 478 in the House. In the 95th congress (1977–1978), the Senate recorded 1,156 votes; the House recorded 1,540 votes. This trend leads to greater accountability for a representative and increases the tendency to vote according to constituent pressures.

Regional concerns are other factors that influence how a member votes. For example, representatives from oil-producing states tended to vote the same way on President Carter's energy programs, regardless of their party affiliation. There is also a growing tendency for members to group together to form voting blocs on given issues based on regional concerns, ethnic relations, or ideological matters. For example, different members will join the Black Caucus, the Export Caucus, Members of Congress for Peace through Law, or the Mushroom Caucus. These informal groupings can influence a member's votes on a limited number of issues.

Another critically important factor is the intangible influence of personalities. Members will support colleagues they like and respect more readily than those they do not know as well. Personal reputations, built up over years of service in Congress, facilitate the legislative proposals of senior members.

Two additional external factors also play a role in how a member votes. The relatively weak party structure enables interest groups to have increased influence. A current political issue concerns the rapid growth during the 1970s of campaign contributions by these groups. These contributions, often made through officially registered political action committees (PACs), frequently are a more significant element in the election of members than their own parties.

These groups have frequent meetings with members and their staffs throughout the legislative process.

A final factor that might influence a member's behavior is the role of the media. Members rely upon the media for the publicity needed to keep their names alive in their districts. Thus, there is more incentive to attend hearings that receive wide coverage. There is also less readiness to take unpopular stands in order to accommodate the leadership or the administration if members believe these positions will be widely reported.

Voting Procedures

Voting on bills may occur repeatedly in different forms before the final vote is taken. As noted, the House votes for a rules bill. One of the procedural methods is a vote to recommit a bill to committee for further study—a vote that, if carried, usually signals the defeat of that bill.

Actual voting may take a number of forms. In a voice vote (viva voce) members respond "Aye" or "No." This method obviously does not give an accurate count, so a division of the house (standing vote) may be requested. Under this method, members stand up and are counted for or against a measure. During a teller vote in the House, members walk past a teller who counts those in favor or opposed. Finally, both chambers resort to recorded votes. The House has an electronic device for machine recording in order to speed the process. Each member has a card he or she may place in the appropriate slot; the machine records the votes and reports the results. In the Senate, an actual call of the roll takes place, with each member responding when his or her name is called.

Action in the Nonoriginating House

After a bill is passed in one house, it is sent to the other chamber. With the exception of revenue bills, it does not matter which chamber originates a given piece of legislation.

The second chamber has a number of options. It may pass or reject the bill in exactly the same form; it may subject the bill to its own legislative proceedings, sending it to the appropriate committees for scrutiny or alteration before bringing it up for a vote; or it may continue work on its own version of a similar bill. To save time, similar bills (often the same bill) are frequently introduced in both chambers simultaneously.

Conference Committees

If the Senate and the House pass different versions of the same bill, these differences can be reconciled by a conference committee. Members of the conference committee are appointed by the Speaker of the House and the president of the Senate, so that both chambers are represented. A majority of the committee members on each side must agree before the conference committee may issue its report and the revised bill. Often, compromises are made by both sides and differences divided. For example, as noted above, in the windfall profits tax bill, the conference figure of $227 billion was halfway between the House version of $277 billion and the Senate figure of $178 billion.

The reports of the conference committee are sent back to the House and Senate, which must vote for the revised bill with no amendments. Each house must approve the conference committee bill in identical form, a difference from the Japanese system, in which the lower house can override an unfavorable vote of the upper house with the consent of two-thirds of the members present.

Presidential Action

After both houses of Congress have passed an identical bill, it is sent to the president. If the president approves, he signs the bill, transforming it into law. Routine measures are usually signed in private. At times, presidential signings are accompanied by a ceremony, with the interested parties present. When an important bill reaches the president's desk, influential members of Congress, cabinet members, and other dignitaries crowd into the president's office to witness the event. The president may use a dozen or more pens to sign so that each guest may have a souvenir of the occasion. Reporters and photographers will cover the event for posterity, and also perhaps for the political benefit of the participants.

A bill may also become law if the president holds it for ten days (excluding Sundays) without signing or vetoing it. This inaction is taken as a signal that the president frowns on the bill but for some reason will not block its passage.

If the president objects strenuously to a bill, he may veto it, returning it to Congress with a message explaining his objections. The bill may still become law if both houses of Congress override the veto with a two-thirds majority; if not, the veto stands and the bill is killed. President Carter vetoed twenty-seven bills; only two of his vetoes were overriden.

A *pocket veto* occurs if a bill reaches the president less than ten days before Congress adjourns and the president does not sign it.

When bills are finally passed and signed, or passed over a veto, they become law and are numbered by Congress chronologically (i.e., P.L. 96–123 is the one hundred twenty-third law passed by the 96th congress).

Conclusions

Although rules and procedures remain relatively constant, the manner and style of Congress is in constant flux, depending on the personality of the members, the issues facing the nation, evolving precedents within Congress, and the state of legislative-executive relations. Since the early 1970s, many changes have taken place. Congress has reacted to Vietnam, Watergate, the growth of executive branch agencies, and what came to be referred to as the "imperial presidency" by instituting a number of reforms designated to restore or increase the powers of the legislature.

The passage of these reforms was facilitated by changes in the composition of Congress. Over one-half of the current members of the House were elected for the first time after 1972; forty-eight members of the Senate are still in their first term. These new, generally younger, and more independent members have been less inclined to follow party leaders or executive branch desires. The 1970 Reorganization Act, which led to a proliferation of the number of subcommittees, enabled many junior members to hold subcommittee chairs. Thus, nearly every member of Congress is either a chairman or a ranking minority member of a committee or subcommittee, with something of an independent power base.

Other trends have developed in recent years. Congress has become a full-time, year-round job; there has been a growing emphasis on dealing with constituent requests, often at the expense of sound legislative policy; Congress, which is composed largely of lawyers, has written more and more detailed regulations for executive agencies, extending the legislative function ever more deeply into the executive; the complexity of issues and the huge congressional workload have led to a proliferation of staff who, often, are lawyers or other specialized professionals; there has been a decline in the cohesiveness of political parties as well as a growth in the power of interest groups, especially those devoted to a single cause; and members of Congress have become acutely aware of the media and often shape their activities to attract media attention.

Many of these changes have been significant in keeping Congress a vibrant, living institution. Its procedures have allowed individual members acting there as individuals to have a direct and often highly significant input into shaping the laws and course of the nation.

10

The Member of the U.S. Congress

Susan Webb Hammond

The individual member of Congress is elected to office and discharges the duties of that office in a political and institutional environment shaped by the U.S. governmental system. The features of the system that are significant for senators and representatives are a presidential and federal system of government, political parties that are loose associations at the national level and a declining force in congressional elections, and an electoral system with a fixed term of office and single-member districts.

Under the presidential system, Congress is a coequal power center with the president. Cooperation is required, but disagreement, conflict, and independence are inevitable. The legislative and executive branches may be controlled by different parties, as was the case between 1969 and 1976 when the Republicans held the White House and the Democrats controlled the Congress. Members of Congress are elected and carry out legislative, representative, and oversight functions as individual representatives of their states or districts; they are not members of the governing or opposition coalition with fortunes tied to the head of government. The president has some effect on congressional elections and may influence a member's voting decisions, but electoral fortunes and policy decisions are also heavily dependent on other factors such as constituency.

The federal system affects both the elections and the duties of federal legislators. State law governs many aspects of election: primaries for candidate selection, the type of ballot, and, for representatives, the boundaries of the congressional district. Once in office, senators and representatives are cognizant and are often reminded of federalism and their local ties. In debate, they are referred to as "The representative (or senator) from (state)." In the House, the state delegation is an important social and policy group. The delegation works with new members to obtain desired committee assignments, makes important introductions, and shares knowledge of legislative processes and procedures. Casework is an important part of the work of every congressional office, as senators and representatives intercede with the federal bureaucracy for constituents on such diverse matters as obtaining social security checks, reversing Medicare eligibility rulings, and assisting with emergency military leave. Federal projects—grants of federal money for construction of dams and hospitals or programs in areas such as education, health, and employment—are handled by more senior staff or, on occasion, by the member of Congress. As the number of federal programs has increased and the federal money available to states and localities has also increased, a significant part of each legislator's job has become obtaining a share of federal grants for the district or state. In developing legislation and in voting, members of Congress are continually aware of their local ties and obligations. The interest of the district or the state is an accepted reason for a member to vote against the party's predominant position. With the expansion of federal programs the formulas for distributing federal funds have turned into battlegrounds. All senators and representatives have worked to assure that generous levels of funding will be available for their constituents. Regionalism has increased, and House members from the same area of the country have, for example, formed groups to work together on matters of common concern. Finally, should candidates for president and vice-president not receive the requisite majority of electoral votes, federalism affects both the president and Congress: members of the House, deciding as separate state groups and casting one vote for each state, elect the president; and senators, casting votes as individuals, elect the vice-president.

Party continues to be an important organizing force both in elections and in Congress. Virtually all senators and representatives are Democrats or Republicans; the occasional congressman who runs as an Independent or on a third-party ticket has caucused with one of the two major parties after election. But party is a declining force in the recruitment and election of members. The typical career pattern of previous years—election first to local party offices, then to the state legislature, and finally to Congress—is changing; a number of members are self-recruited; others are elected after achievements in fields other than politics (senators Glenn and Schmidt, for example, who were both astronauts) or in appointive offices (Senator Moynihan). Current campaign laws and practices reinforce this pattern. Within Congress, party leaders are given important institutional duties.

As the importance of party in recruitment and election has declined, the job of the party leader has become more difficult. Elected without much party experience or assistance, the individual member may follow his or her own inclinations rather than the party leader on policy matters. Party leaders in Congress, in various degrees, rely on rewards, sanctions, and personal persuasion to obtain the individual member's support of the leadership view on issues. Speaker Thomas P. (Tip) O'Neill (D-Mass.) commented on the leader's job to political columnist David Broder: "A good many of the members coming into Congress now never came through the organization, never rang a doorbell in their life, never were a precinct worker, never brought people to an election, weren't brought up in the realm of party discipline. . . . [These new members] don't think about party loyalty."[1]

Nevertheless, members of each party tend to share certain broad beliefs that have some effect on policy choices. Party label may be said to be the most important of several predictors of a member's total voting pattern.

The major features of the electoral system—calendared elections, nomination by primary, parties that are decentralized to the state and local level rather than nationally centered, and the single-member district with plurality voting—affect the selection, duties, and activities of the individual member. All representatives are elected from single-member districts. Although each of the fifty states elects two senators, even in that case the system of election is, in effect, a single-member district system, since the six-year terms are staggered and two senators from the same state are not elected to full terms at the same time. Thus, members of the same party do not compete against each other in the general election.

A consequence of the electoral system is the close relationship the individual member has to his or her constituents. The member speaks for them in Congress and assists them in dealings with the federal bureaucracy. Some senators and representatives also serve as "representatives" for distinct groups in other districts or states who may not be able to elect a representative whom they feel speaks for them. In recent years, for example, black representatives, or the Black Caucus as it is called, have made an effort to speak for black people on a nationwide basis on policy matters.

Senate-House Differences

The four factors—a presidential system, federalism, declining party influence, and the electoral system—shape the environment in which every legislator works. The general institutional and political context is similar for every member of Congress, and senators and representatives have similar legislative responsibilities. However, differences between the Senate and the House of Representatives result in somewhat different working environments.

First, House constituencies, based on population, average about 500,000 persons. In contrast, senators' constituencies vary greatly, since they reflect entire state populations, from 406,000 (Alaska) to 22,694,000 (California). Six states are so sparse in population that they elect only one representative; in those states the representative and the senators serve the same constituency. Representatives' constituencies, because they are geographically smaller and more compact than states, are often quite homogeneous. Thus, New York City is divided into eighteen congressional districts, all urban, several with a large number of constituents with similar concerns. There are a number of predominantly rural districts in the House, also. In contrast, senators' constituencies are far more heterogeneous: New York senators represent 17,648,000 constituents in New York City and other urban areas and in the rural upstate areas. The senators from the state of Illinois represent urban and predominantly Democratic Chicago as well as more rural and Republican downstate areas. As a consequence, the House on occasion appears to be more parochial and more concerned with the local impact of proposed legislation.

In recent years, informal caucuses of representatives (the Steel Caucus, the Textile Caucus, the New England Congressional Caucus) have been established without regard for party to offer information exchange and strategy assistance to pass legislation benefiting similar districts with similar concerns.

For the individual member in the larger and more formally organized House, committee work is especially important. The member's impact on legislation tends to be made primarily through work in committee. Only rarely do freshman House members serve in positions of visibility and enhanced power, for example as subcommittee chairmen or ranking minority members. In the smaller and more egalitarian Senate, a newly elected senator of the majority party will chair a subcommittee. Legislatively, moreover, committee decisions are more likely to be changed during floor debate, with individual senators who are not on the reporting committee leading the effort to make changes. Hence, all senators, in addition to having a vote, have an opportunity to make an impact on policy and programs through committee work or floor debate. Senators are able to become better known to the public than representatives. Many senators develop a national following and can expect extensive media attention. In recent years, the Senate has been called a "breeding ground for presidents."

Recruitment and Selection of Members

The Constitution and federal and state laws set the parameters of the congressional election process. The six-year term for senators and the two-year term for representatives are established by the Constitution. All 435 members of the House of Representatives and one-third of the 100 members of the Senate are elected every two years. House members must be twenty-five years of age, senators thirty. General elections nationwide are held on the first Tuesday after the first Monday in November of even-numbered years. Both Senate and House members are elected by a majority (or in some instances a plurality) of the popular vote. State legislatures generally establish the boundaries of congressional districts; reapportionment occurs after each decennial census. State law also details nomination and election procedures, which may vary considerably from state to state.

Recruitment of Candidates

Recruitment of candidates to office results from a combination of factors. The opportunity structure — that is, the availability of an office — is important:

Is the incumbent retiring? If not, is the incumbent vulnerable? Are elections in the district or state usually won by narrow margins (is it a "marginal district")? Do the possible candidate's personal attributes (political experience, occupation, age, background) tend to fit the profile of the typical winner in a particular constituency?

Candidate desire to run is also important and is based on factors that include personality, ambition, and occupation and career status. At the local level, parties are often active in recruiting candidates to run against strong incumbents — e.g., they recruit the likely losers. By contrast, self-recruitment occurs with regularity, especially if the seat is open or vulnerable. Self-recruited candidates may have extensive experience with local or state elective or appointive office or in party matters. Party leaders will sometimes recruit well-known persons even outside the party to stand for office. Party structure in a locality and the level of party competition appear to be major variables affecting recruitment patterns: competitive districts and states have more varied recruitment patterns than areas that have been dominated by one party.[2]

Nomination

All congressional candidates are nominated by primary election.[3] There are variations among the states in the dates of the primary, in whether a voter must be registered as a Democrat or Republican to participate in that party's primary, in whether the nominee must receive a majority or plurality of the vote, and in whether runoff elections are held.

The nomination process is decentralized, and the national party leaders typically are not involved in nomination decisions, although the national party may make information, as on campaign finance laws, available to all candidates.

Congressional primaries are not always competitive. Incumbent senators running for reelection won 95 percent of their primary contests between 1952 and 1974. Incumbent representatives won renomination 98 percent of the time.[4] On the other hand, in areas where nomination is tantamount to election because of domination by one party, primaries may be very competitive. As in the general election, primary fights are most likely to occur when an incumbent retires or is perceived to be vulnerable to defeat.

The Election Campaign

Campaigns vary from state to state because filing dates for candidacy and nomination procedures are set by state law. The type of constituency — urban or rural, homogeneous or diverse — the geography of the district or state, and the availability of media coverage are among the factors that govern campaign styles and practices.

Campaign financing. The cost of congressional campaigns has increased tremendously in recent years, leading to efforts both to limit expenditures and to provide public financing. During the 1970s, new federal law brought about major changes in the financing of congressional campaigns.[5]

Detailed reporting of campaign contributions and expenditures is required. Candidates for Congress finance their campaigns by drawing on personal funds and raising contributions from individuals, political parties, and political committees. Individuals may contribute no more than $1,000 to a candidate for each election (a primary and a general election are considered separate elections) and no more than $25,000 to all federal candidates. Political committees, including political parties and political action committees (PACs) established by corporations, labor unions, and trade associations to accept voluntary contributions from their membership, may give $5,000 to each candidate in each election. Candidates may use unlimited personal funds in their own campaigns.

In 1976, the average House candidate spent just over $79,000; the average Senate candidate spent $593,000.[6] By 1978, total expenditures by House candidates had increased by 44 percent; Senate expenditures had increased by 72 percent. Thus, the average House candidate spent $113,760 and the typical Senate candidate spent about $1 million in that year. However, expenditures vary widely. In 1978, in one race $7.5 million was spent, or about $12 per vote. Twenty-one candidates spent over $1 million. In the House, expenditures are lower, although in 1978 nine candidates spent more than $500,000. Again in 1978, the average cost of winning a first term in the House was $229,000.[7]

Major expenses are public opinion polling and television and newspaper advertising, as well as staff salaries and campaign literature. The most expensive campaigns occur in competitive districts or districts with open seats, or in cases when the campaign is lengthy.

Members of Congress consider fundraising a never-ending process.[8] In recent elections, political action committees have increased their contributions to campaigns significantly. PACs contributed $23 million to House candidates in 1978, more than 20 percent of all contributions received and an increase from less than 15 percent in 1972.

Candidates need not be wealthy, but personal wealth is helpful. The latest financial statements filed by members of Congress indicate that in 1979, five senators had incomes of more than $500,000; another ten had incomes of $100,000 to $500,000. Only two representatives reported incomes of more than $500,000; thirteen reported incomes of $100,000 to $500,000.[9] Most unearned income derives from significant assets (stocks, bonds, or real estate) held by the members. Nine representatives received no outside income, earned or unearned, and a number reported minimal amounts.

Studies indicate that high campaign spending improves a challenger's chances but does not guarantee victory to either an incumbent or a challenger.[10]

Elections. The timing of regular, calendared congressional elections affects candidates in various ways. First, every House member faces frequent elections. Newly elected members make an effort to organize offices quickly to provide services to their constituents, as a duty and as a way of building support for future elections. They frequently return to their districts to be seen and to be available to their constituents. Senators, with longer terms, carry out similar activities, but they also devote considerable immediate attention to policy matters as well. Typically, senators increase the frequency of trips back to their states during the last two years of the six-year term.

Voter turnout in congressional elections held in a presidential election year is substantially higher—an average of about 17 percent more—than for congressional midterm elections held at the midpoint of a president's four-year term.[11] Midterm elections generally mean the loss of some seats by the president's party in Congress. Midterm elections thus appear to act as a balancing mechanism that reasserts more local concerns after an election with a national focus.

General elections, like primary elections, are decentralized to the state and district level. The national party and the House and Senate congressional campaign committees often provide training, information, and some campaign contributions to party candidates. Party leaders, including the president or presidential candidates, also endorse and often campaign for congressional candidates. Endorsement is helpful in a state or district that supports a presidential candidate strongly, but on occasion candidates absent themselves during presidential visits so as to make clear that they do not necessarily support presidential policies (and do not want to share a president's expected electoral defeat). Endorsement by the party can be helpful; it is rarely withheld, but on occasion close association with a party can be a detriment to election. The practices reflect, once again, the decentralized nature of the parties and the electoral system, as well as the increasing practice of emphasizing incumbency and personal experience rather than the party label.

Third-party candidates for congressional elections are relatively unusual and are mainly a local phenomenon. Third parties in the United States tend to be rare, and they generally operate for only short periods of time. New York, where the local Conservative and Liberal parties regularly nominate candidates—often endorsing the Republican or Democratic candidates—is a major exception.

Characteristics of members of Congress. Traditionally, the characteristics of members of Congress differ from those of their constituencies. They tend to be older, better educated, from higher-status occupations, and with more political experience. In recent years, however, some changes have gradually occurred: the average age has decreased, there are somewhat fewer lawyers and more diverse prior occupations, and fewer have previous political experience. In the 96th congress (1979–1980), the average age of all members was just under fifty; representatives were slightly younger and senators slightly older than fifty. The age of members is decreasing because members elected to their first terms are younger: in both the Senate and the House new members elected in 1978 were, on average, in their early forties. More than 50 percent of the members of the 96th congress were lawyers, a slight decrease from previous years because more than 50 percent of the newly elected representatives were *not* lawyers; 29 percent of all members were in business or were bankers, and 12 percent had backgrounds in education. Sixteen women served in the House, one in the Senate. There is some fluctuation in the number of women members but no clear trend toward increase or decrease since about 1950. There were sixteen black representatives, no black senator; although the number of blacks in Congress has increased since the 1950s, this minority is consistently underrepresented in terms of the United States population. In recent years, the percentage of newly elected senators and representatives who had previously held elective office has decreased to about 67 percent from more than 90 percent in the 1950s, a reflection of declining party strength and increasing independence of candidates as well as of changes in Congress that may encourage the recruitment of nonparty candidates.[12] There is little movement of members among the branches of government. On occasion, members move to cabinet secretarial posts or federal judgeships, but few members move to Congress from these positions.

Senators and representatives reach Congress by diverse career paths. A number of members have previously held elective or appointive office at the state or local level. State legislators and mayors may move on to the House of Representatives; governors, as well as members of the House, tend to run for the Senate. Members have often been active in state or local political parties. Increasingly, prominent local—or national—figures with few party ties or experience in state or local government are standing for office and being elected. Unlike legislators in parliamentary systems, new members generally have not had extensive high-level experience in national policy formulation.

After leaving Congress, members often practice law, serve as lobbyists, enter university teaching, or serve as consultants. Some few are appointed to cabinet or subcabinet positions in the federal executive branch. Some House members run for other office, usually state governorships or Senate seats. If senators seek another office, it is much more likely to be the presidency.

The Member in Office

Serving in the national Congress is a full-time job. Today, Congress is in session throughout the year, although generally in an election year (the second session of the two-year Congress) adjournment occurs prior to the November election. Members often maintain two homes, one in their state or district and one in Washington, D.C., or its suburbs.

The congressional job has various components: law making (legislating), oversight of government programs and agencies, and constituent service. Members are expected to return to their states and districts frequently to meet with constituents, to fulfill speaking engagements, and to keep up their ties with local party and political officials. Until recently, virtually all the commentary and scholarly research on Congress focused on legislative activities in Washington. It is now clear, however, that activities in the constituency are expected by constituents, occupy a significant portion of a representative's time, and are an important factor shaping the member's policy views and Washington activities.[13] Constituent service activities, both in the home state and in Washington, appear to be important to incumbent reelection.[14]

Senators and representatives receive salaries and benefits designed to permit full-time work in Congress. Allowances for the operation of personal offices and a variety of support services are also provided.

Salaries and Benefits

In 1980, senators and representatives were paid a salary of $60,662.50 per year; this amount was more than the salaries paid top-level civil servants in the executive branch, less than the salaries of Supreme Court justices ($75,900) or cabinet officers ($69,630), and equivalent to the salaries of federal appeals court judges.[15] Members may elect to participate in health and life insurance programs available to all federal government employees; a monthly program is paid for by the member. Members may also elect to participate in the federal government retirement program, paying 8 percent of their salary each year to the program; retirement pensions for those who have served in Congress at least five years are based on a formula using the highest salary years to determine annuity but may not exceed 80 percent of the member's final salary. Members may earn additional income through lecturing, writing, and other outside activities. The limits on earned income, first established in 1977 by the House, are based on the belief that serving in Congress is a full-time job that permits only sporadic additional income-earning activities. Many members augment their salaries and allowances with personal funds, and there are no limits on income derived from stocks, bonds, or other business interests. Senators and representatives are required to file statements regularly disclosing income and liabilities as well as statements detailing expenditure of all official allowances. All statements are available for public inspection.

Allowances and Central Services

Senators and representatives receive official money to hire staff aides and to operate offices on Capitol Hill and in their state or district. A number of services are also provided directly to members or their staffs by central legislative and support service agencies and offices in Washington; services provided include mailing and package-wrapping assistance, computer services, legislative research and information, and legislative drafting. The staffing and support services, unique in the world, derive from the governmental system and the role of the member in that system: the legislature as a separate branch of government with policy and representative responsibilities, and members elected from single-member districts with close and continuing ties to the constituency. Allowances permit members to obtain assistance in the discharge of their official duties. Campaign expenses, including campaign staff salaries, must be paid from nonofficial funds. Senior aides often take a leave of absence from a senator's or representative's staff in order to work on the reelection campaign.

In 1980, each representative received an annual "clerk-hire" allowance of $308,328 and was authorized to hire up to 18 full-time and 4 part-time or temporary staff aides. Top aides may earn $50,112 per year. Not all members use the full allowance or employ the full number of aides authorized: in early 1980, members employed an average of 16.5 aides, at an average salary of $16,566.[16]

An official expenses allowance entitles representatives to money to operate offices in Washington, D.C., and in their districts. It is designed to cover the expenses of office equipment, office rental in the district, postage, travel to the district (estimated at thirty-two round trips per year), telephone and telegraph, newsletters and questionnaires, computer services (for legislation information, correspondence, etc.), office supplies, and other office expenses. The member is entitled to $40,000 and variable amounts for travel, telecommunications, and rental of district office space, with the average annual allowance approximately $80,000.

Senators receive the same salaries and benefits (health and life insurance and retirement plan) as representatives. Office allowances for senators—for staff salaries and office expenses—are larger, and the allowances for both staff salaries and office expenses vary among senators. These differences from the House are a consequence of generally larger constituencies and of variation in the size of Senate constituencies.

The administrative, clerical, and legislative assistance allowance authorized for each senator is based on state population and in 1980 ranged from $711,646 for states with less than 2 million population (for example, Alaska, Vermont, Wyoming, and Rhode Island) to $1,259,874 for states with more than 22 million population (California). The allowance included up to $168,468 for hiring aides to assist senators with their committee work.

Senators also receive an official office expense account allowance to cover expenses of telephone and telegraph, postage, stationery, newspaper and magazine subscriptions, and travel. The allowance varies according to the population of the state and the distance from Washington, D.C. (for the travel and telephone component). In 1980, the amount authorized for expenditure ranged from $33,000 per year for the senators from Delaware to $143,000 per year for the senators from Hawaii, who have high travel and telephone expenses. California senators received up to $87,000, and New York senators, with nearly 18 million constituents, received up to $70,000. Senators also may lease a mobile office and receive basic office equipment, space for their state offices in federal buildings, and a paper and envelope allowance. With the exception of the mobile office, these allowances are based on state population.

Members of Congress may also send official mail under the franking privilege. (A facsimile of the member's signature on an envelope is equivalent to a stamp.) Assistance is also available to senators and representatives from three other sources: committee staff, party and leadership offices, and the four legislative support agencies.

Other Assistance

Congressional committees have appointed staff since the mid-1800s, but since 1946, when the Legislative Reorganization Act was passed, committee staffs have increased in size and have become increasingly expert and professional. In 1980 there were about 1,700 staff members on Senate committees and 2,784 in the House. Many subcommittees now have their own staffs and operate, especially in the Senate, as autonomous units. Committee staff members are generally partisan, and although they are formally appointed by the committee's majority or minority caucus, in fact they work for the member who appointed them—the committee or subcommittee chairman or ranking minority member, or in some cases an individual senator or representative. For senators especially, this system of appointment and control augments the personal office staff. Senators who chair committees may be directing the work of 50 to 80 staff aides on their committee, subcommittee, and personal staffs. Committee aides must work on committee matters, but the committee's or subcommittee's priorities are often set by the chairman. When, for example, Senator Magnuson (D-Wash.) chaired the Commerce Committee, the committee staff worked extensively on consumer issues, one of his major interests. Party and leadership offices thus augment the individual member's resources. And either through a committee or on an individual basis, individual members may request special studies or assistance from the four legislative support agencies: the Congressional Research Service that is part of the Library of Congress, and the Congressional Budget Office, the General Accounting Office, and the Office of Technology Assessment.

Personal Office Staff and Organization

Senators' personal staffs average about 35, representatives' 16.5. Staff aides are divided between Washington and one or more offices in the state or district. The typical senator and representative employ several secretaries, several caseworkers, one or more press aides, several (up to six in a Senate office) legislative assistants, a federal projects worker, an office manager, and an administrative assistant. Many also employ one or more field representatives, senior aides who represent the legislator in the district or state, delivering speeches and meeting with constituent groups. Senators' staffs, because they are generally larger than those of representatives, are often organized by departments: mail, press, casework, legislation.

Although most aides are generalists in that they handle broad areas (energy, conservation, or foreign policy issues; general casework), they are increasingly specialized when compared to aides a decade ago. Professional staff, both personal and committee, are recruited from the executive branch, from other legislative offices, or from the private sector: a foreign service officer, for example, may move from the State Department to the Foreign Affairs Committee, or an employee of an environmental interest group will join the personal staff of a senator to handle environmental legislation. Personal staff aides are more likely to be recruited from the legislator's district or state than are committee aides; they may have skill training such as in law, but they have less specific issue expertise. Personal legislative assistants, however, more and more resemble committee professionals both in their training and in their expertise.

Caseworkers are typically aides familiar with federal programs that have an impact directly on the individual constituent. The type of case varies from state to state: Florida senators and representatives, for example, have many older constituents and receive a number of requests for assistance on social security and Medicare matters; other members may receive requests for help primarily from military personnel or miners seeking benefits for black lung disease. Case loads vary. Senators' offices typically handle one thousand to eight thousand or more cases a year. But the offices of senators from the largest states process thirty to fifty thousand cases a year.[17] In the House the average case load is about ten thousand.

Increasingly, both senators and representatives are appointing federal projects aides. These staff aides assist constituent groups — cities, towns, counties, educational institutions — with the grant application process for federal funds for highways, dams, education programs, hospital construction, and so forth. Much of the liaison between the constituency and the federal government agency has come to be handled by staff.

Press aides deal with local and national reporters; draft press releases, newsletters to constituents, and speeches; and make arrangements for radio and television interviews. Many senators and representatives regularly send radio or television tapes commenting on legislation or issues of current concern to stations in their district or state.

Legislative aides are generally trained as lawyers or have specific expertise in an issue area, as, for example, a doctoral degree in Asian studies; many, particularly on committees, have prior experience in government or the private sector. These aides assist in all phases of legislative work: doing background research to identify problems and develop proposals, setting up committee hearings, drawing up witness lists, preparing questions for the members to ask during hearings, drafting testimony, or drawing up legislation and amendments. They may work with staff aides of other senators and representatives in developing compromise legislative language that will be acceptable to a group of members. They are often active in discussions with other senators and representatives to obtain support for a legislative position and in developing strategy and building the necessary coalitions for passage of legislation. Aides also brief members on legislation scheduled for committee or floor action, summarizing arguments, listing those in favor or opposed, noting provisions that may affect a member's state or district, and alerting the members to possible floor amendment. Many aides work quite independently within general guidelines set up by the legislator. In other offices, legislators guide their aides closely. Several studies indicate that aides are increasingly relied on for their expertise and their judgment. Although the voting decision is made by the legislator, a trusted aide can provide information that may be a major influence.

Administrative assistants and executive assistants continue to be generalists in an increasingly specialized office. As the top staffer to the member, the aide generally manages the substantive work of the office, handles difficult personnel and constituent matters, and works on legislation that is particularly controversial or important to the state. In addition, the aide may represent the legislator back in the state or district, meet with constituent groups, and serve as political confidants and advisers.

The member's work. Typically, senators and representatives work long days, attending to duties in Washington and making frequent trips to their constituencies. Senators reported, in 1976, a working day of about eleven hours. It may begin with an early morning breakfast with a group of constituents and end with attendance at an evening reception of a national group. When in Washington, senators spend nearly four hours in committee or subcommittee meetings or on the Senate floor. They spend nearly two hours meeting with constituents and interest groups in their office and another two hours at events (meetings, speeches) outside the office. Two hours are devoted to mail, press work, and similar matters. Two-and-one-half hours are spent with staff or reading staff papers, some of it in committee.[18] Representatives report similar schedules: four-and-one-half hours in committee or on the floor, three hours in the office meeting with constituents or working with staff, two hours at events away from Capitol Hill, nearly two hours in travel or other activities.[19] Both senators and representatives make frequent trips to their states and districts. In addition, there are trips in connection with committee work or to conferences as members of congressional delegations.

The daily schedule is crowded and often unpredictable, and the days are fragmented. The number of committee meetings has been increasing, as has the length of time spent in session. There are more scheduling conflicts. Many members are concerned about the many demands on their time—partially a result of increasing resources and independence. Both Senate and House have attempted to simplify scheduling matters in recent years by limiting the number of committee assignments and by providing scheduling assistance, but many of the problems still remain.

Conclusion

The staff, allowances, and support services available permit a member of Congress to operate quite autonomously, to pursue actively particular legislative interests or concerns, and to have a major impact as an individual reflecting personal or constituent interests on national policy. There is latitude in how the legislator uses allowances, and members have the resources not only to serve as representatives and legislators on policy questions but also to supply constituent services.

Official allowances permit members to hire staff aides, organize and operate offices, and travel largely as the individual member deems necessary. Some members operate four or more offices, one in Washington and the rest in the district or state; as was noted, they may supervise as many as fifty to eighty staff aides in these offices and on committee staffs. They may also obtain assistance from the legislative support agencies and from central support groups within each house. The system permits members to function independently of other members, of party, and of the president.

Legislators have different priorities: some focus primarily on committee work, others spend more time in the ombudsman role, still others make national reputations as legislators on specific national issues or in legislative investigatory work. All members face multiple demands on their time and attention. Constituents appear to be contacting their legislators more frequently for assistance in working with the federal government and about national issues and concerns. They expect their senators and representatives to appear at state and district events regularly. Many groups come to Washington to meet with their legislators. Virtually all senators have heterogeneous constituencies with various interest groups bringing their concerns to their legislators and expecting representation in policy matters. Increase in the number and activity of single-issue interest groups has created additional pressures for legislators.

As the role of party and the power of seniority have decreased and the resources available to the individual legislator have increased, the potential for one individual to affect the course of legislation or the operation of a program has increased. Because of the changes of the 1970s resulting in a more decentralized decision-making process and a wider distribution of more resources, coalition building is less predictable than previously. Individual senators and representatives can operate quite autonomously if they wish, using staff to draft amendments for committee and floor action and to assist them in mapping strategy. Staff also are important in assessing how proposed legislation or the implementation of federal programs affect the legislator's district or state. As a consequence, it has become more difficult to coordinate the work of Congress and to develop unified and consistent national policy.

Members of Congress are subject to an extraordinary number of pressures and demands that are not present in more centralized systems. Members play multiple roles: legislator, representative of constituency and of party, ombudsman. In nearly every action as a legislator a member must balance a number of legitimate but competing demands. Constituents, state delegations, national interest groups, party leaders, and the president all bring pressure.

The role of the individual member is a logical consequence of the system of divided powers. The close ties to the constituency, the resources available to the member, and the organization and procedures of the two houses give the member the potential for significant impact on the content and course of legislation and on federal programs and national policy.

Notes

1. David S. Broder, *Changing of the Guard: Power and Leadership in America* (New York: Simon & Schuster, 1980), pp. 35–36.

2. William J. Keefe and Morris S. Ogul, *The American Legislative Process: Congress and the States*, 4th ed. (Englewood Cliffs, N.J.: Prentice-Hall, 1977), pp. 87–88; see also Leo M. Snowiss, "Congressional Recruitment and Representation," *American Political Science Review* 60 (September 1966): 627–639.

3. Keefe and Ogul, *American Legislative Process*, p. 94.

4. Malcolm E. Jewell and Samuel C. Patterson, *The Legislative Process in the United States*, 3d ed. (New York: Random House, 1977), pp. 88–89.

5. The Federal Election Campaign Act of 1971 (P.L. 92–225), Campaign Act amendments of 1974 (P.L. 93–443), and Campaign Act amendments of 1976 (P.L. 94–283). A number of provisions of the 1974 law were challenged in court; in January 1976 the Supreme Court upheld individual and committee contribution limits and disclosure requirements and overturned the limits on expenditures and candidates' contributions for congressional campaigns (*Buckley* v. *Valeo*). Thus the present system is based on federal law and court order.

6. *Congressional Quarterly Weekly Report*, June 25, 1977, pp. 1292–1294; *Congressional Quarterly Weekly Report*, October 9, 1977, p. 290.

7. *Congressional Quarterly Weekly Report*, September 29, 1979, p. 2157.

8. Ibid., p. 290.

9. *Congressional Quarterly Weekly Report*, p. 2471.

10. *Congressional Quarterly Weekly Report*, September 29, 1979, pp. 2155–2157; Samuel C. Patterson, "The Semi-Sovereign Congress," in *The New American Political System*, ed. Anthony King (Washington, D.C.: American Enterprise Institute, 1978), pp. 151–152.

11. Robert B. Arseneau and Raymond E. Wolfinger, "Voting Behavior in Congressional Elections," paper presented at the meeting of the American Political Science Association, 1973, p. 2.

12. *Congressional Quarterly Weekly Report*, December 30, 1978; *Congressional*

Quarterly Weekly Report, January 20, 1979; *Congressional Quarterly Weekly Report*, January 27, 1979; David J. Vogler, *The Politics of Congress*, 3d ed. (Boston: Allyn & Bacon, 1980), p. 72.

13. Richard R. Fenno, *Homestyle: House Members in Their Districts* (Boston: Little, Brown, 1978).

14. Glenn R. Parker and Roger H. Davidson, "Why Do Americans Love Their Congressmen So Much More Than Their Congress?," *Legislative Studies Quarterly* (1979): 37–66.

15. Party leaders in each house were paid higher salaries: Speaker of the House, $79,125; president pro tempore of the Senate and majority and minority leader of both houses, $68,575.

16. U.S., Congress, House of Representatives, Committee on Appropriations, Subcommittee on Legislative Appropriations, *Hearings on Legislative Branch Appropriations, FY 1981* (Washington, D.C.: Government Printing Office, 1980), p. 299.

17. Janet E. Breslin, "Constituent Service," in *Senators: Offices, Ethics and Pressures*, committee print (Washington, D.C.: Senate Commission on the Operation of the Senate, 1977), p. 21.

18. U.S., Congress, Senate, *Compilation of Reports To Be Filed by Senators, Officers and Employees* (Washington, D.C.: Government Printing Office, 1980), p. 306.

19. U.S., Congress, Senate, Commission on the Operation of the Senate, *Toward A Modern Senate*, committee print, 6 vols. (Washington, D.C.: Senate Commission on the Operation of the Senate, Senate Doc. 94–278, 1977), pp. 16–19.

11

The U.S. Congress
in Budgeting and Finance

Joel Havemann

It is only fitting that for a government that consumes more than half a trillion dollars a year, the budget process of that government should be enormously complex. The current budget process of the U.S. government has evolved over about sixty years, periodically adding new layers of complexity. Insofar as it involves the executive branch, the system is quite similar to the Japanese style of preparing budgets. But the process by which Congress subsequently deals with the budget is far more complex than that used by the Japanese Diet.

For the executive branch of the U.S. government, budget preparation is a never-ending cycle. Almost two years before the beginning of any given fiscal year, the agencies of the executive branch begin preparing their spending plans for that year. About eight months before the fiscal year begins, the president submits to Congress the proposed budget for all these agencies. Even after Congress approves a budget and the fiscal year begins, the agencies continue to make adjustments in their spending plans. Consequently, at most times of the year, the executive branch is working on three budgets at once: the one that governs its current activities, the one that it has proposed to Congress for its next fiscal year's activities, and the one that it is preparing for submission to Congress for the year after that.

From the point of view of Congress, the budget process is scarcely less simple. Every year after the president has submitted a budget, Congress must still take three major actions before the executive branch receives authority to spend money. First, it must approve an overall budget that sets the broad outlines for spending plans for the coming year. Then it must pass authorization bills that permit Congress to appropriate funds for particular programs within the scope of the budget. Finally, it must pass appropriations bills that actually provide the executive branch with the legal authority to spend money.

In the United States, the president submits the executive branch budget to Congress every year in late January. That is a few weeks after the government of Japan sends its budget to the Diet. But whereas the Japanese fiscal year begins on April 1, the fiscal year in the United States does not begin until October 1. Thus, while the Diet has only about three months to put a budget in shape for the new year, Congress has more than eight months. There is another difference: the Diet virtually always finishes work on the budget before the fiscal year begins, but Congress hardly ever does. Usually, Congress takes almost an entire year to put its mark on the federal budget. Its impact, therefore, can be far greater than that of the Diet.

The Public Sector in the United States

In the United States, the national government is the largest layer of government, but below it are many others. The federal government spent about $580 billion in the 1980 fiscal year. That amount represents about 23 percent of the U.S. gross national product of about $2,500 billion. National government consumption in Japan will be about $210 billion, which is about 19 percent of the Japanese gross national product (about $1,100 billion).

In the federal system of the United States, fifty state governments and the District of Columbia, which is the seat of the national government in Washington, rank in the next layer below that of the federal government. At the third level are nearly eighty thousand local government bodies. Some of these (about three thousand) are county governments, which are typically the next biggest governmental jurisdictions after the states, and others (about thirty-six thousand) are governments of cities, townships, and other municipalities within the counties. All these levels of government—states, counties, and municipalities—provide a variety of services for their residents. In addition, there are about forty-one thousand overlapping, single-purpose governmental bodies. Most numerous are about fifteen school districts; other single-purpose governmental bodies have functions such as building roads and eliminating insect pests.

All levels of government rely on one form or another of taxation to raise the money they need to operate, and there is great variety among the forms of taxation in the United States. Local units of government typically rely on a tax assessed on private property. Of the fifty states, forty-five levy a sales tax, forty-four tax personal income, and forty-six impose a corporate income tax. Most of the states also tax various consumer items, particularly gasoline, tobacco, and alcoholic beverages.

At the federal level, three taxes bring in most of the revenue: the personal income tax, the corporate income tax, and the social security tax. In 1980, taxes on personal income will raise about $239 billion, and taxes on business income will raise another $72 billion. A payroll tax shared equally by employers and employees, which is used to support the social security system of pension benefits for retired persons, will bring in another $162 billion. But these are hardly the only taxes. The federal government also adds a tax to the price of such goods and services as gasoline, alcohol, tobacco, telephone calls, and even fishing rods, guns, and bows and arrows. The government collects fees for many of the services it provides, including issuing passports and granting admittance to national parks. There are tariffs on many imports, and there is a new tax on crude oil that is designed to capture some of the so-called windfall profits of the oil companies. Altogether, the government expects to collect about $519 billion in revenue in 1980. Because it expects to spend about $580 billion, it will show a deficit of $61 billion.

The federal government in the United States accounts for about two-thirds of the expenditures in the public sector, which, in all, equals about 36 percent of the gross national product. In addition to the 23 percent of the gross national product that is consumed by the federal government, state and local government budgets will account for another 13 percent. Of that 13 percent, however, about 4 percent will be in the form of payments from the federal government; these payments are also counted in the federal share of the gross national product. When this double counting is eliminated, the total public sector in the United States—federal, state, and local—accounts for about 32 percent of the entire U.S. economy.

Congress and the Budget

To understand the role of Congress in the federal budgetary process, it is necessary to know something about how the executive branch prepares the budget proposals that are submitted to Congress every year.

Until 1921, there was no centralized budget process in the executive branch. The agencies simply submitted their budgets separately to Congress for its approval or modification. Then in 1921, Congress passed the Budget and Accounting Act, which established a bureau of the budget in the Treasury Department to coordinate the budget proposals of all the agencies. In 1939, President Franklin Roosevelt moved the Bureau of the Budget to the Executive Office of the President. For the first time, the president himself was able to fit the budgets of all the agencies of government into his own blueprint for what the government should be doing in the coming year. In 1970, with Congress's approval, President Richard M. Nixon changed the name of the Bureau of the Budget to the Office of Management and Budget (OMB).

Every year, all the agencies submit their spending requests for the coming year to OMB. Consider, for example, the budget for the 1982 fiscal year, which will begin on October 1, 1981. In the spring of 1980, the agencies submitted to OMB a preliminary estimate of their 1982 budget requests. Inevitably, the agencies suggested more spending than OMB felt the government could afford. In the summer of 1980, OMB assigned each agency a budget target, and for most agencies, the target fell below the level the agencies had discussed in their spring estimates. In the fall, the agencies submitted their formal budget requests to OMB, detailing how much money they sought for each of their activities. OMB made cuts from many of the programs; when the agencies objected strongly to a particular reduction, they appealed to the president, who resolved the most difficult issues. The result of this painstaking exercise is the president's budget, which, with modifications growing out of the last election, was submitted to Congress in January 1981, more than eight months before the beginning of fiscal 1982.

Up to this point, budget preparation in the United States is not very much different from the system in Japan. In both countries, the budget that the government submits to the legislature is a consensus document that reflects months of negotiations between government agencies and the government's central budget office (in Japan, the Budget Bureau in the Finance Ministry). But in Japan, the consensus tends to be broader, because the government tries to incorporate the ideas of interest groups and, to some degree, opposition members of the Diet before it formally submits its budget.

By the time the Japanese budget reaches the Diet, most interested parties have had a chance to influence the budget. The budget is modified in the Diet to only a relatively modest extent. In recent years, when the Liberal Democratic party lost some of its tight control of the government, opposition parties introduced their own amendments to the government's budget. But the government had already tried to take the opposition views into account, and its budget generally received the approval of the Diet with only a few modifications.

Such is not the case in the United States. Every year, Congress subjects the president's budget to rigorous review, even when Congress is controlled by the same political party that occupies the White House. Interest groups have many opportunities to pressure Congress to modify the budget to suit their interests. The budget that finally emerges from Congress can be quite different from the one that the president submitted.

Before it emerges from Congress, the budget undergoes three distinct levels of review. The broadest level of review is also the newest: only in 1974 did Congress establish what is known as the congressional budget process. Before 1974, Congress never held up the budget itself. Instead, it enacted individual spending and revenue legislation for the coming year. When it finished legislating, it added up the pieces to find out how much the government would raise through taxes and how much it would spend. The situation was similar to the one that had prevailed in the executive branch before 1921, when there was no presidential budget to bind together the individual budgets of all the federal agencies.

The 1974 Congressional Budget Act established two budget committees, one in the Senate and one in the House, to supervise the congressional budget process. Each budget committee has a staff of about seventy-five people to help its members understand the federal budget. In addition, the Budget Act established the Congressional Budget Office (CBO) to provide Congress with a source of budget expertise somewhat comparable to that of the Office of

Management and Budget in the executive branch. No longer does Congress have to rely on the executive branch, which often plays the role of its adversary in the determination of budget policy, for information about the budget. The CBO, with a staff of about two hundred, provides Congress with independent information about the budget.

The budget committees are not the only committees of the Senate and House that deal with the president's budget. In addition, there are the Senate and House appropriations committees, which are responsible for preparing the legislation that actually gives the executive branch permission to spend money. And about fifteen other committees in both the Senate and the House also play a role, because they are responsible for legislation authorizing federal programs. Until it enacts legislation to authorize programs, Congress does not have the power to appropriate money to operate them.

The budget committees, the appropriations committees, and the authorizing committees are all part of a complex process that occupies Congress for at least eight months between the receipt of the president's budget at the end of January and the beginning of the fiscal year on October 1. As soon as the budget arrives in Congress, all three kinds of committees begin holding hearings designed to help them prepare legislation. If all goes well (which it seldom does), Congress meets a series of deadlines that are calculated to enable it to finish work on the budget before October 1. The following are the crucial dates:

March 15. By this date, all the committees of the Senate and House with jurisdiction over spending or tax legislation report to the budget committees on their plans for legislation that will have an influence on the coming year's budget. Their reports are analogous to the budget requests that the agencies submit to OMB. The reports guide the budget committees as they prepare a budget for the coming year, but the budget committees are not bound by them, and they frequently reject spending requests.

April 1. The CBO submits a report to the budget committees by this date that analyzes the economic and policy consequences of various budget strategies that Congress might adopt for the coming year. But in the early years of the congressional budget process, the budget committees found the CBO report too long to be of much help and timed too late in the process to be very useful. So in recent years, the CBO has instead submitted a series of short reports analyzing particular budget issues.

April 15. This is the deadline for preparation of the Senate and House budget committees' separate versions of a tentative budget for the coming year. The budget takes the form not of an ordinary piece of legislation but of a concurrent resolution, which does not need the signature of the president. The budget provides guidelines for subsequent congressional action on actual spending and tax legislation. Compared with the president's budget, it is nothing more than an outline, consisting of (1) an estimate of total spending and revenue for the coming year, along with the resulting surplus or deficit, and (2) a breakdown of spending money among eighteen broad categories of governmental activity, the largest being income transfer programs, national defense, and health.

May 15. A month after the budget committees complete the preparation of a tentative budget, Congress is to finish the job of actually adopting a budget. During this month, the following steps must take place:

1. The full Senate and House must pass their own versions of the budget by accepting or modifying their budget committees' proposals.
2. A conference committee consisting of members of the Senate and House budget committees must reconcile the differences between the two versions of the budget.
3. The full Senate and House must accept the tentative budget submitted by the conference committee.

May 15 is also the deadline for the first step in one of the other levels of congressional budget action. By this date, the authorizing committees must submit to the Senate and House all their legislation that will authorize spending for the coming year. This legislation allows the Senate and House appropriations committees to begin the third level of congressional budget action—the preparation of appropriations bills.

At this point in the process, Congress still has not voted actually to spend money. It has merely set the stage for the adoption of spending legislation. There are two basic ways in which Congress can vote to spend money.

1. Congress can first pass legislation that authorizes spending and then pass appropriations bills that actually result in spending. This is the classical approach, and it is the most common. The appropriations committees in the Senate and the House, which are responsible for preparing the appropriations bills, have jurisdiction over about two-thirds of the budget. Spending that results from appropriations bills is called *front-door* spending because it follows the traditional path through the appropriations committees.

2. Congress can pass legislation—not appropriations bills—that mandates spending without subsequent action in appropriations bills. For example, many income transfer programs, such as social security, are established by laws that make the payment of federal benefits automatic to persons who qualify to receive them. Spending that results from automatic spending legislation is called *back-door* spending because it avoids the front door represented by appropriations committees.

Committees of Congress may begin work on spending legislation at any time of the year. But spending legislation may not be brought to vote on the Senate or House floor until Congress adopts its budget by May 15. The reason for this timing is that the budget is intended to guide the Senate and House as they debate spending legislation. The budget is merely advisory; Congress may choose to vote for a spending bill that exceeds its own budget. But if it does, the public is aware that Congress is "busting" its own budget. Congress cannot pass spending legislation without being fully aware of the impact of the legislation on the overall budget.

For nearly four months after May 15, Congress completes work on all its spending legislation for the coming year. Back-door spending bills may move through the Senate and House at any time during that period. Appropriations bills generally move toward the end of the period. Only after May 15, when all the authorizing bills have been prepared by their committees, can the appropriations committees begin to shape their appropriations bills. The appropriations bills may not go to the Senate and House until Congress has enacted the legislation that authorizes the appropriations. Legislation to change the tax laws also must wait until after Congress adopts its budget by May 15 before such legislation can be put to a vote by the Senate and House.

Early September. After a summer of work on spending and tax legislation, the next deadline in the congressional budget process falls a week after Labor Day, which is the first Monday in September. By this date, Congress is to have completed work on all spending and tax bills for the coming year.

September 15. Fifteen days before the beginning of the new fiscal year, Congress is to revise the budget that is adopted in May. The revised budget may be identical to the tentative budget. Or it may modify the tentative budget according to changing economic circumstances or demands on the federal budget. Like the tentative budget, the revised budget consists of total spending and revenue and the resulting surplus or deficit, and a breakdown of spending into eighteen categories. But unlike the tentative budget, the revised budget is binding. After it adopts its revised budget, Congress may not enact a tax bill that cuts revenue below the budget's total. Nor may it enact a spending bill that sends total spending above the budget's total. The spending categories in the revised budget, however, are still only advisory; Congress may vote for more spending in one category if it makes compensating cuts elsewhere.

September 25. Congress may choose in its revised budget not to make room for all the spending increases or tax cuts that it may have adopted during the summer. In such a case, it must reduce spending or increase tax revenue to bring these revisions in line with the dictates of the revised budget. The budget itself directs committees of the Senate and House to prepare legislation to reconcile total spending and tax revenue with the budget. The reconciliation legislation must be adopted by September 25.

The beginning of the new fiscal year is not necessarily the end of the annual congressional budget cycle, even if Congress has met all its deadlines. After the fiscal year begins, Congress may decide that economic conditions require a quick tax cut or spending increase. Or an emergency may arise—the most extreme possibility is a war—for which Congress needs to make money available immediately. In such a case, Congress may vote for more spending or less tax revenue than was permitted by its revised budget. But first, it must revise its budget again, by adopting what is known as a third budget resolution. In theory, Congress may revise its budget an indefinite number of times before the fiscal year ends.

A Case Study

The complex federal budget process can perhaps be best understood by studying one small part of the budget. Planetary exploration, a minor part of the budget of the National Aeronautics and Space Administration (NASA), provides a good example. NASA, which sent men to the moon in the 1960s, has become smaller and less ambitious since then; but it still spent more than $4 billion in the 1980 fiscal year. The agency's biggest project, budgeted at more than $1 billion in that year, is the space shuttle, an orbiting space laboratory, and launching pad that was sent into earth's orbit on April 19, 1980. By contrast, planetary exploration was budgeted at only $220 million in fiscal 1980. NASA used that money to collect data from nine spacecraft that have been launched toward the sun and four of the planets to collect information about the solar system. More important from a budgetary standpoint, it used part of its planetary exploration budget in connection with the launch of two probes of Jupiter from the space shuttle.

Fiscal 1980 began on October 1, 1979, but planning for NASA's 1980 planetary exploration budget began long before then. As early as 1975, NASA's five-year spending plans began showing the amount of money it expected to spend for planetary exploration in 1980. The serious planning, aimed at developing a firm 1980 budget total, began in early 1978, nearly two years before the first day of the fiscal year. Here are the important steps in the process that resulted in NASA's 1980 planetary exploration budget:

Early 1978. NASA officials got a tentative idea of the funds they could use for planetary exploration in 1980. Officials at the agency's five space flight centers and six research centers around the country submitted their estimates to NASA headquarters in Washington.

April 1978. The Office of Management and Budget (OMB) conducted its spring review of NASA's budget. The staff of OMB and NASA informally discussed the issues that the 1980 budget was likely to raise. Then the OMB staff met with the OMB director to prepare documents showing the president the highlights of the NASA budget.

July 1978. OMB notified NASA and all the other agencies of how much, in OMB's estimation, their 1980 budgets should be. NASA, like all the other agencies, was officially provided with a single amount to represent its entire 1980 budget. For NASA, that amount was about $4.7 billion. But on an informal basis, the OMB staff told the NASA staff the components that were used to arrive at the overall total.

September 1978. NASA submitted to OMB its request for its 1980 budget. Like almost all other agencies, NASA asked for more than OMB had suggested. Its total budget request of $4.9 billion included $238 million for planetary exploration.

January 1979. After OMB had negotiated its differences with the agencies, with final decisions by the president on the toughest issues, the president submitted his annual budget request to Congress. For NASA, he asked for some $4.7 billion, about the amount that OMB had originally suggested. OMB cut about $200 million from NASA's budget request, including $17.8 million for planetary exploration. The biggest single cut was of $10 million that NASA had requested to begin planning for unmanned flights to Venus. The president's budget included $220.2 million for planetary exploration.

February 1979. Authorizing committees in the House and Senate began work on NASA's budget, which Congress authorizes anew each year. House committees typically plunge into greater detail, and in this case the House Science and Applications Committee's Subcommittee on Space Science and Applications compiled a hearing record that consumes four volumes and more than 2,300 pages. In the Senate, the Commerce, Science, and Transportation Committee's Subcommittee on Science, Technology, and Space produced a three-volume hearing record of 1,350 pages.

February 1979. Well before Congress finished work on the authorization bill, subcommittees of the Senate and House appropriations committees began work on the NASA appropriation for 1980. NASA's budget was included in an appropriations bill that also provided money for the Housing and Urban Development Department and a variety of other agencies.

March 1979. The appropriations committees notified the budget committees of their estimates of the money that would be needed for all programs under their jurisdiction, including NASA's. Both appropriations committees endorsed the president's request of $4.7 billion, and they requested an additional $100 million for the space shuttle. Their estimates for NASA generally did not address planetary exploration specifically.

Also in March, the House passed a $4.76 billion NASA authorization bill that included the full $220.2 million requested by the president for planetary exploration.

May 1979. Congress adopted a tentative fiscal 1980 budget that included a $5.5 billion target for general science, space, and technology, a category that included not only NASA but also the National Science Foundation and a few other small agencies. The total for the category was large enough to accommodate the requests of the appropriations committees for $100 million more for NASA than the president had requested.

June 1979. The Senate passed a $5 billion NASA authorization bill, which like the House bill included $220.2 million for planetary exploration. A conference committee of members of the Senate and House authorizing committees was appointed to reconcile the difference between the two versions of the bill.

Even before the Congress completed work on the authorization bill, the House passed an appropriations bill that included $4.91 billion for NASA. Part of that total was $219.9 million for planetary exploration, $300,000 less than the maximum permitted by both versions of the authorization bill. The cut was from the use of automatic data processing equipment.

July 1979. The Senate and House accepted a compromise NASA authorization bill worked out by the conference committee. The final bill authorized $4.95 billion, including $220.2 million for planetary exploration. In the same month, the Senate passed an appropriations bill that included $4.943 billion for NASA, $219.9 million of it for planetary exploration.

August 1979. President Carter signed the NASA authorization bill. The bill did not empower NASA to spend money; it merely authorized Congress to appropriate money in the separate appropriations bill.

October 1979. After another Senate-House conference committee had reached a compromise between the two versions of the appropriations bill that included money for NASA, the Senate and House passed the bill in final form. For NASA, the bill included $4.943 billion, the figure in the original Senate bill. For planetary exploration, it included $219.9 million, $300,000 less than the full authorization.

November 1979. President Carter signed the appropriations bill into law. The action came more than a month after the beginning of fiscal 1980; in the meantime, NASA had continued to operate at its fiscal 1979 spending level.

In November, two months after its deadline, Congress adopted a revised budget that included $5.7 billion for the category of general science, space, and technology. That total was large enough to accommodate the NASA appropriation.

The 1981 Budget: A Year of Tumult

The preparation of the fiscal 1981 budget was marked by a series of policy reversals and innovative procedures, all designed to cope with an erratic economy that resisted the best efforts of federal policy makers.

In January, President Carter submitted to Congress a budget calling for outlays of $616 billion and a deficit of $16 billion. But a few weeks later, the inflation rate for the month of January was reported to have reached an annual rate of 18 percent, an alarming level in the United States. Carter immediately decided to combat the new round of inflation with a more restrictive fiscal policy, and he took the extraordinary step of revising his own budget. He ordered OMB to identify spending programs that could be cut, and he asked the Treasury Department for proposals for increasing taxes. In March, he gave Congress a new budget with spending of about $611 billion, a figure that actually reflected about $15 billion worth of spending cuts because the estimate of the costs of existing programs had risen by about $10 billion since January. Thanks to a variety of proposed tax increases, including a $.10-per-gallon increase in the federal gasoline tax, the $16 billion deficit in the January budget was turned into a $16 billion surplus in March.

The rising inflation rate also put pressure on Congress to adopt a balanced budget. The Senate and House budget committees, just beginning to prepare the tentative congressional budget, felt that strong measures would be necessary to force the rest of Congress to accept spending cuts. In the previous year, the tentative congressional budget assumed enactment of a variety of cost-cutting bills that would have saved several billion dollars. But with few exceptions, the committees with jurisdiction over the programs targeted for spending cuts refused to act, and the revised congressional budget had to be enlarged accordingly. So this year, the budget committees decided they had to take firmer action. They decided upon the unprecedented strategy of using the tentative budget to achieve spending cuts through the process of reconciliation.

According to the 1974 Congressional Budget Act, reconciliation was part of the revised budget. If the revised budget did not make room for all the spending that Congress had already enacted, Congress would have to reconcile its spending bills to the budget by reducing them. Until 1980, Congress had not tried the procedure of reconciliation; it had balked at forcing itself to make cuts from legislation that it had already enacted. But this year, the budget committees decided to resort to the reconciliation process in the tentative budget. They prepared a tentative budget that directed ten committees in the Senate and eight committees in the House to prepare legislation cutting spending by $6.4 billion. The budget also directed the tax-writing committees in the Senate and the House to prepare a bill increasing revenue by $4.2 billion.

The spending priorities of the budget proved just as controversial as the fiscal policy behind it. The House version of the tentative budget included $148 billion for defense, not much different from the $150 billion that President Carter requested in his March budget. But in the Senate, Ernest F. Hollings, an advocate of more defense spending, took over the chair of the Budget Committee when Carter appointed Edmund S. Muskie, a moderate on defense spending, as secretary of state. Under Hollings's leadership, the Senate voted $156 billion for defense. Hollings largely prevailed in the conference committee that reconciled the House and Senate versions of the budget, and the conference committee approved $154 billion for defense.

The controversies over fiscal policy and defense spending delayed congressional action on the tentative budget. Only on June 12, four weeks after its May 15 deadline, did Congress finally adopt a budget. The budget set a spending target of $614 billion, not much more than President Carter's March budget request. But because Congress was already in the process of rejecting Carter's $.10-per-gallon gasoline tax, the congressional budget included less revenue than Carter's March budget. But Congress made sure that its budget was balanced; in fact, the budget showed a (relatively) tiny surplus of $200 million.

Unfortunately for Congress, the balanced budget evaporated almost immediately. The economy turned sharply downward in the second quarter of 1980. That change meant that estimates of tax revenue, which depend heavily on personal and corporate income, also turned down. In addition, the slumping economy pushed up the estimates of the costs of such programs as unemployment compensation and welfare benefits. The economy provided an object lesson in the uncontrollability of the federal budget. Through events entirely outside of Congress's control, the small surplus of the tentative budget quickly turned into a hefty deficit. Congress might have been able to eliminate that deficit by cutting spending and raising taxes, but such steps would probably only have deepened the recession. Indeed, during the summer, many members of Congress endorsed a tax cut as a means of stimulating the economy.

Even for the U.S. government, the year of the formulation of the 1981 budget was a tumultuous one. To a Japanese observer, every year must seem marked by a striking degree of discord. There is little in the formulation of the president's budget request that would not seem familiar to a Japanese, but the congressional process must appear extraordinary indeed. Unlike the Diet, Congress views itself as an adversary of the executive branch, even when the same political party controls both. The Diet makes much of its imprint on the budget privately, before the government formally submits its budget. But Congress, which has no voice in the formulation of the president's budget, attacks that budget annually with renewed vigor. It is a noisy, raucous, time-consuming process. But out of it usually comes a budget that somehow seems to reflect the public will.

12

The U.S. Congress
in Foreign Relations, Trade, and Defense

Charles E. Morrison

Introduction

This chapter will discuss the functions and powers of the U.S. Congress as they relate to foreign political and economic policy and to defense policy. It will also consider the evolution of the relationship between the Congress and the executive branch in these policy areas and the process by which Congress carries out its responsibilities.

Before going into these questions, however, some of the general and very fundamental differences between the U.S. Congress and most parliamentary bodies discussed in previous chapters should be reiterated.

First, the U.S. Constitution designed the Congress and the Office of the President to check and balance each other. It is not the constitutional responsibility of the Congress, nor even of the members of the president's own party in Congress, to support the president and the executive branch. Rather, the Constitution intends that Congress exercise its own independent judgment on legislative and policy matters, giving due consideration, of course, to the proposals and policies of the president. Individual members of the Congress and the body as a whole may support or oppose the president on specific issues. In a sense, the entire Congress often acts as something akin to a "loyal opposition" to the president.

Second, because the Congress is an independent branch of the federal government, it has felt the need to develop its own sources of information, especially in recent years. Congress has, therefore, created for itself large staffs—17,000 individuals working for the members and committees of Congress as well as 20,000 others in subsidiary agencies, such as the Congressional Research Service, the General Accounting Office, the Office of Technology Assessment, and the Congressional Budget Office. Anyone familiar with other legislative bodies would find that the U.S. Congress is not just a political body but has also become very bureaucratic in its attention to detail, its procedures for evaluating issues, and its many public reports on foreign as well as domestic issues.

Third, party considerations play a relatively minor role in the congressional consideration of foreign relations, trade, and defense matters. In the trade area, the economic composition of a member's constituency—whether it is primarily agricultural or industrial, and what kinds of industries—is a more important factor in determining that member's voting than his party affiliation. In the case of foreign policy and defense policy, the member's ideological orientation and constituent pressures are key factors on most votes. For these reasons, members of the same party frequently oppose each other, and successful legislation often requires a coalition of majority and minority party members. Minority party members can be very effective and successful legislators if they know how to build coalitions across party lines, while other members, even if they are in the majority party, may be regarded as "lightweights" because of their inability in this respect.

The Evolution of Congressional-Executive Relations

The Constitution provides only the most sketchy of guides to the respective powers of the Congress and the president in foreign relations, trade, and defense. Most of the president's powers are implied rather than stated; those of the Congress largely proceed from its general legislative role rather than from the identification of specific functions. Such powers as are referred to in the Constitution are shared by the two branches. The president "makes treaties," but only with the "advice and consent" of two-thirds of the Senate can treaties be ratified. Under the Constitution, the president appoints and receives ambassadors, but the Senate must confirm the appointments of U.S. envoys. The president is the commander in chief of the armed forces, but the Congress has the power "to declare war." The Congress shall raise and maintain armies and navies, "provide for the common defense," and "regulate commerce with foreign nations." These powers it must exercise through legislation, and like all legislation, this legislation is subject to the veto of the president and to administration by the president. The Constitution, therefore, necessitates a working relationship between the Congress and the executive branch; neither can successfully make or implement foreign or defense policies without the support or concurrence of the other.

One constitutional scholar has called the U.S. Constitution "an invitation to struggle for the privilege of directing American foreign policy." During the years after World War II, however, there was a remarkable degree of consensus on the basic foreign policy and trade goals of the United States, which was reflected in a high degree of presidential leadership and congressional concurrence. Given the unity born of World War II and the subsequent need for unity in the face of the cold war, this pattern of executive dominance–congressional concurrence not only seemed appropriate but was sustained by a body of carry-over legislation and practice from the war, which had vested in the president powers in foreign relations. The 1970s, however, witnessed a resurgence in congressional involvement in foreign policy and congressional efforts to exert greater control over the actions of the president.

This resurgence has been reflected in many different ways. In some instances, as in the case of the August 1973 prohibition against military operations in Indochina, the 1974 termination of military aid to Turkey, and the 1976 Clark amendment ending military aid to political factions in Angola, Congress forced rather abrupt and immediate changes in U.S. policies. In other instances, Congress established new procedures to assure its involvement in future crucial foreign policy and national security issues. Those procedures included the 1973 War Powers Resolution, adopted over the president's veto, which requires congressional authorization of any use of U.S. military forces for longer than sixty days and permits congressional termination of the use of such forces in the interim by concurrent resolution. In addition, new legislation permitted legislative vetoes of other executive branch decisions, as in the case of major military weapons sales and the sale of nuclear material. Congress also augmented its staff and research capabilities, improving its ability to oversee executive branch activities. A new Congressional Budget Office was established, and the House of Representatives and the Senate created intelligence committees to oversee the operations of intelligence agencies. Congress also insisted on closer consultations with the executive branch on major issues and negotiations and in the case of the Tokyo round of the multilateral trade negotiations (MTN) actually placed staff at the U.S. negotiating mission in Geneva.

This reassertion of congressional involvement in foreign policy has not been without controversy in the United States. Executive branch officials complain that Congress's interest is fitful at best and that too often members of Congress vote on the basis of domestic political considerations and parochial constituency interests rather than on the basis of enlightened and broader national interests. Congress, according to its critics, has intruded too deeply into the administration of policy. Its questioning and occasional reversal of the policies of the executive branch, again according to critics, have undermined the credibility of U.S. foreign policies, created inconsistencies, and weakened the international effectiveness of the president. Supporters of a more activist congressional role, however, regard this role as central to popular and democratic control of foreign policy. They argue that congressional involvement and watchfulness help assure that policies with broad support will be adopted and that this means, in the long run, a more effective foreign policy. They also point out that the involvement of the Congress requires the executive branch to think through its policies more carefully in order to justify and explain them before the Congress.

The debate regarding the proper role of Congress in foreign policy continues.

Although there is some evidence that the perception of a more dangerous international environment in the 1980s is leading the United States back in the direction of more presidential discretion, it is likely that Congress will continue to play a very active role in foreign policy.

One of the reasons for the reassertion of congressional interest in foreign policy is the heightened influence that U.S. involvement with the rest of the world has on the individual citizen's life and livelihood. This influence has been particularly evident in the Middle East, where war or civil unrest can mean substantially higher prices at the gasoline pump. It is also evident in foreign trade, where imports now account for about 8 percent of American GNP, a figure double that of the early 1960s. Moreover, starving Khmer refugees, shown on television screens, prompt public humanistic demands that assistance be provided. Pictures of Japanese fishermen killing porpoises or whales provoke a flood of mail to members of Congress, urging them to make statements of outrage or to write to the prime minister of Japan, or perhaps to introduce legislation to boycott Japanese products. Since such matters are important to the public in the United States, members of Congress cannot afford to ignore them. Moreover, publicity-conscious politicians can see ways of utilizing such issues to strengthen their political position by commenting about or introducing legislation regarding an issue even before they hear from their constituents. In fact, many issues relating to foreign policy may be politically "safer" to comment upon than domestic issues. A member can hardly lose in a domestic political sense, for example, by opposing dolphin killing in Japan.

Another major reason congressional involvement in foreign relations is likely to continue is the lack of a consensus on foreign policy among Americans. The destruction of the "cold war consensus" in the wake of public dissatisfaction with the Vietnam War is often cited as a principal cause of Congress's more active role in the 1970s. Although the Congress had appeared to authorize, through the vague Gulf of Tonkin resolution, some measure of presidential action in Indochina and although it voted appropriations for the war, the public also saw the Congress as the most likely tool for terminating U.S. involvement. Congressional opponents of the war, especially Chairman Fulbright and other members of the Foreign Relations Committee, used their prestige and public positions to articulate dissent.

The ending of the Vietnam War, however, did not end the debate about many other aspects of U.S. foreign policy. Another dispute involved the role of intelligence agencies, with some members appalled by the lack of accountability of intelligence agencies and by revelations of CIA activities in contravention of the agency's charter. Other members believed that the use of covert activities in the past was justified by international circumstances and argue that the intelligence agencies need a freer hand to protect U.S. interests. Foreign aid is another controversial issue. Some favor more foreign assistance channeled increasingly through international organizations to ensure that developmental, rather than political, considerations are paramount; others believe that aid should be reduced. The latter members have fought to restrict disbursement of U.S.-donated funds to international development banks and other international organizations and have sought, instead, to channel it to governments friendly to the United States. Similar cleavages exist in regard to defense spending and foreign trade policy.

Congress, reflecting the plurality of U.S. society, is the primary political arena where such battles are waged. The executive branch is also a battleground, but the Congress is the most accessible branch of government. Of its 535 members, some will be found to espouse the interests or position of any major group within the society. Ethnic Greeks, for example, were able to mount a lobbying campaign that helped persuade the Congress to force the executive branch, at least for a time, to cut off military aid to Turkey in the wake of the Turkish invasion of Cyprus.

Means of Influencing Policy

There are many tools by which Congress influences the making of U.S. foreign and defense policy, including legislation, hearings, oversight functions, informal consultations, treaty approval, and the legislative veto. In the following pages, some of these tools are examined and illustrated with specific events.

Legislation

In the United States, much policy is explicitly defined in law. Congress's legislative role, therefore, is its most definitive and powerful vehicle for shaping U.S. policies. The Taiwan Relations Act of 1979 provides a useful illustration of how Congress can modify a policy proposed by the president. In this instance, the president, using his unique constitutional power to receive ambassadors, recognized the People's Republic of China and withdrew recognition from Taiwan. At the same time, the administration had introduced legislation to establish a private organization to carry out the functions of the U.S. embassy in Taipei and assure that most treaty and commercial relations could be maintained on the same basis with Taiwan even though it was not recognized as an independent country. The Congress substantially modified the bill to reflect the concern of many members of the Congress that the U.S. reaffirm its interest in Taiwan's security. The amended version of the legislation declared that, as a matter of policy, the United States would consider any nonpeaceful action against Taiwan, including boycotts and embargoes, as a threat to the peace of the western Pacific and of grave concern to the United States. It also stated that U.S. policy is to provide Taiwan with enough defensive arms to maintain its self-defense capability and to maintain a U.S. capacity to resist any resort to force that might jeopardize Taiwan. Although the executive branch resisted the congressional language, suggesting that the U.S. security commitment remained despite the abrogation of the U.S.-Taiwan security treaty, the president signed the bill for fear that otherwise no bill would be forthcoming.

The Taiwan Relations Act was confined to a single foreign policy issue. The annual multifaceted authorization bills for the Department of State, foreign assistance, and defense, by contrast, generally collect numerous statements and alterations of U.S. policy on their way through the Congress. Another chapter discusses the budget process in detail; here the main point is that authorization and appropriations bills must be acted upon by the committees and the full bodies of each house, and there are very strong incentives for the president to sign the final result even though specific congressional additions or changes may not be to his liking. If these alterations were introduced separately as bills or resolutions, they might never see the light of day. But, attached to authorizing or appropriations legislation, they have some chance of succeeding or, at least, of receiving some publicity.

The powers of the Congress to modify the legislative proposals of the president are virtually unlimited. In fact, it is to be expected that every major authorization or appropriations bill will be amended in the course of passage through the Congress. New programs or spending may be authorized and appropriated, other programs may be entirely eliminated, budget figures may be changed, broad policy statements may be added, or very technical changes may be made. Examples of recent successful amendments added in Congress include the preservation of eleven U.S. consulates in several European, African, and Asian cities (which the Department of State was closing down for budgetary reasons), a statement that diplomatic recognition of countries should be perceived as an acknowledgement of their existence and not as approval of their governmental policies, funding of increased aid for Khmer refugees, and new funding for larger numbers of fighter aircraft and naval vessels.

Many of these amendments originate during committee or subcommittee consideration or mark up. There has often been prior consultation with the Department of State or Department of Defense, and in fact, an amendment may be supported by substantial elements within these departments even when the "official" executive branch policy is to oppose it. For the executive branch, floor amendments tend to be more dangerous. They are often offered by members not on the committee who are less familiar with foreign policy matters. They are subject to a vote by the full house of Congress, and it is much more difficult to present the executive branch arguments to the full house than to a committee. Floor amendments may also be presented with no advance warning. On the other hand, floor amendments are generally easier to eliminate in conference committees because they are likely to have been adopted in only one house and because only committee members on the conference committees vote on them.

During debate on the 1978 foreign aid authorization bill in the House of

Representatives, for example, an amendment was offered on the floor and quickly adopted that prohibited direct U.S. aid or U.S. aid supplied indirectly through international organizations to Cuba, Cambodia, Uganda, and Vietnam. The executive branch objected that it was inappropriate to prohibit assistance that went through international organizations, and since that objection was sustained by the Senate, the conference committee agreed that only direct aid to these four countries should be prohibited by the legislation.

One of the most significant foreign policy amendments in recent years was the Jackson-Vanik amendment to the Trade Act of 1974. This amendment prohibited most-favored-nation treatment and export credits to non–market economy countries that did not allow free emigration. The amendment was directed at the Soviet Union's refusal to allow free emigration of Soviet Jews. It was backed by Jewish organizations in the United States and also supported by members of Congress opposed to freer trade with the Soviet Union. Because the amendment was introduced early in the consideration of the Trade Act, there was time to work out a delicate compromise with the executive branch providing for a waiver or lifting of the restriction if the president found that the non–market economy country was making progress towards freer emigration. The secretary of state communicated the substance of the modified amendment to the Soviet Union, and it was believed to be acceptable to the USSR. Floor amendments to the Export-Import Bank Authorization Act, however, severely limited any credits that might have been extended to the Soviet Union even if the waiver were exercised; the executive branch found itself unable to prevent the lower credit ceilings, and the Soviet Union canceled the existing trade agreement with the United States. In this instance, Congress destroyed a major pillar of the administration's détente policy toward the Soviet Union.

The Legislative Veto

The modified Jackson-Vanik amendment contained a provision permitting the Congress, by a two-house concurrent resolution not requiring the president's signature, to annul a decision to grant a waiver lifting the prohibitions against most-favored-nation and export credits. This kind of legislative technique, although not envisaged in the Constitution, has become increasingly important as a tool for providing a means for Congress to be the final judge of significant decisions initially delegated to the president. Very rarely, however, has Congress vetoed an executive branch decision, and the inhibitions against so doing are much stronger in the foreign policy area than in matters of domestic policy. The Congress, however, came close to overturning the 1978 decision of President Carter to sell jet fighters to Saudi Arabia and Egypt and his 1980 decision to permit the sale of nuclear material to India. In both cases, resolutions of disapproval were defeated by narrow margins in the Senate.

Usually, the principal effect of the legislative veto has been to require the president to consider his decision much more carefully and assure himself that he has enough support within the public and Congress to sustain his position against serious challenge. Reconsideration often involves a compromise with potential opponents before the decision is actually made or, more rarely, a modification prior to a congressional vote. In the case of the Middle East arms sales, for example, the president announced his intention to sell additional F-15s to Israel in 1983–1984 two weeks prior to the Senate vote. Such compromises are often an important element in import relief cases. If the president chooses not to provide the kind of relief recommended by the International Trade Commission (ITC), the Congress may, by concurrent resolution, overturn the president's decision and reinstate the recommendations of the ITC. The president, therefore, is unlikely to provide no relief to the domestic industry. He may not provide as much relief as the ITC recommends, but because of the possibility of a legislative veto, he will generally seek a compromise with the industry and its congressional supporters prior to a decision.

The Senate's Treaty Powers

The requirement that the Senate must approve a treaty by a two-thirds vote acts, in a sense, as a form of legislative veto. In this instance, however, the powers of the Senate extend far beyond simple approval or disapproval of the president's decision to enter into a treaty relationship. In the course of its consideration of a treaty, the Senate can make amendments in the treaty language (requiring new negotiations with the other party), attach reservations modifying U.S. obligations and also requiring the consent of the other party, add "understandings" clarifying the U.S. interpretation of the treaty, or amend the resolution of ratification to affect future negotiations or establish policies regarding implementation of the treaty.

The Senate has very rarely rejected a treaty outright (only 16 treaties have been rejected by the Senate vote from 1789 while 1,393 treaties have been approved). The Senate, however, has failed to act on 100 other treaties, and 38 treaties have not entered into force because of Senate modifications unacceptable to the other treaty partner.

The treaty power has led to the most dramatic foreign policy confrontations between the president and the Congress. Important and controversial treaties, like the Versailles Treaty following World War I and the Panama Canal treaties of 1978, stand as symbols of the president's foreign policy and domestic effectiveness. For the president's political opponents in the Senate, such treaties offer unique opportunities to weaken the position of the president while garnering only one-third of the votes of the Senate.

The Versailles Treaty was perhaps the most controversial treaty in U.S. history. It was strongly supported by President Wilson, who had played an important role in its negotiation; but the Senate Foreign Relations Committee recommended forty-five amendments and four reservations. Since the amendments would have required renegotiation of the multiparty treaty, they were rejected by the Senate; but a total of fourteen reservations were approved, substantially modifying the terms of the U.S. agreement. The president opposed approval with the reservations added. In four separate votes on the treaty with various combinations of reservations, the treaty never received the two-thirds vote necessary for approval.

More recently, the Senate approved by a two-vote margin two treaties providing for the return of the Panama Canal Zone to the Republic of Panama and establishing a permanent regime of neutrality. Because there was very vocal and widespread public opposition to the treaties, senators who supported the treaties desired modifications that they argued were improvements on the negotiated versions. In this instance, Senate approval was largely secured by Panamanian acceptance of two Senate amendments providing that the United States could take independent action to defend the canal and that its naval vessels could "go to the head of the line" in a military emergency. The political importance of these amendments was demonstrated when the Senate Foreign Relations Committee voted to recommend them without attaching them to the Neutrality Treaty in committee. This action permitted them to be adopted on the Senate floor, with many senators not on the committee also sharing in the credit of cosponsoring them. Even so, the executive branch (and Panama) had to accept additional reservations and understandings to secure the necessary two-thirds vote.

The Senate's treaty power can have an important influence on the treaty negotiating process. The president must negotiate with one eye on the Senate, and in the case of potentially controversial treaties, the executive branch frequently consults with interested senators to assure their support. The SALT treaties are illustrative. SALT I was approved by the Senate in 1972 after an amendment was adopted to the resolutions of ratification making it clear that in the next SALT treaty, the Senate expected that both the Soviet Union and the United States should have equal numbers of missile launchers. This amendment set very important parameters on the president's negotiating flexibility; his ignoring those parameters, even if that had been logical for other reasons, almost certainly would have become an issue in itself and guaranteed disapproval of the SALT II treaty. Although a formula was found and agreed upon on an equal number of launchers and a SALT II treaty was signed, the late 1979 Soviet invasion of Afghanistan created an international and domestic political climate in which Senate ratification would have been most unlikely. Even though the Afghanistan invasion was unrelated to strategic weapons systems, the president and Senate leadership agreed that Senate consideration of the treaty should be suspended.

Hearings and Reports

Hearings are an integral part of the legislative process. If a committee considers a bill, it invites executive branch witnesses and interested outside parties to make comments. The fact that a committee holds hearings, however, does not necessarily mean that it intends to recommend the bill's adoption. Often hearings are intended simply to "test the waters" to learn whether the bill will find public support. Sometimes it is well known that a majority of the committee members oppose the bill, but they want to give the bill's sponsor an opportunity to make his or her position known. These situations often arise in trade legislation, where protectionist bills frequently are the subject of hearings and rarely receive any further consideration.

Committees may also hold hearings with no specific legislation as a focus but rather for the purpose of exploring an issue, examining executive branch implementation of laws (oversight), or building up a case for a particular policy position. Members may use hearings to try to influence policy when actual legislation is unlikely to be successful. Congressional criticism of the Vietnam War, for example, began with 1966 hearings in the Senate Foreign Relations Committee, which gave opponents a forum long before there was any chance of changing policy by legislation. Similarly, in 1980 it was clear that binding legislation curtailing foreign automobile imports could not pass the Congress. Hearings by a number of congressional committees, however, allowed individual members of Congress to express their concern for the plight of the domestic industry, to state positions, and to urge certain actions on the executive branch. Hearings, in this sense, are regarded as a way of influencing public sentiments and building a case, but they may also serve as a safety valve for the venting of grievances. After the United Nations General Assembly passed a resolution equating Zionism with racism, there were outraged demands from the U.S. public and Congress for U.S. withdrawal from the United Nations. The Foreign Relations Committee's promise to hold hearings on whether or not the United States should continue as a U.N. member served to satisfy these demands until tempers had cooled.

Congressional hearings are printed and are made available to the public. Another form of making views known is through congressional reports. There are many kinds of reports; for example, every bill reported to the floor by a committee is accompanied by a committee report describing the bill, explaining the committee's recommendations and the meaning of each provision in the bill, assessing the budgetary cost, and detailing committee action. The report may also contain separate views or minority views by members of the committee who oppose the bill or who wish to emphasize particular aspects. In such a report, the committee may desire to state its position on an issue or urge a course of action on the executive branch without making legislative changes. For example, for many years the Senate Appropriations Committee criticized what it regarded as excessive salaries paid to officials of international organizations and development banks and urged the executive branch to use U.S. influence to hold down salary increases.

A congressional report, however, may simply discuss an issue. Such reports are popular in the foreign policy field where creating actual legislation is difficult or impossible. Congress, for example, may not be able to pass a law creating a Pacific economic community organization, but a member of Congress favoring such an organization can have a report prepared for him or her on this subject. Congress cannot make laws for Japan, but the reports of the special task force of the House Ways and Means Committee on U.S.-Japan trade relations (the Jones reports) contain recommendations to the Japanese as well as the U.S. government.

Reports may be prepared not only by the committee members and staff but also by outside consultants hired by the committee, the Congressional Research Service, the Congressional Budget Office, or the General Accounting Office. Some are very technical (e.g., on the cost of a particular weapons system or the reason food aid intended for Chad rotted on the piers in Dakar); others, like the General Accounting Office's *United States-Japan Trade: Issues and Problems*, are very broad. For the most fundamental issues, Congress may establish a special outside study group, or commission, such as the 1974–1975 Commission on the Organization for the Conduct of Foreign Policy.

Reports rarely have a decisive influence on foreign policy or defense issues, but they often serve an important role in consensus building. A 1979 report of the Senate Armed Services Committee opposing further U.S. troop withdrawals from Korea, for example, was one of a number of considerations leading to an abandonment of the withdrawal program.

Consultations

Aside from the visible work of Congress—legislation, hearings, and reports—there are daily consultations between members of Congress and the executive branch on all matters of foreign policy, trade policy, and defense. Usually particularly close consultative relationships exist between the executive agencies and the committees that oversee their activities. For executive branch officials, consultations help explain executive branch policy or provide advice and support. Consultations allow the executive branch to anticipate and perhaps correct for any potential political problems. It is particularly essential in the early stages of a proposal to assure support within the committees of jurisdiction because a majority in the committees is crucial to enactment of any necessary legislation and in defending that legislation before the full house. Often executive branch members complain that members of Congress, and even their staffs, have little time or desire for in-depth consultations. Occasionally, members do not want to be consulted for fear of making real or implied commitments. However, those members who do want to play an active role in the formative stages of policy making can sometimes have an important impact.

Members of the Senate Foreign Relations Committee and House Foreign Affairs Committee are regularly briefed, often in closed (or confidential) session, on the status of major negotiations or on international events. On truly important issues, such as the Iranian hostage crisis, the secretary of state may make himself available to all members. In addition, there are frequent consultations between the president and the congressional leaders.

Party affiliation makes very little difference when it comes to consultations on international and defense matters. Since successful legislation and policies require the support of both majority and minority members, the executive branch prefers to brief both.

Members of Congress have a broad right to information from the executive branch. For those on the committees of jurisdiction, this right is derived from their oversight role; and, of course, it is in the interests of each department to keep the members of the committees of jurisdiction informed and satisfied. Thus members of the Senate Finance Committee and the House Ways and Means Committee receive special attention from the Office of the Special Trade Representative, and members of the armed services committees are well attended to by the Defense Department and military services. But members not on the committees of jurisdiction also vote and can introduce bills or amendments affecting any executive branch agency. Although the agencies' treatment of members not on the committees of jurisdiction may not be quite as forthcoming, especially on sensitive issues, the agencies have an incentive and obligation to respond.

Members are most likely to contact agencies regarding problems brought up by constituents. Letters on foreign affairs issues may be referred to the Department of State for reply. The department may also be contacted about employment opportunities, visa problems, briefings for a constituent going overseas, or a constituent's relative who is in jail in a foreign country. These inquiries are generally handled through a congressional liaison office, and the responses provided are largely the same for all members regardless of party affiliation or other considerations.

Travel

In 1979, 293 (of 535) members of Congress traveled abroad. A far greater number of trips were made by the congressional staff. These trips serve a variety of purposes, first and foremost of which is to inform the member of international issues of legislative import. Many members of the Senate, for example, travelled to Panama shortly before the Panama Canal treaties debate. Their trips gave them opportunities to see the facility and talk with Panamanian leaders and with U.S. officials and other interested parties in Panama or the Canal Zone. Members, particularly those members favoring the treaties, regarded such trips as politically beneficial. They believed they could better defend whichever position they took if they were able to say that they had been on the scene.

Congressional travel can be very useful in concentrating the member's valuable time on a single issue, such as a negotiation. Travel may clarify the executive branch's explanation of the international context of its policy (the member is likely to be much more familiar with the domestic context). Because of their greater independence, members of Congress may serve a useful role in opening up new U.S. channels of communication where an effort to do so by the executive branch would create diplomatic problems. Members of Congress, for example, have visited North Korea and Heng Samrin's Kampuchea, countries with which the United States does not have relations. Members may also be useful in explaining to foreign leaders U.S. domestic constraints. A trip by Senator Daniel Inouye in 1978 to the Philippines, for example, is often credited with helping convince President Marcos that certain Philippine demands for foreign assistance in base negotiations with the United States were unrealistic in terms of congressional approval. A trip by the majority and minority leaders of the Senate to Panama before the treaties debate was instrumental in achieving the acquiescence of the Panamanian leaders to the proposed Senate amendments to the neutrality treaty.

Congressional travel has its limitations, however. Some trips are boondoggles, with little learning going on. In some cases, the members of Congress may come away with distorted views, having discussed issues with only government officials (or, in some cases, only opposition leaders).

Congress and Trade Policy

As mentioned above, the Constitution gives Congress the power to regulate commerce with foreign nations. Because of the special nature of this constitutional provision and the importance of U.S. trade policy for U.S.-Japanese relations, Congress's role in trade deserves special consideration.

Some trade matters, such as the commercial provisions of friendship, commerce, and navigation treaties, are handled in treaty form and referred to the Senate Committee on Foreign Relations. Most trade agreements, however, are subject to legislative action by both houses of Congress; they are handled in the House of Representatives by the Ways and Means Committee and in the Senate by the Finance Committee. For years, Congress legislated all tariff levels; but in 1930, the Congress made what came to be seen as a disastrous mistake by enacting extremely high tariffs, thus contributing to the severity and longevity of the Great Depression. After this, Congress tried a new approach; it periodically delegated to the president advance authority to negotiate, on a reciprocal basis, tariff reductions within limits established by Congress. This authority permitted the President to enter into the Tokyo round of the multilateral trade negotiations.

Congress has also delegated to the executive branch and to an independent U.S. agency, the International Trade Commission, the duties for dealing with instances of dumping, export subsidies, and escape clause import relief. Congress periodically changes the applicable law and procedures, as it did in amending the antidumping and countervailing duty statutes in both the Trade Act of 1974 and the Trade Act of 1979.

Although the Congress has delegated much of its authority in the foreign trade field, it can by legislation set new tariffs, establish import quotas, or mandate negotiations leading to orderly marketing agreements. At a time when a domestic industry is suffering serious unemployment problems, a member of Congress from the affected area may introduce legislation to establish import restraints or make threatening statements about establishing restraints.

The chance of passage of far-reaching restrictive legislation, however, is limited. First, tariff and quota measures are considered revenue matters, which, under the Constitution, must be initiated in the House of Representatives. Such measures have not been popular with the prevailing sentiment in the House Ways and Means Committee. Secondly, there has been a long trend in Congress toward dealing with the broader trade policy issues and procedures and allowing administrative mechanisms to resolve specific industry trade issues. Thus, the question of whether the U.S. automobile industry receives import protection is likely to be decided by the International Trade Commission, not by the Congress.

Committees

As the foregoing indicates, committees play a crucial role in the process by which Congress influences policies. Although ultimate power resides in the two houses, the committees conduct hearings, recommend bills, and — in most instances — issue reports. Committees also conduct investigations, carry on oversight of executive branch activities, and serve as the vehicles for much of the consultation that occurs between the executive branch and the Congress. Since, with rare exceptions, bills and resolutions are referred to committees, these committees hold the keys to their success or failure. Normally, the Foreign Relations Committee can kill a treaty simply by never reporting it to the full Senate. Committees also play a crucial intermediary role between the full houses of Congress and the executive branch. The latter relies on committee members and staff for political advice and to explain executive branch goals and programs to the full houses.

Each congressional committee has a defined area of jurisdiction; most legislation and executive branch programs involving foreign relations, trade, and defense fall within the jurisdiction of five committees in each house of Congress. The Senate Foreign Relations Committee and the House Foreign Affairs Committee have jurisdiction over foreign political relations, foreign assistance programs, and some international economic matters. The armed services committees have comprehensive jurisdiction over defense programs, although they share oversight of defense intelligence with the intelligence committees. All appropriations bills are referred to the appropriations committees of each house. Finally, the Senate Finance Committee and the House Ways and Means Committee have jurisdiction for tariffs, reciprocal trade agreements, and import relief and adjustment assistance programs. Other aspects of international economic policy are shared by many other committees. In the Senate, for example, the Committee on Banking, Housing, and Urban Affairs has jurisdiction over Export-Import Bank legislation and export controls, the Committee on Agriculture has jurisdiction over agricultural trade matters (with the exception of sugar and international commodity agreements), and the Commerce Committee has jurisdiction over most Commerce Department programs, including export promotion.

Each of these committees has subcommittees that may be more or less active depending on the internal structure of the committee, the willingness of the chairman of the full committee to refer bills to the subcommittee, and the aggressiveness and vigor of subcommittee chairmen. The Senate Armed Services Committee, with seventeen members, has six subcommittees: arms control, general procurement, manpower and personnel, military construction and stockpiling, procurement policy and reprograming, and research and development. The Senate Foreign Relations Committee, with fifteen members, has seven subcommittees, including a subcommittee on Asia and the Pacific. The House Foreign Affairs Committee, with thirty-four members, has eight subcommittees.

The subcommittees of the Senate Foreign Relations Committee and the Finance Committee hold hearings, but actual voting on bills is done by the full committee. The Subcommittee on International Trade of the House Ways and Means Committee, therefore, will initially vote on a piece of trade policy legislation (for example, a proposed resolution of disapproval of the president's decision in an import relief case), and if that legislation is reported to the full Ways and Means Committee, there will be a second vote by the full committee before the bill or resolution is reported to the full house. In contrast, the Subcommittee on International Trade of the Finance Committee will only hold a hearing on the legislation; the actual vote will occur in the full Finance Committee, and that vote will be by all members of the committee.

Since jurisdictional lines among committees often overlap, it is possible for almost every committee of the Congress to involve itself in one way or another in international issues. The Senate Governmental Affairs Committee and the House Committee on Government Operations, for example, have very broad jurisdiction to investigate the administration of the laws and the relations among various branches of the government. In exercising this jurisdiction they have held, within the past few years, hearings on intelligence operations, trade and foreign aid reorganization, and U.S. participation in international organizations.

When committee members, for political reasons, find it expedient to hold hearings on an issue, almost any committee can develop an angle on the issue within its jurisdiction. Problems of the U.S. automobile industry, for example, can be looked at in the Senate by the Committee on Banking, Housing, and Urban Affairs (on financial assistance to the industry), by the Committee on Commerce, Science, and Transportation (on transportation aspects), by the Finance Committee (on trade problems of the industry), by the Committee on Environment and Public Works (on automobile emissions and how emission standards have affected the health of the industry), by the Judiciary Committee (on the impact of antitrust legislation on the industry), by the Foreign Relations Committee (on how the plight of the industry has affected U.S.-Japan relations), and by the Committee on Labor and Human Resources (on unemployment). Although the committee's (or subcommittee's) own special area of jurisdiction serves as the jurisdiction for the hearing, the actual scope and the members' questions may range very widely.

Conclusion

Although the U.S. Congress cannot bring down a government, as an independent branch of the U.S. government its powers in foreign policy as well as all aspects of domestic policy are very considerable indeed. Congress reflects public sentiments, shapes public debate, makes very specific changes in laws and budgets, and sometimes serves as the final arbiter of domestic policy struggles. Much of what becomes policy first percolates in the congressional cauldron. Human rights as an issue in foreign policy, for example, was long of concern to the Congress before it was embraced by the executive branch when Jimmy Carter was elected president. In the late 1970s and early 1980s, congressional sentiment for an expanded defense budget anticipated executive branch proposals for real growth in defense spending.

There are, however, many limitations on the role Congress plays. First of all, as a collegial body of equals, Congress is not well equipped to undertake specific policy initiatives. There is no one voice that speaks for Congress, and the influence of the leaders of Congress, including committee chairmen, has steadily declined. Foreign policy initiatives are usually undertaken by the president in the form of specific proposals or doctrines. Congress may respond positively or negatively or not at all.

Second, the internal organization of Congress often complicates its consideration of policy issues. The committee structure tends to discourage explicit consideration of tradeoffs or encourage a more comprehensive view of an issue. The committees that handle environmental legislation, for example, are unlikely to be very sensitive to the international trade implications of environmental protection laws. The Finance Committee and Ways and Means Committee are relatively insensitive to the diplomatic aspects of trade policy, and the Senate Foreign Relations Committee is much more interested in the political and security aspects of U.S. relations with foreign nations. As previously mentioned, jurisdiction over international economic policy, in particular, is widely scattered among committees, making a comprehensive overview of trade policy or even of export promotion virtually impossible in the Congress.

Perhaps the most fundamental weakness of Congress in foreign relations is its domestic orientation. Members are elected by the voters in their states and districts, and their first consideration is usually their reelection. It is often hard to reconcile the demands, needs, and prejudices of any particular constituency of voters with the requirements of an interdependent world. Some members of Congress act on foreign policy issues as if they were domestic issues without larger ramifications. Clearly, it is a very important function of the Congress to bring to bear a domestic perspective on consideration of international issues. But there is also a national interest that is more than simply the representation of the interests of a particular constituency, which is sometimes overlooked in this process.

Conference Participants

Steering Committee

Jed Johnson, Jr.	Member of Congress, 1965–1967
William S. Mailliard	Member of Congress, 1953–1974
Fumio Matsuo	Kyodo News Service, Tokyo
John S. Monagan	Member of Congress, 1959–1973
Francis B. Tenny	Director, Japan-U.S. Friendship Commission
Nathaniel Thayer	Director, Asian Studies, Johns Hopkins University
Francis R. Valeo	Secretary, U.S. Senate, 1966–1977
Tadashi Yamamoto	Director, Japan Center for International Exchange

U.S. Advisory Board

Robert C. Angel	Director, United States Japan Trade Council
Robert W. Barnett	Carnegie Endowment for International Peace
Ernest S. Griffith	Former Director, Congressional Research Service, Library of Congress
Robert S. Ingersoll	U.S. Ambassador to Japan, 1972–1974
Robert Kilmarx	Georgetown University
Ellis Krauss	Professor, Western Washington University
Edwin O. Reischauer	U.S. Ambassador to Japan, 1961–1966
Vincent Rock	Executive Director, Commission on the Operation of the U.S. Senate
Robert Scalapino	Professor, University of California
William B. Spong, Jr.	Member of Congress, 1966–1973
Neil Staebler	Member of Congress, 1963–1965
Justin Williams, Sr.	Author

Writers on the Japanese Diet

Shoichi Izumi	National Diet Library
Koji Kakizawa	Member of the Diet
Shuzo Kimura	Senior Researcher, Committee on Foreign Affairs, House of Councillors
Koichi Kishimoto	Editor, Jiji Press
Kan Ori	Professor of Political Science, Sophia University
Hiroshi Yamato	Assistant to Diet Member

Writers on the U.S. Congress

Susan Webb Hammond	Professor, Department of Political Science, The American University
Joel Havemann	*National Journal*
Charles E. Morrison	Fellow, Culture Learning Institute, East-West Center
Ralph D. Nurnberger	Georgetown Center for Strategic Studies
Robert L. Peabody	Professor, Department of Political Science, Johns Hopkins University
James L. Sundquist	The Brookings Institution

Additional Conference Participants and Observers

Kazuo Aichi	Parliamentary Vice-Minister, Japanese Diet
R. P. Anand	Research Associate, Culture Learning Institute, East-West Center
J. Glenn Beall, Jr.	Member of Congress, 1969–1977
Verner C. Bickley	Director, Culture Learning Institute, East-West Center
Joseph R. Biden, Jr.	Member of U.S. Senate
Charles B. Brownson	Member of Congress, 1951–1959
Satsuki Eda	Member of the Diet
Arlen Erdahl	Member of U.S. House of Representatives
Charles K. Fletcher	Member of Congress, 1947–1949
Lee Hamilton	Member of U.S. House of Representatives
Robert P. Hanrahan	Member of Congress, 1973–1975
Ichiro Hino	Member of the Diet

Walter H. Judd	Member of Congress, 1943–1963
Hiroshi Peter Kamura	Japan Center for International Exchange
Paul Kattenburg	Professor, James Byrnes International Center
Martha Keys	Member of Congress, 1975–1979
James A. Kuhlman	Director, James Byrnes International Center
Alex Lacy	President, Sangamon State University
Sachiko Matsumoto	Japan Center for International Exchange
D. Bailey Merrill	Member of Congress, 1953–1955
Frank E. Moss	Member of Congress, 1959–1977
Hidenao Nakagawa	Member of the Diet
Sakihito Ozawa	Assistant to Diet Member
James M. Quigley	Member of Congress, 1955–1961
William V. Roth, Jr.	Member of U.S. Senate
Hugh Scott	Member of Congress, 1941–1977
Henry P. Smith III	Member of Congress, 1965–1975
Robert Taft, Jr.	Member of Congress, 1963–1971
John Walsh	Research Associate, Culture Learning Institute, East-West Center

Contributors

Susan Webb Hammond, Professor, The American University

Joel Havemann, Deputy Editor, *National Journal*

Shoichi Izumi, Director, Planning and Training Division, National Diet Library

Koji Kakizawa, Senior Researcher, Committee on Foreign Affairs, House of Councillors, Japanese Diet

Shuzo Kimura, Senior Researcher, Committee on Foreign Affairs, House of Councillors, Japanese Diet

Koichi Kishimoto, Chief Editor of Political Section, Jiji Press

Charles E. Morrison, Fellow, East-West Center

Ralph D. Nurnberger, Center for Strategic and International Studies

Kan Ori, Professor of Political Science, Sophia University

Robert L. Peabody, Professor, Johns Hopkins University

James L. Sundquist, The Brookings Institution

Francis R. Valeo, Secretary of Senate, 1966–1977

Hiroshi Yamamoto, Assistant to Diet Member Tokusaburo Kosaka, House of Representatives, Japanese Diet

Tadashi Yamamoto, Director, Japan Center of International Exchange

Index

Duplicate subject entries are categorized as follows: (J) for Japan, (UK) for United Kingdom, and (US) for United States.

Administrative agreements
in Japan, 100–101
See also Treaties (J); Treaties (US)
Administrative branch (J). *See* Bureaucracy (J)
Administrative Procedures Act, 119
"Agreement on a Plan for Coalition Government," 28
Analysis of International Relations, The, 110
Ashida, Hitoshi, 57, 82(table)

Baerwald, Hans, 22
Baker, Howard, 138
Benjamin, Roger, 20, 22
Bills. *See* Legislative process (US), types of legislation
Blacks
in Congress, 162
Board of Audit, 18
Board of Elections, 67, 68
Broder, David, 156
Brussels tariff nomenclature treaty, 101
Buckley v. Valeo, 118
Budget Act, 146
Budget and Accounting Act, 120, 173
Budgetary process (J), 6, 171–172, 174, 182
administrative level, 84, 86–87
bureaucracy and, 85, 86–89, 95–96
cabinet and, 86, 88, 90–91
changes in, 92–97, 93(fig.)
committee systems and, 89–92
defense, 105–106
expenditures growth, 97(n1, n2)
foreign aid, 105
House of Councillors and, 90
House of Representatives and, 89–90
influences on, 88–89
LDP and, 20–21, 89, 91–92, 94–96

1947 Constitution and, 89, 90
PARC and, 87, 95
policy level, 87–89
political parties and, 20–21, 89, 91–92, 94–96
prime minister and, 89
review and approval, 89–92
revisions, 95–96
Budgetary process (US), 6, 126, 146 171–182
appropriations bills, 176, 177
calendar, 175–178
case study, 178–180
committee system and, 174–175, 181
defense policy and, 181–182
executive branch and, 120, 171, 173–175
expenditures growth, 97(n1, n2)
fiscal 1981, 180–182
spending legislation, 176–177
Bureaucracy (J), 12–13, 19, 79–97
appointments in, 80
budget and, 85, 86–89, 95–96
foreign policy and, 6–7
LDP and, 29–30
legislative process and, 16, 17, 19–20, 50–51, 53, 81
PARC and, 33
policy formation and, 30–31
political parties and, 37
prewar, 79
supervision of, 18
See also Committee systems (J)
Bureaucracy (US)
congressional oversight of, 119–120
See also Committee systems (US)
Byrd, Robert C., 135, 138, 139

Cabinet (J), 14–15, 16, 18, 30, 46–47
budget and, 86, 88, 90–91

committee systems and, 43
House of Representatives and, 57–59
Legislation Bureau, 51
legislative process and, 104
policy formation and, 103
prewar, 38
treaties and, 99, 101–102
See also Parliamentary-cabinet system (J)
Cabinet (US)
confirmation of, 119
Campaigns. *See* Electoral process (J);
    Electoral process (US)
Campbell, John Preighton, 97(n3)
Carter, Billy, 146
Carter, Jimmy, 117, 124, 125, 131, 144,
    146, 198
energy program, 141–143, 145, 151
fiscal 1981 budget, 180–181
foreign policy, 189
CBO. *See* Congressional Budget Office
Central Intelligence Agency (CIA), 186
CGP. *See* Clean Government party
Checks and balances
in Japan, 18, 39
in U.S., 115, 116–120, 124–126, 183
China. *See* People's Republic of China;
    Taiwan
CIA. *See* Central Intelligence Agency
Cicco, John A., Jr., 20, 22
Clean Government party (CGP), 15, 26,
    27–28, 66, 94
campaign financing, 69
defense policy and, 36–37
Diet members, 71–72
Diet staff and, 74
foreign policy and, 36–37
leadership, 48
Cloture, 135, 150
Commerce, Department of (US), 197
Committee on Audit, 45
Committee on Budget, 45
Committee on Discipline, 44–45
Committee systems (J), 15, 16–18, 22,
    23(n10), 28–29, 43–46, 44(table),
    63, 97(n7)
budgetary process and, 89–92
cabinet and, 43
defense policy and, 108–111
foreign policy and, 108–111
leadership in, 49
legislative process and, 50, 51, 53, 81,
    83
PARC and, 32–33
staffs, 75
treaties and, 101–102
Committee systems (US), 63, 119, 196–199

bill investigation and, 148–149
budgetary process and, 174–175, 181
changes in, 154
conference committees, 152–153
foreign policy and, 188, 191–194
hearings, 191–193
House of Representatives, 158
investigative function, 146–147
leadership in, 165
legislative process and, 141–142,
    144–145, 148–149, 188, 191–193
party leadership and, 133, 134
political parties and, 136
Senate, 134
special interests and, 149
staffs, 75, 165–166
Confederation of Labor, 15, 26, 69
Congress
caucuses, 151, 158
checks on, 118
constituencies, 155–156, 157, 162–163
democratization of, 137–139
expense accounts in, 164
investigative function, 146–147
Joint Economic Committee, 121
members of, 4–6, 154, 155–170, 186
nature of, 2, 3
oversight function, 119–120, 124–125,
    192, 194, 197
regionalization and, 156
reports, 192–193
salaries and benefits in, 163–164
services to, 163–165
staff, 75, 126, 144–145, 156, 163,
    165–167, 183
travel by, 194–195
See also House of Representatives (US);
    Senate
Congressional Budget Act, 174, 181
Congressional Budget Office (CBO), 119,
    124, 144, 174–175, 185, 193
Congressional oversight. *See* Congress,
    oversight function
Congressional Record, 148, 151
Constitution. *See* Meiji Constitution; 1947
    Constitution; U.S. Constitution
Constitutional Convention, 113
Constitutional Liberal party, 37
Constitutional Progressive party, 37
Council of Economic Advisers, 121
Curtis, Gerald L., 77(n4)
Czechoslovakia, 26

Defense Agency, 110
Defense Agency Establishment Law, 104,
    109

Defense, Department of (US), 188, 194
Defense policy (J), 1, 6–7, 99–111
    budget, 105–106
    committee systems and, 108–111
    LDP and, 25–26, 106
    legislation, 104–105
    opposition parties and, 36–37
    political parties and, 36–37, 103–104
    resolutions, 106, 107(table)
Defense policy (US), 1, 7
    budget, 181–182
    Constitution and, 121
    president and, 121–122
Democratic party, 117, 123
    Senate floor leader, 133–134
    Steering and Policy Committee, 137
Democratic Socialist party (DSP), 15, 26,
        27–28, 66, 94
    campaign financing, 69
    defense policy and, 36–37
    Diet members, 71–72
    foreign policy and, 36–37
    leadership, 48
Deutsch, Karl W., 110
Diet
    Budget Committee, 15, 18
    constituencies, 76, 83
    democratization of, 61
    functions of, 18–19, 22, 39–40, 108–111
    investigative function, 108–111
    members of, 4–6, 22, 23(n10), 61–77
    nature of, 3
    organization of, 46–50
    oversight function, 18, 22
    prewar, 11–13, 23(n1), 37–38, 39,
        45–46, 51, 53, 59, 61, 62, 79
    public attitude toward, 20, 62, 63,
        76–77
    representation function, 18–19
    salaries in, 75–76, 77(n9)
    second-generation members, 71–72, 75
    sessions of, 46–48, 62
    staff, 21, 31, 46, 74–75, 83
    See also House of Councillors; House of
        Representatives (J)
Diet Law, 43, 62
Dirksen, Everett, 138
Domei. *See* Confederation of Labor
DSP. *See* Democratic Socialist party

Eisenhower, Dwight D., 117
Elder Statesmen, 13, 57
Electoral process (J)
    campaign financing, 62, 68, 69, 77(n4)
    campaign restrictions, 67–68
    candidate selection, 65–67, 77(n3)
    districts, 64–65, 66, 77(n2)

    legal requirements, 64
    media and, 68
    support groups, 67, 69
Electoral process (US), 156, 157
    campaign financing, 159–160
    candidate recruitment, 158–159
    constituencies, 161
    general elections, 160–161
    incumbency and, 138, 159
    party leadership and, 136
    political parties and, 161
    primaries, 159
Electoral System Commission, 65
Emperor, 11–12, 23(n1), 79, 99
Employment Act, 121
E-2C patrol plane, 106
Executive branch (US)
    appointments in, 119
    budgetary process and, 120, 171,
        173–175
    Bureau of the Budget, 121, 173
    congressional consultations with, 193–194
    See also President
Export-Import Bank Authorization Act, 189

Federal Election Campaign Act
    amendments, 169(n5)
Federal government (US)
    states and, 116–117
Filibuster, 135, 150
Ford, Gerald R., 117, 124, 131, 137
Foreign Affairs Committee (J). *See* House
        of Councillors, Committee on Foreign
        Affairs
Foreign aid (J), 100
    budget, 105
    See also Foreign policy (J)
Foreign aid (US), 186–187, 188–189. *See
        also* Foreign policy (US)
Foreign policy (J), 99–111
    bureaucracy and, 6–7
    committee systems and, 108–111
    LDP and, 33–34, 106
    legislation, 104–105
    omnidirectional, 33–34
    opposition parties and, 36–37
    PARC and, 33–34
    political parties and, 36–37, 103–104
    resolutions, 106, 107(table)
    See also Foreign aid (J)
Foreign policy (US), 7, 125–126, 145–146,
        183–195, 198–199
    committee systems and, 188, 191–194
    congressional travel and, 194–195
    Constitution and, 121, 184
    legislation, 187–189
    legislative veto and, 189–190

media and, 186
political parties and, 184
president and, 121–122, 184–186
See also Foreign aid (US)
Friends of Constitutional Government
  Association, 38
Fukuda, Takeo, 30, 32, 82(table)
Fulbright, William, 186

General Accounting Office, 119, 144, 193
General Council of Trade Unions, 15, 69
"General Plan for a Democratic Coalition
  Government," 28
"General Plan for Popular Coalition
  Government," 28
Genro. See Elder Statesmen
Glenn, John, 156
Government scandals
  in Japan, 38
  in U.S., 146
Great Achievement Society, 37
Great Britain, 4, 28, 64
Great Depression, 116, 122, 195
Great Society, 117
Green Breeze Society, 55, 70–71
Grumman Corporation, 106

Halleck, Charles, 137
Hamilton, Alexander, 129
Hammond, Susan Webb, 2
Hara, Kei, 38
Hatoyama, Ichiro, 56, 82(table)
Havemann, Joel, 3
Hebert, F. Edward, 137
Heng, Samrin, 195
Hiroshi, Yamato, 2
Hollings, Ernest F., 181
House of Commons (UK), 14
House of Councillors, 4, 13–14, 29, 40–46,
  59, 61
  budget and, 90
  Cabinet Committee, 109
  Committee on Foreign Affairs, 108–109,
    110
  Committee on House Management, 16,
    46, 54
  committee system, 43–46, 108–109
  election of members, 77(n11)
  electoral district system and, 64–65
  leadership, 41–43, 44–45, 47–49
  legislative process, 52(table), 55
  members of, 40–41, 70–71
  Official Bulletin, 54
  power of, 14
  Special Committee on Security, Okinawa,
    and Northern Problems, 109

staff, 46
treaties and, 101
House of Peers (UK), 40, 41
House of Representatives (J), 3, 4, 11–12,
  13–14, 39, 40–46
  Budget Committee, 89–90, 91–92
  cabinet and, 57–59
  Cabinet Committee, 108
  Committee on Foreign Affairs, 101, 108,
    110
  Committee on House Management, 16,
    54, 101
  committee system, 43–46, 49, 108–109
  dissolution of, 58–59
  electoral district system and, 64–65
  leadership, 41–43, 44–45, 47–49
  legislative process, 52(table), 55
  members of, 40–41, 70–71
  Official Bulletin, 54
  parliamentary-cabinet system and, 57–58
  power of, 14
  prewar, 61
  prime minister and, 57–58
  Special Committee on Security, 109
  staff, 46
  Standing Committee on Social and Labor
    Affairs, 29
  treaties and, 101
House of Representatives (US), 3, 4, 7, 14
  Armed Services Committee, 196
  Committee of the Whole, 150
  Committee on Government Operations,
    197
  committee system, 158
  constituencies, 157–158
  democratization of, 137–138, 139
  floor leaders, 131–132
  Foreign Affairs Committee, 193, 196, 197
  leadership, 130–133, 170(n15)
  legislative scheduling in, 149–150
  members of, 138, 144, 158
  party whips, 132
  power hierarchy, 136–137
  retirement from, 138
  Rules Committee, 150
  salaries in, 170(n15)
  speaker, 130–131, 170(n15)
  staff, 131
  state delegations, 155–156
  structure of, 127–128
  Ways and Means Committee, 137, 194,
    195, 196, 197, 198
Huitt, Ralph K., 133, 134
Human rights, 198

Ikeda, Hayato, 26, 30, 82(table)
Imperial Rule Assistance Association, 38

Impoundment Control Act, 124
Inouye, Daniel, 195
Interest articulation. *See* Special interests
(J); Special interests (US)
International Trade Commission (ITC), 190,
195–196
Inukai cabinet, 38
Isibashi, Tanzan, 82(table)
ITC. *See* International Trade Commission
Ito, Hirobumi, 37, 38
Izumi, Shoichi, 2

Jackson, Henry M., 142
Japan
agriculture policy, 1
constitution. *See* Meiji Constitution;
1947 Constitution
defense policy. *See* Defense policy (J)
Diet. *See* Diet
fiscal policy, 1, 17
foreign policy. *See* Foreign policy (J)
industry, 25
modernization of, 79
political power in, 3–4, 14–15, 19–20,
96–97
social structures, 26–27
trade policy, 6–7
U.S. occupation of, 3, 80
See also Japan-U.S. relations
Japan Communist party (JCP), 25, 27–28,
38, 66, 94, 109
campaign financing, 69
Diet members, 71–72
Diet staff and, 74
Japan Foundation Act, 104
Japan Immigration Service Law (JIS), 104
Japan International Cooperation Agency
Law, 104
Japan–Republic of Korea Continental Shelf
Agreement, 101
Japan-ROK treaty, 101–102, 103, 104
Japan Socialist party (JSP), 15, 25, 27–28,
41, 55, 66, 94, 109
campaign financing, 69
Diet members, 71–72
LDP and, 36
leadership, 48
Japan-U.S. relations, 2, 193, 195
economic, 1
"Nixon shocks," 26, 105
Japan-U.S. security treaty, 101, 103, 104
JCP. *See* Japan Communist party
Jefferson, Thomas, 129
Jimii. See Budgetary process (J),
administrative level
JIS. *See* Japan Immigration Service Law
Johnson, J. Bennett, 142

Johnson, Lyndon B., 117, 121, 137, 138
JSP. *See* Japan Socialist party

Kakizawa, Koji, 3
Kampuchea, 195
Katayama, Tetsu, 57, 82(table)
Kato cabinet, 38
Kennedy, John F., 117
Kimura, Shuzo, 3
Kishi, Nobusuke, 82(table)
Koenkai. *See* Electoral process (J),
support groups
Koichi, Kishimoto, 2
Konin. See Liberal Democratic party,
candidate selection
Korea. *See* North Korea; South Korea

Law for Determining Names and Locations
of Diplomatic and Consular Offices
Abroad, 104
Law for the Establishment of the Ministry
of Foreign Affairs, 104
LDP. *See* Liberal Democratic party
Legislative branch (US)
powers of, 128
Legislative process (J), 29, 50–56,
52(table), 63
amendments, 53–54
bureaucracy and, 16, 17, 19–20, 50–51,
53, 81
cabinet and, 104
committee systems and, 50, 51, 53, 81,
83
enactment, 83, 104–105
LDP and, 21, 54–55
PARC and, 32–33
political parties and, 20–21, 54–55
Legislative process (US), 141–154
amendments, 188–189
bill introduction, 148
committee systems and, 141–142,
144–145, 148–149, 188, 191–193
compromise in, 142–143, 152–153,
189–190
constituencies and, 151
debate in, 150
enactment, 118–119
floor action, 149–152
hearings, 191–193
media and, 152
political parties and, 134–135
president and, 122, 145–146, 153
riders, 118
scope of, 144–145
special interests and, 143–144
types of legislation, 147

veto and, 118, 153
voting, 151–152
Legislative Reorganization Act, 165
Legislative veto, 125, 126, 189–190
Liberal Democratic party, 5, 15–16, 19, 41, 56, 103
  budget and, 20–21, 89, 91–92, 94–96
  bureaucracy and, 29–30
  campaign financing, 69
  candidate selection, 65–67, 77(n3)
  defense policy and, 25–26, 106
  Diet leadership and, 48–49
  Diet members, 71–72
  Diet Policy Committee, 29, 33, 37, 51
  Executive Council, 29, 33, 51
  factions within, 31, 34–35, 66
  foreign policy and, 33–34, 106
  JSP and, 36
  leadership, 87, 97(n5)
  legislative process and, 21, 54–55
  National Political Association, 69
  opposition parties and, 26–27, 36
  Policy Affairs Research Council. *See*
    Policy Affairs Research Council
  policy formation and, 18, 30–31
  special interests and, 31–32
Library of Congress
  Congressional Research Service, 75, 119, 144, 193
  See also National Diet Library
Lobbying
  in Japan, 31–32, 64
  See also Special interests (J);
    Special interests (US)
Lockheed elections, 27

MacArthur, Douglas, 28, 80, 146
Madison, James, 129
Magnuson, Warren, 165
Mansfield, Mike, 135, 138
Marcos, Ferdinand, 195
Matsushita, Keiichi, 109
Matthews, Donald R., 133
McDonnell Douglas Corporation, 106
Media (J), 23(n6)
  Diet members and, 62, 63, 70
  electoral process and, 68
Media (US)
  foreign policy and, 186
  legislative process and, 152
  senators and, 158
Meiji Constitution, 11, 37, 38, 39, 40, 41, 45, 47
  prime minister and, 57
  treaties and, 99
Meiji period, 3, 20, 79
Miki, Takeo, 32, 35, 82(table)

Ministries. *See* Cabinet (J)
Ministry of Finance (MOF), 20, 31
  budget and, 84, 86–88, 92
  Budget Bureau, 18, 95
Ministry of Foreign Affairs, 110
Ministry of Health and Welfare, 29
Ministry of Justice, 67
Ministry of Posts and Telecommunications, 28
Ministry of War scandal, 38
MOF. *See* Ministry of Finance
Morrison, Charles E., 3
Moynihan, Daniel P., 156
MTN. *See* Multilateral trade negotiations
Multilateral trade negotiations (MTN), 185
Mushakoji, Kinhide, 111
Muskie, Edmund S., 181

NASA. *See* Budgetary process (US), case study
National Aeronautics and Space Administration (NASA). *See* Budgetary process (US), case study
National Defense Council, 105
National Diet Library, 21, 41, 46, 75
  Research and Legislative Reference Department, 110
  See also Library of Congress
Nationalist Liberal party, 37
National Security Council, 121
Nemawashi, 33
Neutrality Treaty, 191, 195
New Deal, 116, 117
New Frontier, 117
New Liberal Club, 27, 66, 97
  campaign financing, 69
Newspapers. *See* Media (J); Media (US)
1947 Constitution, 13–15, 17, 39, 40, 41, 47
  budget and, 89, 90
  revision of, 56
Nixon, Richard M., 117, 131, 146, 173
  presidential powers and, 123–126
"Nixon shocks," 26, 105
North Korea, 195
Nuclear weapons, 1
Nurnberger, Ralph D., 2

Office of Management and Budget (OMB), 97(n3), 173, 174–175
Office of Technology Assessment, 119, 144
Ohira, Masayoshi, 30, 32, 58, 82(table)
Oil crisis (1973), 26
Okinawa reversion agreement, 102, 103, 104
Okuma cabinet, 38
OMB. *See* Office of Management and Budget

O'Neill, Thomas P., 139, 156
Ori, Kan, 2, 20, 22

PACs. *See* Political Action Committees
Panama. *See* Republic of Panama
Panama Canal treaties, 190–191, 194, 195
PARC. *See* Policy Affairs Research Council
Parliamentary-cabinet system (J), 28–29, 30, 39, 49–50
  House of Representatives and, 57–59
  policy formation and, 103
  See also Cabinet (J)
Patman, William, 137
Peabody, Robert L., 2
People's Republic of China (PRC), 26, 187
Philippines, 195
"Plan for a Middle-of-the-Road Coalition Government," 28, 37
"Plan for a Middle-of-the-Road Reform Coalition," 28
"Plan for Progressive Coalition for Democratic Government," 28
Poage, W. R., 137
Pocket veto. *See* Legislative process (US), veto and
Policy Affairs Research Council (PARC), 16, 18, 21, 51, 63
  budget and, 87, 95
  foreign policy and, 33–34
  policy formation and, 30–31, 32, 33–34, 35
  Social Affairs Division, 29
Policy Deliberation Commission, 32, 33
Policy formation (J), 17–18, 42–43
  bureaucracy and, 30–31
  cabinet and, 103
  LDP and, 18, 30–31
  opposition parties and, 36–37
  PARC and, 30–31, 32, 35
  political parties and, 18, 28–32, 35–37
  See also Defense policy (J); Foreign policy (J)
Policy formation (US), 187–195, 198
  political parties and, 135
  See also Defense policy (US); Foreign policy (US)
Political action committees (PACs), 130, 151
  campaign financing and, 160
Political Funds Regulation Law, 69
Political parties (J), 13, 14–16, 17, 25–38
  budgetary process and, 20–21, 89, 91–92, 94–96
  bureaucracy and, 37
  campaign financing, 69
  candidate selection and, 65–67

defense policy and, 36–37, 103–104
foreign policy and, 36–37, 103–104
legislative process and, 20–21, 54–55
lobbying role of, 31–32
opposition, 5, 6, 15, 17, 19, 21, 22, 25, 26–28, 29–30, 35–37, 37–38, 42(table), 65–66, 91, 92, 94, 103–104.
  See also names of individual parties
parity, 19, 26–27, 36, 37, 42(table), 43, 48, 50, 95
policy formation and, 18, 28–32, 35–37
proletarian, 38
scandal and, 38
See also names of individual parties
Political parties (US), 4–5, 15, 17, 115–116, 122–123, 126
  committee systems and, 136
  congressional leadership and, 130–137
  development of, 128–129
  electoral process and, 161
  foreign policy and, 184
  leadership, 133, 156–157
  legislative process and, 134–135
  policy formation and, 135
  power of, 156
  role of, 129–130
  third-, 156, 160
  See also Democratic party; Republican party
PRC. *See* People's Republic of China
President, 3, 7
  checks on, 118–120, 124–126
  checks on Congress, 118
  defense policy and, 121–122
  economy and, 121
  foreign policy and, 121–122, 184–186
  legislative process and, 122, 145–146, 153
  powers of, 120–122, 123–126, 184–185
  Supreme Court appointments, 117
  trade policy and, 195
  See also Executive branch (US)
Primaries. *See* Electoral process (US), primaries
Prime minister, 7, 50, 79, 80, 81, 82(table)
  budget and, 89
  election of, 47
  House of Representatives and, 57–58
  Meiji Constitution and, 57
Privy Council, 13
Public Finance System Council, 86, 97(n4)
Public Office Election Law, 58, 64, 65, 67, 68, 77(n4)

Radio. *See* Media (J); Media (US)
Railway scandal, 38

Rayburn, Sam, 139
Reagan, Ronald, 117, 125, 126
Reorganization Act, 154
Republican party, 117, 123, 139
  Senate floor leader, 134
Republic of Korea. *See* South Korea
Republic of Panama, 191
Resolutions. *See* Legislative process (US),
  types of legislation
Revised Health Insurance Law, 94
Revised Social Security Law, 94
Roosevelt, Franklin D., 116, 117, 120,
  121, 122, 125, 173
Roosevelt, Theodore, 120
Ryoufukai. *See* Green Breeze Society

SALT treaties, 191
San Francisco peace treaty, 25, 80
Sato, Eisaku, 30, 82(table)
Schmidt, William, 156
Scott, Hugh, 138
SEC. *See* Securities and Exchange
  Commission
Securities and Exchange Commission (SEC),
  106
Seisaku. See Budgetary process (J), policy
  level
Self-Defense Forces, 37, 104–105, 109
Senate, 4, 7
  Appropriations Committee, 192
  Armed Services Committee, 193, 196, 197
  Commerce Committee, 197
  Committee on Agriculture, 197
  Committee on Banking, Housing, and
    Urban Affairs, 197
  Committee on Foreign Relations, 190,
    191, 192, 193, 195, 196, 197,
    198–199
  committee system, 134
  confirmation hearings, 119
  democratization of, 138–139
  Finance Committee, 194, 195, 197, 198
  floor leaders, 133–137
  foreign policy and, 190–191
  Governmental Affairs Committee, 197
  leadership, 133–137
  legislative scheduling in, 149–150
  members of, 138, 144, 158
  power hierarchy, 136–137
  retirement from, 138
  salaries in, 170(n15)
  structure of, 127–128
  treaty powers, 190–191
Shidehara, Kijuro, 82(table)
Socialism, 26
Social Mass party, 38

Sōhyō. *See* General Council of
  Trade Unions
Soka Gakkai, 15, 26
South Korea, 100, 101–102, 103, 104
Soviet Union, 26, 101, 189
Special interests (J), 15–16, 33, 63–64
  LDP and, 31–32
  lobbying by, 31–32
Special interests (US), 151–152
  committee systems and, 149
  legislative process and, 143–144
Standing Committee on the Cabinet, 28
State, Department of (US), 147, 188, 194
State governments (US)
  jurisdictions of, 116–117
Strategic Arms Limitation Talks. *See* SALT
  treaties
Suffrage
  in Japan, 12
Suisen. See Liberal Democratic party,
  candidate selection
Sundquist, James L., 2
Supreme Court (J)
  electoral districts and, 77(n2)
Supreme Court (US), 116
  check on Congress, 117–118
  checks on, 117–118
Suzuki, Zenko, 65, 82(table)
Synfuels legislation
  in U.S., 142–143

Taishō era, 13
Taiwan, 187
Taiwan Relations Act, 187
Tanaka, Kakuei, 32, 82(table)
Taxation
  in U.S., 172–173, 177–178
Tax System Investigation Commission, 86,
  97(n4)
Television. *See* Media (J); Media (US)
Tojo, Hideki, 38
Tokyo District Court, 65
Tokyo municipal assembly scandal, 38
Trade. *See* Japan, trade policy; Japan-U.S.
  relations, economic; United States,
  trade policy
Trade Act (1974), 189, 196
Trade Act (1979), 196
Treasury, Department of the (US), 173
Treaties (J), 99–103
  committee system and, 101–102
  Diet alteration of, 102
  See also Foreign policy (J)
Treaties (US), 190–191. *See also* Foreign
  policy (US)
Truman, Harry S, 117, 146

United Kingdom. *See* Great Britain
United Nations, 192
United Social Democratic party, 27
United States
  agriculture policy, 1
  Congress. *See* Congress
  Constitution. *See* United States—
    Constitution
  defense policy. *See* Defense policy (US)
  electoral district system in, 64–65. *See also* Electoral process (US)
  energy policy, 141–143, 145, 151
  fiscal policy, 1
  foreign aid. *See* Foreign aid (US)
  foreign policy. *See* Foreign policy (US)
  industry, 1
  political power in, 3–4
  president. *See* President
  public sector, 172–173
  trade policy, 195–196
  See also Japan-U.S. relations
United States–Japan relations. *See* Japan-U.S. relations

United States–Japan Trade, 193
United States—Constitution, 143, 183
  defense and, 121
  foreign policy and, 121, 184
  presuppositions of, 128
U.S.-Japan security treaty, 25–26, 37
USSR. *See* Soviet Union

"Value-Creation Society." *See* Soka Gakkai
Versailles Treaty, 190–191
Veto. *See* Legislative process (US), veto and; Legislative veto
Vietnam War, 26, 121–122, 186, 192

War Powers Resolution, 124, 126, 185
Watergate scandal, 146
Wilson, Woodrow, 120, 190
Women
  in Congress, 162
  in Diet, 72–73

Yoshida, Shigeru, 30, 56, 57, 58, 82(table)